William Paley

A View of the Evidences of Christianity

In Three Parts

William Paley

A View of the Evidences of Christianity
In Three Parts

ISBN/EAN: 9783337026042

Printed in Europe, USA, Canada, Australia, Japan

Cover: Foto ©Lupo / pixelio.de

More available books at **www.hansebooks.com**

A

VIEW

OF THE

EVIDENCES OF CHRISTIANITY.

IN THREE PARTS.

PART I. Of the direct Historical Evidence of Christianity, and wherein it is distinguished from the Evidence alledged for other **Miracles**.

PART II. Of the Auxiliary Evidences of Christianity.

PART III. A brief Consideration of some popular Objections.

BY WILLIAM PALEY, M. A.

ARCHDEACON OF CARLISLE.

THE SECOND EDITION,

IN TWO VOLUMES.—VOL. II.

LONDON:

PRINTED FOR R. FAULDER, NEW BOND-STREET.

M.DCC.XCIV.

CONTENTS

OF THE

SECOND VOLUME.

PART II.

OF THE AUXILIARY EVIDENCES OF CHRISTIANITY.

CHAP.

CHAP. VI.

CHAP. VII.

CHAP. VIII.

CHAP. IX.

PART III.

A BRIEF CONSIDERATION OF SOME POPULAR OBJECTIONS.

CHAP. I.

CHAP. II.

CHAP. III.

CHAP.

[vii]

C H A P. IV.

C H A P. V.

C H A P. VI.

C H A P. VII.

C H A P. VIII.

PART II.

OF THE AUXILIARY EVIDENCES OF CHRISTIANITY.

CHAP. I.

Prophecy.

If. lii. 13. liii. " BEHOLD, my fervant fhall deal prudently, he fhall be exalted, and extolled, and be very high. As many were aftonifhed at thee; his vifage was fo marred more than any man, and his form more than the fons of men: fo fhall he fprinkle many nations; the kings fhall fhut their mouths at him; for that which had not been told them fhall they fee; and that which they had not heard fhall they confider. Who hath believed our report? and to whom is the arm of the Lord revealed?

For

For he fhall grow up before him as a tender plant, and as a root out of a dry ground : he hath no form nor comelinefs ; and when we fhall fee him, there is no beauty that we fhould defire him. He is defpifed and rejected of men, a man of forrows, and acquainted with grief : and we hid, as it were, our faces from him ; he was defpifed, and we efteemed him not. Surely he hath borne our griefs, and carried our forrows : yet we did efteem him ftricken, fmitten of God, and afflicted. But he was wounded for our tranfgreffions, he was bruifed for our iniquities : the chaftifement of our peace was upon him ; and with his ftripes we are healed. All we like fheep have gone aftray ; we have turned every one to his own way ; and the Lord hath laid on him the iniquity of us all. He was oppreffed, and he was afflicted, yet he opened not his mouth : he is brought as a lamb to the flaughter, and as a fheep before her fhearers is dumb, fo he openeth not his mouth. He was taken from prifon and from judgement ; and who fhall declare his generation ? for he was cut

off

off out of the land of the living: for the
tranfgreffion of my people was he ftricken.
And he made his grave with the wicked,
and with the rich in his death; becaufe he
had done no violence, neither was any deceit
in his mouth. Yet it pleafed the Lord to
bruife him; he hath put him to grief.
When thou fhalt make his foul an offering
for fin, he fhall fee his feed, he fhall prolong
his days, and the pleafure of the Lord fhall
profper in his hand. He fhall fee of the
travail of his foul, and fhall be fatisfied: by
his knowledge fhall my righteous fervant
juftify many; for he fhall bear their iniquities. Therefore will I divide him a portion with the great, and he fhall divide the
fpoil with the ftrong; becaufe he hath
poured out his foul unto death: and he was
numbered with the tranfgreffors; and he
bare the fin of many, and made interceffion
for the tranfgreffors."

Thefe words are extant in a book, purporting to contain the predictions of a writer,

who

who lived feven centuries before the Chriftian æra.

That material part of every argument
from prophecy, namely, that the words
alledged were actually fpoken or written before the fact, to which they are applied, took
place, or could by any natural means be forefeen, is, in the prefent inftance, inconteftable.
The record comes out of the cuftody of adverfaries. The Jews, as an ancient father
well obferved, are our librarians. The paffage is in their copies as well as in ours.
With many attempts to explain it away,
none has ever been made by them to dif-
credit its authenticity.

And, what adds to the force of the quotation is, that it is taken from a writing
declaredly prophetic; a writing, profeffing
to defcribe fuch future tranfactions and
changes in the world, as were connected
with the fate and interefts of the Jewifh
nation. It is not a paffage in an hiftorical
or devotional compofition, which, becaufe it

turns

turns out to be applicable to some future events, or to some future situation of affairs, is presumed to have been oracular. The words of Isaiah were delivered by him in a prophetic character, with the solemnity belonging to that character; and what he so delivered, was all along understood by the Jewish reader to refer to something that was to take place after the time of the author. The public sentiments of the Jews, concerning the design of Isaiah's writings, are set forth in the book of Ecclesiasticus: " He saw, by an excellent spirit, what should come to pass at the last, and he comforted them that mourned in Sion. He shewed what should come to pass for ever, and secret things or ever they came." (ch. xlviii. v. 24.)

It is also an advantage which this prophecy possesses, that it is intermixed with no other subject. It is entire, separate, and uninterruptedly directed to one scene of things.

The

The *application* of the prophecy to the evangelic hiftory is plain and appropriate. Here is no double fenfe: no figurative language, but what is fufficiently intelligible to every reader of every country. The obfcurities, by which I mean the expreffions that require a knowledge of local diction, and of local allufion, are few, and not of great importance. Nor have I found that varieties of reading, or a different conftruing of the original, produce any material alteration in the fenfe of the prophecy. Compare the common tranflation with that of Bifhop Lowth, and the difference is not confiderable. So far as they do differ, Bifhop Lowth's corrections, which are the faithful refult of an accurate examination, bring the defcription nearer to the New Teftament hiftory than it was before. In the fourth verfe of the fifty-third chapter, what our Bible renders " ftricken," he tranflates " judicially ftricken:" and in the eighth verfe, the claufe " he was taken from prifon and from judgement," the Bifhop gives " by an oppreffive judgement he was taken off."

The

The next words to thefe, " who fhall declare his generation ?" are much cleared up in their meaning by the Bifhop's verfion, "his manner of life who would declare," *i. e.* who would ftand forth in his defence ? The former part of the ninth verfe, " and he made his grave with the wicked, and with the rich in his death," which inverts the circumftances of Chrift's paffion, the Bifhop brings out in an order perfectly agreeable to the event ; " and his grave was appointed with the wicked, but with the rich man was his tomb." The words in the eleventh verfe, " by his knowledge fhall my righteous fervant juftify many," are in the Bifhop's verfion " by the *knowledge of him* fhall my righteous fervant juftify many."

It is natural to enquire what turn the Jews themfelves give to this prophecy*. There is

* " Vaticinium hoc Efaiæ eft carnificina Rabbinorum, de quo aliqui Judæi mihi confelli funt, Rabbinos fuos ex propheticis fcripturis facile fe extricare potuiffe, *modo Efaias tacuiffet.*" Hulfe Theol. Jud. p. 318. quoted by Poole in loc.

good proof that the ancient Rabbins explained it of their expected Messiah*; but their
modern expositors concur, I think, in re-
presenting it, as a description of the cala-
mitous state and intended restoration of the
Jewish people, who are here, as they say,
exhibited under the character of a single
person. I have not discovered that their exposition rests upon any critical arguments, or
upon these in any other than a very minute
degree. The clause in the ninth verse,
which we render " for the transgression of
my people was he stricken," and in the
margin " was the stroke upon him," the
Jews read, " for the transgression of my people was the stroke upon *them*." And what
they alledge in support of the alteration
amounts only to this, that the Hebrew pro-
noun is capable of a plural, as well as of a
singular signification, that is to say, is capable of their construction as well as ours†.

And

---

* Hulse Theol. Jud. p. 430.

† Bishop Lowth adopts in this place the reading
of the seventy, which gives smitten *to death*, " for the
transf-

And this is all the variation contended for: the reſt of the prophecy they read as we do.

The

tranſgreſſion of my people was he ſmitten to death." The addition of the words "to death," makes an end of the Jewiſh interpretation of the clauſe. And the authority, upon which this reading (though not given by the preſent Hebrew text) is adopted, Dr. Kennicot has ſet forth by an argument, not only ſo cogent, but ſo clear and popular, that I beg leave to tranſcribe the ſubſtance of it into this note. "Origen, after having quoted at large this prophecy concerning the Meſſiah, tells us, that having once made uſe of this paſſage, in a diſpute againſt ſome that were accounted wiſe among the Jews, one of them replied, that the words did not mean one man, but one people, the Jews, who were ſmitten of God, and diſperſed among the Gentiles for their converſion; that he then urged many parts of this prophecy, to ſhew the abſurdity of this interpretation, and that he ſeemed to preſs them the hardeſt by this ſentence—"for the tranſgreſſion of my people was he ſmitten to death." Now, as Origen, the author of the Hexapla, muſt have underſtood Hebrew, we cannot ſuppoſe that he would have urged this laſt text as ſo deciſive, if the Greek verſion had not agreed here with the Hebrew text; nor that theſe wiſe Jews would have been at all diſtreſſed by this quotation, unleſs the Hebrew text had read agreeably to the words "to death," on which the argument principally depended; for by quoting it immediately, they would have triumphed

over

The probability, therefore, of their expe-
fition is a fubject of which we are as capable
of judging as themfelves. This judgement
is open indeed to the good fenfe of every
attentive reader. The application which
the Jews contend for, appears to me to labour under infuperable difficulties; in particular, it may be demanded of them to
explain, in *whofe* name or perfon, if the
Jewifh people be the fufferer, does the prophet fpeak, when he fays, " he hath borne
our griefs, and carried *our* forrows, yet *we*

over him, and reprobated his Greek verfion. This,
whenever they could do it, was their conftant practice
in their difputes with the Chriftians. Origen himfelf,
who laborioufly compared the Hebrew text with the
Septuagint, has recorded the neceffity of arguing with
the Jews, from fuch paffages only, as were in the Septuagint agreeable to the Hebrew. Wherefore, as
Origen had carefully compared the Greek verfion of
the Septuagint with the Hebrew text; and as he puz-
zled and confounded the learned Jews, by urging upon
them the reading " to death" in this place; it feems
almoft impoffible not to conclude, both from Origen's
argument, and the filence of his Jewifh adverfaries,
that the Hebrew text at that time actually had the word
agreeably to the verfion of the feventy." Lowth's Ifaiah,
p. 242.

did

did efteem him ftricken, fmitten of God and
afflicted; but he was wounded for *our* tranfgreffions, he was bruifed for *our* iniquities,
the chaftifement of *our* peace was upon him,
and with his ftripes *we* are healed." Again,
the defcription in the feventh verfe, " he
was oppreffed and he was afflicted, yet he
opened not his mouth; he is brought as a
lamb to the flaughter, and as a fheep before
her fhearers is dumb, fo he openeth not his
mouth," quadrates with no part of the Jewifh hiftory with which we are acquainted.
The mention of the " grave," and the
" tomb," in the ninth verfe, is not very
applicable to the fortunes of a nation; and
ftill lefs fo is the conclufion of the prophecy
in the twelfth verfe, which exprefsly reprefents the fufferings as *voluntary*, and the
fufferer as interceding for the offenders,
" becaufe he hath poured out his foul unto
death, and he was numbered with the tranfgreffors, and he bare the fin of many, and
made interceffion for the tranfgreffors."

———————

There are other prophecies of the Old
Teftament,

Teſtament, interpreted by Chriſtians to relate to the goſpel hiſtory, which are deſerving both of great regard, and of a very
attentive conſideration: but I content my-
ſelf with ſtating the above, as well becauſe
I think it the cleareſt and the ſtrongeſt of
all, as becauſe moſt of the reſt, in order
that their value be repreſented with any to-
lerable degree of fidelity, require a diſcuſſion
unſuitable to the limits and nature of this
work. The reader will find them diſpoſed
in order, and diſtinctly explained in Biſhop
Chandler's treatiſe upon the ſubject: and he
will bear in mind, what has been often, and,
I think, truly, urged by the advocates of
Chriſtianity, that there is no other eminent
perſon, to the hiſtory of whoſe life ſo many
circumſtances can be made to apply. They
who object, that much has been done by
the power of chance, the ingenuity of accommodation, and the induſtry of reſearch,
ought to try whether the ſame, or any thing
like it, could be done, if Mahomet, or any
other perſon, were propoſed as the ſubject
of Jewiſh prophecy.

II. A

II. A fecond head of argument from prophecy, is founded upon our Lord's predictions concerning the deftruction of Jerufalem, recorded by three out of the four evangelifts.

Luke xxi. 5—25. " And as fome fpake of the temple, how it was adorned with goodly ftones and gifts, he faid, As for thefe things which ye behold, the days will come, in the which there fhall not be left one ftone upon another, that fhall not be thrown down. And they afked him, faying, Mafter, but when fhall thefe things be? and what fign fhall there be when thefe things fhall come to pafs? And he faid, Take heed that ye be not deceived, for many fhall come in my name, faying, I am Chrift; and the time draweth near. Go ye not therefore after them. But, when ye fhall hear of wars and commotions, be not terrified ; for thefe things muft firft come to pafs, but the end is not by and by. Then faid he unto them, Nation fhall rife againft nation, and kingdom againft kingdom, and great earth-

earthquakes fhall be in divers places, and famines and peftilences : and fearful fights, and great figns fhall there be from heaven. But before all thefe, they fhall lay their hands on you, and perfecute you, delivering you up to the fynagogues, and into prifons, being brought before kings and rulers for my name's fake. And it fhall turn to you for a teftimony. Settle it therefore in your hearts, not to meditate before what ye fhall anfwer; for I will give you a mouth and wifdom, which all your adverfaries fhall not be able to gainfay nor refift. And ye fhall be betrayed both by parents and brethren, and kinsfolk and friends ; and fome of you fhall they caufe to be put to death. And ye fhall be hated of all men for my name's fake. But there fhall not an hair of your head perifh. In your patience poffefs ye your fouls. And when ye fhall fee Jerufa-lem compaffed with armies, then know that the defolation thereof is nigh. Then let them which are in Judea flee to the moun-tains ; and let them which are in the midft of it depart out ; and let not them that are

in

in the countries enter thereinto. For thefe be the days of vengeance, that all things which are written may be fulfilled. But woe unto them that are with child, and to them that give fuck, in thofe days; for there fhall be great diftrefs in the land, and wrath upon this people. And they fhall fall by the edge of the fword, and fhall be led away captive into all nations; and Jeru-falem fhall be trodden down of the Gen-tiles, until the time of the Gentiles be ful-filled."

In terms nearly fimilar, this difcourfe is related in the twenty-fourth chapter of Mat-thew, and the thirteenth of Mark. The profpect of the fame evils drew from our Saviour, upon another occafion, the follow-ing affecting expreffions of concern, which are preferved by St. Luke (xix. 41): "And when he was come near, he beheld the city, and wept over it, faying, If thou hadft known, even thou, at leaft in this thy day, the things which belong unto thy peace; but now they are hid from thine eyes, for

the

the days fhall come upon thee, that thine
enemies fhall caft a trench about thee, and
compafs thee round, and keep thee in on
every fide, and fhall lay thee even with the
ground, and thy children within thee, and
they fhall not leave in thee one ftone upon
another, becaufe thou kneweft not the time
of thy vifitation." Thefe paffages are direct
and explicit predictions. References to the
fame event, fome plain, fome parabolical,
or otherwife figurative, are found in divers
other difcourfes of our Lord *.

The general agreement of the defcription
with the event, viz. with the ruin of the
Jewifh nation, and the capture of Jerufalem
under Vefpafian, thirty-fix years after Chrift's
death, is moft evident : and the accordancy
in various articles of detail and circumftance
has been fhewn by many learned writers. It
is alfo an advantage to the enquiry, and to
the argument built upon it, that we have

---

* Mat. xxi. 33—46. xxii. 1—7. Mark xii. 1—12.
Luke xiii. 1—9. xx. 9—20. xxi. 5—13.

received

received a copious account of the tranfaction
from Jofephus, a Jewifh and contemporary
hiftorian. This part of the cafe is perfectly
free from doubt. The only queftion which,
in my opinion, can be raifed upon the fubject, is whether the prophecy was really delivered *before* the event. I fhall apply, therefore, my obfervations to this point folely.

1. The judgement of antiquity, though
varying in the precife year of the publication of the three gofpels, *concurs* in affign-
ing them a date prior to the deftruction of
Jerufalem *.

2. This judgement is confirmed by a
ftrong probability arifing from the courfe of
human life. The deftruction of Jerufalem
took place in the feventieth year after the
birth of Chrift. The three evangelifts, one
of whom was his immediate companion,
and the other two affociated with his companions, were, it is probable, not much

---

* Lardner, vol. xiii.

younger than he was. They muft, confequently, have been far advanced in life
when Jerufalem was taken; and no reafon
has been given why they fhould defer writing their hiftories fo long.

3. * If the evangelifts, at the time of
writing the gofpels, had known of the deftruction of Jerufalem, by which cataftrophe
the prophecies were plainly fulfilled, it is
moft probable, that, in recording the predictions, they would have dropped fome
word or other about the completion; in like
manner as Luke, after relating the denun-
ciation of a dearth by Agabus, adds, " which
came to pafs in the days of Claudius Cæ-
far † :" whereas the prophecies are given
diftinctly in one chapter of each of the three
firft gofpels, and referred to in feveral different paffages of each, and, in none of all
thefe places, does there appear the fmalleft
intimation that the things fpoken of were

---

* Le Clerc, Diff. III. de Quat. Ev. num. vii. p. 541.
† Acts xi. 28.

come

come to pafs. I do admit that it would have
been the part of an impoftor, who wifhed
his readers to believe that his book was
written before the event, when in truth it
was written after it, to have fuppreffed any
fuch intimation carefully. But this was not
the character of the authors of the gofpel.
Cunning was no quality of theirs. Of all
writers in the world, they thought the leaft
of providing againft objections. Moreover,
there is no claufe in any one of them, that
makes a profeffion of having written prior
to the Jewifh wars, which a fraudulent purpofe would have led them to pretend. They
have done neither one thing nor the other.
They have neither inferted any words,
which might fignify to the reader that their
accounts were written *before* the deftruction
of Jerufalem, which a fophift would have
done; nor have they dropped a hint of the
completion of the prophecies recorded by
them, which an *undefigning* writer, writing
after the event, could hardly, on fome or
other of the many occafions that prefented
themfelves, have miffed of doing.

4. The

4. The admonitions * which Chrift is reprefented to have given to his followers to fave themfelves by flight, are not eafily accounted for upon the fuppofition of the prophecy being fabricated after the event. Either the Chriftians, when the fiege approached, did make their efcape from Jerufalem, or they did not: if they did, they muft have had the prophecy amongft them: if they did not know of any fuch prediction at the time of the fiege, if they did not take notice of any fuch warning, it was an improbable fiction, in a writer publifhing his

* Luke xxi. 20, 21. " When ye fhall fee Jerufalem compaffed with armies, then know that the defolation thereof is nigh ; then let them which are in Judea flee to the mountains, and let them which are in the midft of it depart out, and let not them that are in the countries enter thereinto."

Mat. xiv. 18. " When ye fhall fee Jerufalem compaffed with armies, then let them which be in Judea flee unto the mountains ; let him which is on the houfe top not come down to take any thing out of his houfe, neither let him which is in the field return back to take his clothes."

7   work

work near to that time (which, upon any
even the loweft and moft difadvantageous
fuppofition, was the cafe with the gofpels
now in our hands), and addreffing his work
to Jews and to Jewifh converts (which
Matthew certainly did), to ftate that the followers of Chrift had received admonitions,
of which they made no ufe when the occafion arrived, and of which, experience then
recent proved, that thofe, who were moft
concerned to know and regard them, were
ignorant or negligent. Even if the prophecies came to the hands of the evangelifts
through no better vehicle than tradition, it
muft have been by a tradition which fub-
fifted prior to the event. And to fuppofe,
that, without any authority whatever, without fo much as even any tradition to guide
them, they had forged thefe paffages, is to
impute to them a degree of fraud and impofture, from every appearance of which
their compofitions are as far removed as
poffible.

5. I think that, if the prophecies had been

C 3   com-

compoſed after the event, there would have
been more ſpecification. The names or deſcriptions of the enemy, the general, the
emperor, would have been found in them.
The deſignation of the time would have
been more determinate. And I am fortified
in this opinion by obſerving, that the counterfeited prophecies of the Sybilline oracles,
of the twelve patriarchs, and, I am inclined
to believe, moſt others of the kind, are mere
tranſcripts of the hiſtory moulded into a
prophetic form.

It is objected that the prophecy of the
deſtruction of Jeruſalem, is mixed, or connected with, expreſſions, which relate to the
final judgement of the world; and ſo connected, as to lead an ordinary reader to
expect, that theſe two events would not be
far diſtant from each other. To which I
anſwer, that the objection does not concern
our preſent argument. If our Saviour actually foretold the deſtruction of Jeruſalem,
it is ſufficient; even although we ſhould
allow, that the narration of the prophecy

had

had combined together what had been faid by him upon kindred fubjects, without accurately preferving the order, or always noticing the tranfition of the difcourfe.

CHAP.

CHAP. II.

The morality of the gospel.

IN ftating the morality of the gofpel as an argument of its truth, I am willing to admit two points; firft, that the teaching of morality was not the primary defign of the miffion; fecondly, that morality, neither in the gofpel, nor in any other book, can be a fubject, properly fpeaking, of difcovery.

If I were to defcribe in a very few words the fcope of Chriftianity, as a *revelation* *, I fhould fay, that it was to influence the

---

* Great and ineftimably beneficial effects may accrue from the miffion of Chrift, and efpecially from his death, which do not belong to Chriftianity as a *revelation*; that is, they might have exifted, and they might have been accomplifhed, though we had never, in this life, been made acquainted with them. Thefe effects may be very extenfive. They may be interefting even to other orders of intelligent beings.

conduct

conduct of human life, by eſtabliſhing the
proof of a future ſtate of reward and puniſhment—" to bring life and immortality to
light." The direct object, therefore, of the
deſign is, to ſupply motives, and not rules;
ſanctions, and not precepts. And theſe were
what mankind ſtood moſt in need of. The
members of civilized ſociety can, in all ordinary caſes, judge tolerably well how they
ought to act; but without a future ſtate,
or, which is the ſame thing, without credited evidence of that ſtate, they want a *motive*
to their duty; they want at leaſt ſtrength of
motive, ſufficient to bear up againſt the
force of paſſion, and the temptation of preſent advantage. Their rules want authority.
The moſt important ſervice that can be rendered to human life, and that, conſequently,
which, one might expect beforehand, would
be the great end and office of a revelation
from God, is to convey to the world au-
thoriſed aſſurances of the reality of a future
exiſtence. And although, in doing this, or
by the miniſtry of the ſame perſon by which
this is done, moral precepts, or examples,
or

or illuftrations of moral precepts, may be occafionally given, and be highly valuable, yet ftill they do not form the original purpofe of the miffion.

Secondly, morality, neither in the gofpel, nor in any other book, can be a fubject of difcovery, properly fo called. By which propofition, I mean that there cannot, in morality, be any thing fimilar to what are called difcoveries in natural philofophy, in the arts of life, and in fome fciences; as the fyftem of the univerfe, the circulation of the blood, the polarity of the magnet, the laws of gravitation, alphabetical writing, decimal arithmetic, and fome other things of the fame fort; facts, or proofs, or contrivances, before totally unknown and unthought of. Whoever therefore expects, in reading the New Teftament, to be ftruck with difcoveries in morals, in the manner in which his mind was affected, when he firft came to the knowledge of the difcoveries above mentioned; or rather in the manner in which the world was affected by

them,

them, when they were firſt publiſhed; expects what, as I apprehend, the nature of
the ſubject renders it impoſſible that he
ſhould meet with. And the foundation of
my opinion is this, that the qualities of actions depend entirely upon their effects,
which effects muſt all along have been the
ſubject of human experience.

When it is once ſettled, no matter upon
what principle, that to do good is virtue,
the reſt is calculation. But ſince the calculation cannot be inſtituted concerning each
particular action, we eſtabliſh intermediate
rules: by which proceeding, the buſineſs of
morality is much facilitated, for then, it is
concerning our rules alone that we need enquire, whether in their tendency they be
beneficial; concerning our actions we have
only to aſk, whether they be agreeable to
the rules. We refer actions to rules, and
rules to public happineſs. Now, in the
formation of theſe rules, there is no place
for diſcovery properly ſo called, but there is
ample

ample room for the exercise of wisdom, judgement, and prudence.

As I wish to deliver argument rather than panegyric, I shall treat of the morality of the gospel, in subjection to these observations. And after all, I think it such a morality, as, considering from whom it came, is most extraordinary; and such, as, without allowing some degree of reality to the character and pretensions of the religion, it is difficult to account for: or to place the argument a little lower in the scale, it is such a morality, as completely repels the supposition of its being the tradition of a barbarous age or of a barbarous people, of the religion being founded in folly, or of its being the production of craft; and it repels also, in a great degree, the supposition of its having been the effusion of an enthusiastic mind.

The division, under which the subject may be most conveniently treated of, is that

of

of the things taught, and the manner of teaching.

Under the firſt head, I ſhould willingly, if the limits and nature of my work admitted of it, tranſcribe into this chapter the whole of what has been ſaid upon the morality of the goſpel, by the author of *the internal evidence of Chriſtianity*; becauſe it perfeÐly agrees with my own opinion, and becauſe it is impoſſible to ſay the ſame things ſo well. This acute obſerver of human nature, and, as I believe, ſincere convert to Chriſtianity, appears to me to have made out ſatisfactorily the two following poſitions, viz.

I. That the goſpel omits ſome qualities, which have uſually engaged the praiſes and admiration of mankind, but which, in reality, and in their general effeÐs, have been prejudicial to human happineſs.

II. That the goſpel has brought forwards ſome virtues, which poſſeſs the higheſt intrinſic trinfic value, but which have commonly been overlooked and contemned.

The firft of thefe propofitions he exemplifies, in the inftances of friendfhip, patriotifm, active courage ; in the fenfe in which thefe qualities are ufually underftood, and in the conduct which they often produce.

The fecond, in the inftances of paffive courage or endurance of fufferings, patience under affronts and injuries, humility, irrefiftance, placability.

The truth is, there are two oppofite defcriptions of character, under which mankind may generally be claffed. The one poffeffes vigour, firmnefs, refolution ; is daring and active, quick in its fenfibilities, jealous of its fame, eager in its attachments, inflexible in its purpofe, violent in its refentments.

The other, meek, yielding, complying, forgiving ; not prompt to act but willing to

8   fuffer,

suffer, silent and gentle under rudenefs and insult, suing for reconciliation where others would demand satisfaction, giving way to the pushes of impudence, conceding and indulgent to the prejudices, the wrong-headednefs, the intractability of thofe with whom it has to deal.

The former of thefe characters is, and ever hath been, the favourite of the world. It is the character of great men. There is a dignity in it which univerfally commands refpect.

The latter is poor-fpirited, tame, and abject. Yet fo it hath happened, that, with the founder of Chriftianity, this latter is the fubject of his commendation, his precepts, his example ; and that the former is fo, in no part of its compofition. This, and nothing elfe, is the character defigned in the following remarkable paffages : " Refift not evil, but whofoever fhall fmite thee on the right cheek, turn to him the other alfo ; and if any man will fue thee at the law, and

take

take away thy coat, let him have thy cloke
alfo; and whofoever fhall compel thee to
go a mile, go with him twain; love your
enemies, blefs them that curfe you, do good
to them that hate you, and pray for them
which defpitefully ufe you and perfecute
you." This certainly is not common-place
morality. It is very original. It fhews at
leaft (and it is for this purpofe we produce
it) that no two things can be more different
than the Heroic and the Chriftian character.

Now the author, to whom I refer, has
not only remarked this difference more
ftrongly than any preceding writer, but has
proved, in contradiction to firft impreffions,
to popular opinion, to the encomiums of
orators and poets, and even to the fuffrages
of hiftorians and moralifts, that the latter
character poffeffes the moft of true worth,
both as being moft difficult either to be acquired or fuftained, and as contributing moft
to the happinefs and tranquillity of focial
life. The ftate of his argument is as follows:

I. If

I. If this difpofition were univerfal, the cafe is clear: the world would be a fociety of friends. Whereas, if the other difpofition were univerfal, it would produce a fcene of univerfal contention. The world could not hold a generation of fuch men.

II. If, what is the fact, the difpofition be partial; if a few be actuated by it, amongft a multitude who are not; in whatever degree it does prevail, in the fame proportion it prevents, allays, and terminates quarrels, the great difturbers of human happinefs, and the great fources of human mifery, fo far as man's happinefs and mifery depend upon man. Without this difpofition enmities **muft** not only be frequent, but, once begun, muft be eternal; for each retaliation being a frefh injury, and, confequently, requiring a frefh *fatisfaction*, no period can be affigned to the reciprocation of affronts, and to the progrefs of hatred, but that which clofes the lives, or at leaft the intercourfe, of the parties.

I would only add to thefe obfervations,

that, although the former of the two characters above deſcribed may be occaſionally
uſeful; although, perhaps, a great general,
or a great ſtateſman, may be formed by it,
and theſe may be inſtruments of important
benefits to mankind, yet is this nothing
more than what is true of many qualities,
which are acknowledged to be vicious.
Envy is a quality of this ſort. I know not
a ſtronger ſtimulus to exertion. Many a
ſcholar, many an artiſt, many a ſoldier, has
been produced by it. Nevertheleſs, ſince
in its general effects it is noxious, it is properly condemned, certainly is not praiſed,
by ſober moraliſts.

It was a portion of the ſame character as
that we are defending, or rather of his love
of the ſame character, which our Saviour
diſplayed, in his repeated correction of the
ambition of his diſciples; his frequent admonitions, that greatneſs with them was to
conſiſt in humility; his cenſure of that love
of diſtinction, and greedineſs of ſuperiority,
which the chief **perſons** amongſt his countrymen

trymen were wont, on all occafions, great
and little, to betray. " They (the fcribes
and pharifees) love the uppermoft rooms at
feafts, and the chief feats in the fynagogues,
and greetings in the markets, and to be
called of men, Rabbi, Rabbi. But be not
ye called Rabbi, for one is your mafter,
even Chrift, and all ye are brethren ; and
call no man your father upon the earth, for
one is your father, which is in heaven ;
neither be ye called mafters, for one is your
mafter, even Chrift ; but he that is greateft
among *you* fhall be your fervant, and whofoever fhall exalt himfelf fhall be abafed,
and he that fhall humble himfelf fhall be
exalted *." I make no farther remark upon
thefe paffages, (becaufe they are, in truth,
only a repetition of the doctrine, different
expreffions of the principle, which we have
already ftated) except that fome of the paffages, efpecially our Lord's advice to the
guefts at an entertainment, (Luke xiv. 7.)
feem to extend the rule to what we call

* Mat. xxiii. 6. See alfo Mark xii. 39. Luke xx.
43. xiv. 7.

manners ;

manners; which was, both regular in point of confiftency, and not fo much beneath the dignity of our Lord's miffion as may at firft fight be fuppofed, for bad manners are bad morals.

It is fufficiently apparent, that the precepts we have recited, or rather the difpofition which thefe precepts inculcate, relate to perfonal conduct from perfonal motives; to cafes in which men act from impulfe; for themfelves, and from themfelves. When it comes to be confidered, what is neceffary to be done for the fake of the public, and out of a regard to the general welfare, (which confideration, for the moft part, ought exclufively to govern the duties of men in public ftations) it comes to a cafe to which the rules do not belong. This diftinction is plain; and, if it were lefs fo, the confequence would not be much felt, for it is very feldom that, in the intercourfe of private life, men act with public views. The perfonal motives, from which they do act, the rule regulates.

The

The preference of the patient to the heroic character, which we have here noticed, and which the reader will find explained at large in the work to which we have referred him, is a peculiarity in the Christian institution, which I propose as an argument of wisdom, very much beyond the situation and natural character of the person who delivered it.

II. A *second* argument, drawn from the morality of the New Testament, is the stress which is laid by our Saviour upon the regulation of the thoughts. And I place this consideration next to the other, because they are connected. The other related to the malicious passions ; this to the voluptuous. Together they comprehend the whole character.

" Out of the *heart* proceed evil thoughts, murders, adulteries, fornications, &c.———— These are the things which defile a man." Mat. xv. 19.

D 3   " Wo

" Wo unto you fcribes and pharifees, hy-
pocrites, for ye make clean the outfide of
the cup and of the platter, but *within* they
are full of extortion and excefs.—Ye are
like unto whited fepulchres, which indeed
appear beautiful outward, but are within full
of dead men's bones, and of all uncleannefs;
even fo ye alfo outwardly appear righteous
unto men, but *within* ye are full of hypo-
crify and iniquity." Mat. xxiii. 25. 27.

And more particularly that ftrong expreffion, (Mat. v. 28.) " Whofoever looketh
on a woman to luft after her, hath committed adultery with her already in his
heart."

There can be no doubt with any reflect-
ing mind, but that the propenfities of our
nature muft be fubjected to regulation ; but
the queftion is, *where* the check ought to be
placed, upon the thought, or only upon
action. In this queftion, our Saviour, in
the texts here quoted, has pronounced a
decifive judgment. He makes the control

of

of thought effential. Internal purity with him is every thing. Now I contend that this is the only difcipline which can fucceed; in other words, that a moral fyftem, which prohibits actions, but leaves the thoughts at liberty, will be ineffectual, and is therefore unwife. I know not how to go about the proof of a point, which depends upon experience, and upon a knowledge of the human conftitution, better than by citing the judgement of perfons, who appear to have given great attention to the fubject, and to be well qualified to form a true opinion about it. Boerhaave, fpeaking of this very declaration of our Saviour, " Whofoever looketh on a woman to luft after her, hath already committed adultery with her in his heart," and underftanding it, as we do, to contain an injunction to lay the check upon the thoughts, was wont to fay, that " our Saviour knew mankind better than Socrates." Haller, who has recorded this faying of Boerhaave's, adds to it the following remarks of his own*: " It did not efcape the obfer-

---

* Letters to his Daughter.

D 4　　　　　　　　vation

vation of our Saviour, that the rejection of any evil thoughts was the beft defence againft vice; for, when a debauched perfon fills his imagination with impure pictures, the licentious ideas which he recalls, fail not to ftimulate his defires with a degree of violence which he cannot refift. This will be followed by gratification, unlefs fome external obftacle fhould prevent him from the commiffion of a fin, which he had internally refolved on." "Every moment of time (fays our author) that is fpent in meditations upon fin, increafes the power of the dangerous object which has poffeffed our imagination." I fuppofe thefe reflections will be generally affented to.

III. Thirdly, had a teacher of morality been afked concerning a general principle of conduct, and for a fhort rule of life; and had he inftructed the perfon who confulted him, " conftantly to refer his actions to what he believed to be the will of his Creator, and conftantly to have in view, not his own intereft and gratification alone, but

the

the happinefs and comfort of thofe about him," he would have been thought, I doubt not, in any age of the world, and in any, even the moft improved ftate of morals, to have delivered a judicious anfwer: becaufe, by the firft direction, he fuggefted the only motive which acts fteadily and uniformly, in fight and out of fight, in familiar oc-currences and under preffing temptations; and in the fecond, he corrected, what, of all tendencies in the human character, ftands moft in need of correction, *felfifhnefs*, or a contempt of other men's conveniency and fatisfaction. In eftimating the value of a moral rule, we are to have regard, not only to the particular duty, but the general fpirit; not only to what it directs us to do, but to the character which a compliance with its direction is likely to form in us. So, in the prefent inftance, the rule here recited will never fail to make him who obeys it, *confiderate*, not only of the rights, but of the feelings of other men, bodily and men-tal, in great matters **and** in fmall; of the eafe, the accommodation, **the** felf-compla-
cency

cency of all with whom he has any concern, efpecially of all who are in his power, or dependent upon his will.

Now what, in the moft applauded philofopher of the moft enlightened age of the world, would have been deemed worthy of his wifdom, and of his character, to fay, our Saviour hath faid, and upon juft fuch an occafion as that which we have feigned.

" Then one of them, which was a lawyer, afked him a queftion, tempting him, and faying, Mafter, which is the great commandment in the law ? Jefus faid unto him, Thou fhalt love the Lord thy God, with all thy heart, and with all thy foul, and with all thy mind; this is the firft and great commandment ; and the fecond is like unto it, Thou fhalt love thy neighbour as thyfelf : on thefe two commandments hang all the law and the prophets." Mat. xxii. 35—40.

The fecond precept occurs in St. Matthew, on another occafion fimilar to this

(xix.

(xix. 16.), and both of them upon a third
fimilar occafion in Luke (x. 27). In thefe
two latter inftances, the queftion propofed
was, " What fhall I do to inherit eternal
life ?"

Upon all thefe occafions, I confider the
words of our Saviour as expreffing precifely
the fame thing as what I have put into the
mouth of the moral philofopher. Nor do I
think that it detracts much from the merit
of the anfwer, that thefe precepts are extant
in the Mofaic code : for his laying his fin-
ger, if I may fo fay, upon thefe precepts ;
his drawing them out from the reft of that
voluminous inftitution ; his ftating of them,
not fimply amongft the number, but as the
greateft and the fum of all the others ; in a
word, his propofing of them to his hearers
for their rule and principle, was our Saviour's own.

And what our Saviour had faid upon the
fubject, appears to me to have *fixed* the fen-
timent amongft his followers.

5

St.

St. Paul has it exprefsly, " If there be any other commandment, it is briefly comprehended in this faying, Thou fhalt love thy neighbour as thyfelf*;" and again, " For all the law is fulfilled in one word, even in this, Thou fhalt love thy neighbour as thyfelf †."

St. John, in like manner, " This commandment have we from him, that he who loveth God, love his brother alfo ‡."

St. Peter, not very differently, " Seeing that ye have purified your fouls in obeying the truth, through the fpirit, unto unfeigned love of the brethren, fee that ye love one another with a pure heart fervently §."

And it is fo well known, as to require no citations to verify it, that this love, or charity, or, in other words, regard to the welfare of others, runs in various forms through all the preceptive parts of the apo-

---

* Rom. xiii. 7.   † Gal. v. 14.
‡ 1 John iv. 21.   § 1 Pet. i. 22.

ftolic

ftolic writings. It is the theme of all their exhortations, that with which their morality begins and ends, from which all their details and enumerations fet out, and into which they return.

And that this temper, for fome time at leaft, defcended in its purity to fucceeding Chriftians, is attefted by one of the earlieft and beft of the remaining writings of the apoftolical fathers, the epiftle of the Roman Clement. The meeknefs of the Chriftian character reigns throughout the whole of that excellent piece. The occafion called for it. It was to compofe the diffenfions of the church of Corinth. And the venerable hearer of the apoftles does not fall fhort, in the difplay of this principle, of the fineft paffages of their writings. He calls to the remembrance of the Corinthian church its former character, in which "ye were all of you (he tells them) humble minded, not boafting of any thing, defiring rather to be fubject than to govern, to give than to receive, being content with the portion God

had

had difpenfed to you, and hearkening dili-
gently to his word ; ye were enlarged in
your bowels, having his fufferings always
before your eyes. Ye contended day and
night for the whole brotherhood, that with
compaffion and a good confcience the number of his elect might be faved. Ye were
fincere, and without offence, towards each
other. Ye bewailed every one his neighbour's fins, efteeming their defects your
own*." His prayer for them was for the
" return of peace, long fuffering, and pa-
tience†." And his advice to thofe, who
might have been the occafion of difference
in the fociety, is conceived in the true fpirit,
and with a perfect knowledge, of the Chriftian character. " Who is there among you
that is generous ? Who that is compaffionate ?
Who that has any charity ? Let him fay,
if this fedition, this contention, and thefe
fchifms, be upon my account, I am ready
to depart, to go away whitherfoever ye
pleafe, and do whatfoever ye fhall command

---

* Ep. Clem. Rom. c. 2. Abp. Wake's Tranflation.
† Ib. c. 58.

me,

me, only let the flock of Chrift be in peace,
with the elders who are fet over it. He
that fhall do this, fhall get to himfelf a very
great honour in the Lord; and there is no
place but what will be ready to receive him,
for the earth is the Lord's, and the fullnefs
thereof. Thefe things they, who have their
converfation towards God, not to be repent-
ed of, both have done, and will always be
ready to do*."

This facred principle, this earneft recommendation of forbearance, lenity, and forgivenefs, mixes with all the writings of that
age. There are more quotations in the
apoftolical fathers of texts which relate to
thefe points, than of any other. Chrift's
fayings had ftruck them. "Not rendering
(faith Polycarp, the difciple of John) evil
for evil, or railing for railing, or ftriking for
ftriking, or curfing for curfing†." Again,
fpeaking of fome whofe behaviour had given
great offence, "Be ye moderate (fays he)
upon this occafion, and look not upon fuch

* Ep. Clem. Rom. c. 54.　　† Pol. Ep. ad Phil. c. 2.

as

as enemies, but call them back as suffering
and erring members, that ye save your whole
body*."

" Be ye mild at their anger (saith Ignatius,
the companion of Polycarp), humble at their
boastings, to their blasphemies return your
prayers, to their error your firmness in the
faith; when they are cruel, be ye gentle;
not endeavouring to imitate their ways, let
us be their brethren in all kindness and moderation, but let us be followers of the Lord,
for who was ever more unjustly used, more
destitute, more despised?"

IV. A fourth quality, by which the morality of the gospel is distinguished, is the
exclusion of regard to fame and reputation.

" Take heed that ye do not your alms
before men, to be seen of them, otherwise
ye have no reward of your father which is
in heaven.†"

* Pol. Ep. ad Phil. c. 11.   † Mat. vi. 1.

" When

" When thou prayeſt, enter into thy
cloſet, and when thou haſt ſhut thy door,
pray to thy father which is in ſecret; and
thy father, which ſeeth in ſecret, ſhall reward thee openly*."

And the rule by parity of reaſon is extended to all other virtues.

I do not think, that either in theſe, or in
any other paſſage of the New Teſtament,
the purſuit of fame is ſtated as a vice; it is
only ſaid that an action, to be virtuous, muſt
be independent of it. I would alſo obſerve,
that it is not publicity, but oſtentation, which
is prohibited; not the mode, but the motive
of the action, which is regulated. A good
man will prefer that mode, as well as thoſe
objects of his beneficence, by which he can
produce the greateſt effect; and the view of
this purpoſe may dictate ſometimes publication, and ſometimes concealment. Either
the one or the other may be the *mode* of

* Mat. vi. 6.

the action, according as the end to be promoted by it appears to require. But from
the *motive*, the reputation of the deed, and
the fruits and advantage of that reputation
to ourfelves, muft be fhut out, or, in whatever proportion they are not fo, the action
in that proportion fails of being virtuous.

This exclufion of regard to human opinion, is a difference, not fo much in the
duties, to which the teachers of virtue would
perfuade mankind, as in the manner and
topics of perfuafion. And in this view the
difference is great. When *we* fet about to
give advice, our lectures are full of the advantages of character, of the regard that is
due to appearances and to opinion; of what
the world, efpecially of what the good or
great, will think and fay; of the value of
public efteem, and of the qualities by which
men acquire it. Widely different from this
was our Saviour's inftruction: and the difference was founded upon the beft reafons.
For, however the care of reputation, the
authority of public opinion, or even of the

opinion

opinion of good men, the fatisfaction of being well received and well thought of, the
benefit of being known and diftinguifhed,
are topics, to which we are fain to have recourfe in our exhortations, the true virtue
is that which difcards thefe confiderations
abfolutely; and which retires from them all
to the fingle internal purpofe of pleafing
God. This at leaft was the virtue which
our Saviour taught. And in teaching of
this, he not only confined the views of his
followers to the proper meafure and principle of human duty, but acted in confiftency with his office as a monitor from
heaven.

Next to what our Saviour taught, may
be confidered the manner of his teaching;
which was extremely peculiar, yet, I think,
precifely adapted to the peculiarity of his
character and fituation. His leffons did not
confift of difquifitions; of any thing like
moral effays, or like fermons, or like fet
treatifes upon the feveral points which he
mentioned. When he delivered a precept,

it

it was feldom that he added any proof or argument; ftill feldomer, that he accompanied it with, what all precepts require, limitations and diftinctions. His inftructions were conceived in fhort emphatic fententious rules, in occafional reflections, or in round maxims. I do not think that this was a natural, or would have been a proper method, for a philofopher or a moralift; or that it is a method which can be fuccefsfully imitated by us. But I contend that it was fuitable to the character which Chrift affumed, and to the fituation in which, as a teacher, he was placed. He produced himfelf as a meffenger from God. He put the truth of what he taught upon authority *. In the choice, therefore, of his mode of teaching, the purpofe by him to be confulted was *impreffion* ; becaufe conviction, which forms the principal end of our difcourfes, was to arife in the minds of his fol-

---

* *I* fay unto you, Swear not at all; *I* fay unto you, Refift not evil; *I* fay unto you, Love your enemies †.

† Mat. v. 34. 39. 44.

lowers

lowers from a different fource, from their
refpect to his perfon and authority. Now,
for the purpofe of impreffion fingly and exclufively (I repeat again, that we are not
here to confider the convincing of the underftanding) I know nothing which would
have fo great force, as ftrong ponderous
maxims, frequently urged, and frequently
brought back to the thoughts of the hearers.
I know nothing that could in this view be
faid better, than " Do unto others, as ye
would that others fhould do unto you ; the
firft and great commandment is, Thou fhalt
love the Lord thy God ; and the fecond is
like unto it, Thou fhalt love thy neighbour
as thyfelf." It muft alfo be remembered,
that our Lord's miniftry, upon the fuppofition either of one year or of three, compared with his work, was of fhort duration ;
that, within this time, he had many places
to vifit, various audiences to addrefs ; that
his perfon was generally befieged by crowds
of followers ; that he was, fometimes, driven
away from the place where he was teaching,
by perfecution, and, at other times, thought

fit

fit to withdraw himself from the commotions of the populace. Under these circumstances, nothing appears to have been so practicable, or likely to be so efficacious, as leaving, wherever he came, concise lessons of duty. These circumstances at least shew the necessity he was under of comprising what he delivered within a small compass. In particular, his sermon upon the mount ought always to be considered with a view to these observations. The question is not, whether a fuller, a more accurate, a more systematic, or a more argumentative discourse upon morals might not have been pronounced, but whether more could have been said in the same room, better adapted to the exigencies of the hearers, or better calculated for the purpose of impression. Seen in this light, it hath always appeared to me to be admirable. Dr. Lardner thought that this discourse was made up of what Christ had said at different times, and upon different occasions, several of which occasions are noticed in St. Luke's narrative. I can perceive no reason for this opinion. I
believe

believe that our Lord delivered this difcourfe at one time and place, in the manner related by St. Matthew, and that he repeated the fame rules and maxims at different times, as opportunity or occafion fuggefted ; that they were often in his mouth, were repeated to different audiences, and in various con-verfations.

It is incidental to this mode of moral in-ftruction, which proceeds not by proof but upon authority, not by difquifition but by precept, that the rules will be conceived in abfolute terms, leaving the application, and the diftinctions that attend it, to the reafon of the hearer. It is likewife to be expected, that they will be delivered in terms, by fo much the more forcible and energetic, as they have to encounter natural or general propenfities. It is further alfo to be re-marked, that many of thofe ftrong inftances, which appear in our Lord's fermon, fuch as " If any man will fmite thee on the right cheek, turn to him the other alfo : If any man will fue thee at the law, and take away

E 4 thy

thy coat, let him have thy cloke alfo: Whofoever fhall compel thee to go a mile, go
with him twain;" though they appear in
the form of fpecific precepts, are intended
as defcriptive of difpofition and character.
A fpecific compliance with the precepts
would be of little value, but the difpofition
which they inculcate is of the higheft. He
who fhould content himfelf with waiting
for the occafion, and with literally obferving the rule when the occafion offered,
would do nothing, or worfe than nothing;
but he who confiders the character and difpofition which is hereby inculcated, and
places that difpofition before him as the
model to which he fhould bring his own,
takes, perhaps, the beft poffible method of
improving the benevolence, and of calming
and rectifying the vices of his temper.

If it be faid that this difpofition is unat-
tainable, I anfwer, fo is all perfection;
ought therefore a moralift to recommend
imperfections? One excellency, however,
of our Saviour's rules is, that they are
                                    either

either never miftaken, or never fo miftaken
as to do harm. I could feign a hundred
cafes, in which the literal application of the
rule, " of doing to others as we would that
others fhould do unto us," might miflead
us : but I never yet met with the man who
was actually mifled by it. Notwithftanding that our Lord bid his followers " not to
refift evil," and " to forgive the enemy,
who fhould trefpafs againft them, not till
feven times but till feventy times feven,"
the Chriftian world has hitherto fuffered little by too much placability or forbearance.
I would repeat once more, what has already
been twice remarked, that thefe rules were
defigned to regulate perfonal conduct from
perfonal motives, and for this purpofe
alone.

I think that thefe obfervations will affift
us greatly in placing our Saviour's conduct,
as a moral teacher, in a proper point of
view; efpecially when it is confidered, that
to deliver moral difquifitions was no part of
his defign, to teach morality at all was only
a fub-

a fubordinate part of it, his great bufinefs being to fupply, what was much more wanting than leffons of morality, ftronger moral fanctions, and clearer affurances of a future judgement *.

The *parables* of the New Teftament are, many of them, fuch as would have done honour to any book in the world, I do not

---

* Some appear to require in a religious fyftem, or in the books which profefs to deliver that fyftem, minute directions for every cafe and occurrence that may arife. This, fay they, is neceffary to render a revelation perfect, efpecially one which has for its object the regulation of human conduct. Now, how prolix, and yet how incomplete and unavailing, fuch an attempt muft have been, is proved by one notable example: " The Indoo and Muffulman religion are inftitutes of civil law, regulating the minuteft queftions both of property, and of all queftions which come under the cognizance of the magiftrate. And to what length details of this kind are neceffarily carried, when once begun, may be underftood from an anecdote of the Muffulman code, which we have received from the moft refpectable authority, that not lefs than *feventy-five thoufand* traditional precepts have been promulgated." Hamilton's tranflation of the Hedaya, or Guide.

mean

mean in ftyle and diction, but in the choice of the fubjects, in the ftructure of the narratives, in the aptnefs, propriety, and force of the circumftances woven into them; and in fome, as that of the good Samaritan, the prodigal fon, the pharifee and the publican, in an union of pathos and fimplicity, which, in the beft productions of human genius, is the fruit only of a much exercifed and well-cultivated judgement.

The Lord's prayer, for a fucceffion of folemn thoughts, for fixing the attention upon a few great points, for fuitablenefs to every condition, for fufficiency, for concifenefs without obfcurity, for the weight and real importance of its petitions, is without an equal or a rival.

From whence did thefe come? Whence had this man this wifdom? Was our Saviour, in fact, a well-inftructed philofopher, whilft he is reprefented to us as an illiterate peafant? Or fhall we fay that fome early Chriftians of tafte and education compofed

thefe

thefe pieces, and afcribed them to Chrift?
Befide all other incredibilities in this account, I anfwer, with Dr. Jortin, that they
could not do it. No fpecimens of compofition, which the Chriftians of the firft century have left us, authorize us to believe
that they were equal to the tafk. And how
little qualified the Jews, the countrymen
and companions of Chrift, were to affift him
in the undertaking, may be judged of from
the traditions and writings of theirs which
were the neareft to that age. The whole
collection of the Talmud is one continued
proof, into what follies they fell whenever
they left their Bible; and how little capable
they were of furnifhing out fuch leffons as
Chrift delivered.

But there is ftill another view, in which
our Lord's difcourfes deferve to be confidered; and that is, in their *negative* character, not in what they did, but in what they
did not contain. Under this head, the following reflections appear to me to poffefs
fome weight.

I. They

I. They exhibit no particular defcription
of the invifible world. The future happinefs of the good, and the mifery of the bad,
which is all we want to be affured of, is
directly and pofitively affirmed, and is reprefented by metaphors and comparifons,
which were plainly intended as metaphors
and comparifons, and as nothing more. As
to the reft, a folemn referve is maintained.
The queftion concerning the woman who
had been married to feven brothers, " Whofe
fhall fhe be on the refurrection ?" was of a
nature calculated to have drawn from Chrift
a more circumftantial account of the ftate
of the human fpecies in their future exiftence. He cut fhort, however, the enquiry
by an anfwer, which at once rebuked in-
truding curiofity, and was agreeable to the
beft apprehenfions we are able to form
upon the fubject, viz. " That they who are
accounted worthy of that refurrection, fhall
be as the angels of God in heaven." I lay
a ftrefs upon this referve, becaufe it repels
the fufpicion of enthufiafm ; for enthufiafm
is wont to expatiate **upon** the condition of
the

the departed, above all other fubjects; and
with a wild particularity. It is moreover
a topic which is always liftened to with
greedinefs. The teacher, therefore, whofe
principal purpofe is to draw upon himfelf
attention, is fure to be full of it. The Koran
of Mahomet is half made up of it.

II. Our Lord enjoined no aufterities. He
not only enjoined none as abfolute duties,
but he recommended none as carrying men
to a higher degree of divine favour. Place
Chriftianity, in this refpect, by the fide of
all inftitutions which have been founded in
the fanaticifm, either of their author, or of
his firft followers : or rather compare, in
this refpect, Chriftianity as it came from
Chrift, with the fame religion after it fell
into other hands; with the extravagant merit very foon afcribed to celibacy, folitude,
voluntary poverty; with the rigours of an
afcetic, and the vows of a monaftic life;
the hair fhirt, the watchings, the midnight
prayers, the obmutefcence, the gloom and
morti-

mortification, of religious orders, and of thofe who afpired to religious perfection.

III. Our Saviour uttered no impaffioned devotion. There was no heat in his piety, or in the language in which he expreffed it; no vehement or rapturous ejaculations, no violent urgency in his prayers. The Lord's prayer is a model of calm devotion. His words in the garden are unaffected ex-preffions, of a deep indeed, but fober piety. He never appears to have been worked up into any thing like that elation, or that emotion of fpirits, which is occafionally ob-ferved in moft of thofe, to whom the name of enthufiaft can in any degree be applied. I feel a refpect for methodifts, becaufe I believe that there is to be found amongft them, much fincere piety, and availing, though not always well-informed, Chriftia-nity: yet I never attended a meeting of theirs, but I came away with the reflection, how different what I heard was from what I read; I do not mean in doctrine, with
which,

which, at prefent, I have no concern, but in manner; how different from the calmnefs, the fobriety, the good fenfe, and, I may add, the ftrength and authority, of our Lord's difcourfes.

IV. It is very ufual with the human mind, to fubftitute forwardnefs and fervency in a particular caufe, for the merit of general and regular morality; and it is natural, and politic alfo, in the leader of a fect or party, to encourage fuch a difpofition in his followers. Chrift did not overlook this turn of thought: yet, though avowedly placing himfelf at the head of a new inftitution, he notices it only to condemn it. " Not every one that faith unto me, Lord, Lord, fhall enter into the kingdom of heaven, but he that doeth the will of my Father which is in heaven: many will fay unto me in that day, Lord, Lord, have we not prophefied in thy name? and in thy name have caft out devils? and in thy name done many wonderful works? and then will I profefs

unto

unto you, I never knew you, depart from me, *ye that work iniquity* *." So far was the author of Chriſtianity from courting the attachment of his followers by any ſacrifice of principle, or by a condeſcenſion to the errors which even zeal in his ſervice might have inſpired! This was a proof both of ſincerity and judgement.

V. Nor, fifthly, did he fall in with any of the depraved faſhions of his country, or with the natural biaſs of his own education. Bred up a Jew, under a religion extremely technical, in an age, and amongſt a people, more tenacious of the ceremonies, than of any other part of that religion, he delivered an inſtitution, containing leſs of ritual, and that more ſimple, than is to be found in any religion, which ever prevailed amongſt mankind. We have known, I do allow, examples of an enthuſiaſm, which has ſwept away all external ordinances before it. But this ſpirit certainly did not dictate our Saviour's conduct, either in his treatment of

* Mat. vii. 21, 22.

the religion of his country, or in the formation of his own inftitution. In both he difplayed the foundnefs and moderation of his judgement. He cenfured an overftrained fcrupuloufnefs, or perhaps an affectation of fcrupuloufnefs, about the fabbath; but how did he cenfure it? not by contemning or decrying the inftitution itfelf, but by declaring that " the fabbath was made for man, not man for the fabbath;" that is to fay, that the fabbath was to be fubordinate to its purpofe, and that that purpofe was the real good of thofe who were the fubjects of the law. The fame concerning the nicety of fome of the pharifees, in paying tithes of the moft trifling articles, accompanied with a neglect of juftice, fidelity, and mercy. He finds fault with them for mifplacing their anxiety. He does not fpeak difrefpectfully of the law of tithes, or of their obfervance of it, but he affigns to each clafs of duties its proper ftation in the fcale of moral importance. All this might be expected perhaps from a well-inftructed, cool, and judicious philofopher, but was

not

not to be looked for from an illiterate Jew, certainly not from an impetuous enthusiaft.

VI. Nothing could be more quibbling, than were the comments and expofitions of the Jewifh doctors, at that time; nothing fo puerile as their diftinctions. Their evafion of the fifth commandment, their expofition of the law of oaths, are fpecimens of the bad tafte in morals which then prevailed. Whereas in a numerous collection of our Saviour's apothegms, many of them referring to fundry precepts of the Jewifh law, there is not to be found one example of fophiftry, or of falfe fubtlety, or of any thing approaching thereunto.

VII. The national temper of the Jews was intolerant, narrow-minded, and excluding. In Jefus, on the contrary, whether we regard his leffons or his example, we fee not only benevolence, but benevolence the moft enlarged and comprehenfive. In the parable of the good Samaritan, the very point of the ftory is, that the perfon re-

lieved

lieved by him, was the national and religious enemy of his benefactor. Our Lord
declared the equity of the divine admini-
ſtration, when he told the Jews (what, probably, they were ſurpriſed to hear) " That
many ſhould come from the eaſt and weſt,
and ſhould ſit down with Abraham, Iſaac,
and Jacob, in the kingdom of heaven, but
that the children of the kingdom ſhoud be
caſt into outer darkneſs *." His reproof of
the haſty zeal of his diſciples, who would
needs call down fire from heaven to re-
venge an affront put upon their Maſter,
ſhews the lenity of his character, and of
his religion; and his opinion of the manner
in which the moſt unreaſonable opponents
ought to be treated, or at leaſt of the manner in which they ought not to be treated.
The terms, in which his rebuke was conveyed, deſerve to be noticed :—" Ye know
not what manner of ſpirit ye are of †."

VIII. Laſtly, amongſt the negative quali-

---

* Mat. viii. 11.   † Luke ix. 55.

ties of our religion, as it came out of the
hands of its founder and his apoftles, we
may reckon its complete abftraction from
all views either of ecclefiaftical or civil policy; or, to meet a language much in fafhion
with fome men, from the politics either of
priefts or ftatefmen. Chrift's declaration,
that " his kingdom was not of this world,"
recorded by John; his evafion of the queftion, whether it was lawful or not to give
tribute unto Cefar, mentioned by the three
other evangelifts; his reply to an application
that was made to him, to interpofe his authority in a queftion of property, " Man,
who made me a ruler or a judge over you?"
afcribed to him by St. Luke; his declining
to exercife the office of a criminal judge in
the cafe of the woman taken in adultery, as
related by John, are all intelligible fignifica-
tions of our Saviour's fentiments upon this
head. And with refpect to *politics*, in the
ufual fenfe of that word, or difcuffions concerning different forms of government,
Chriftianity declines every queftion upon
the fubject. Whilft politicians are difputing

about

about monarchies, ariftocracies, and republics, the gofpel is alike applicable, ufeful, and friendly to them all ; inafmuch as, 1ft, it tends to make men virtuous, and as it is eafier to govern good men than bad men under any conftitution : as, 2dly, it ftates obedience to government in ordinary cafes, to be not merely a fubmiffion to force, but a duty of confcience : as, 3dly, it induces difpofitions favourable to public tranquillity, a Chriftian's chief care being to pafs quietly through this world to a better : as, 4thly, it prays for communities, and for the governors of communities, of whatever defcription or denomination they be, with a folicitude and fervency proportioned to the influence which they poffefs upon human happinefs. All which, in my opinion, is juft as it fhould be. Had there been more to be found in fcripture of a political nature, or convertible to political purpofes, the worft ufe would have been made of it, on whichever fide it feemed to lie.

When, therefore, we confider Chrift as a

moral

moral teacher (remembring that this was only a secondary part of his office; and that morality, by the nature of the subject, does not admit of discovery, properly so called); when we consider, either what he taught, or what he did not teach, either the substance or the manner of his instruction; his preference of solid to popular virtues, of a character which is commonly despised, to a character which is universally extolled; his placing, in our licentious vices, the check in the right place, viz. upon the thoughts; his collecting of human duty into two well devised rules, his repetition of these rules, the stress he laid upon them, especially in comparison with positive duties, and his fixing thereby the sentiments of his followers; his exclusion of all regard to reputation in our devotion and alms, and, by parity of reason, in our other virtues: when we consider that his instructions were delivered in a form calculated for impression, the precise purpose in his situation to be consulted; and that they were illustrated by parables, the choice and structure of which

would

would have been admired in any compoſi-
tion whatever : when we obſerve him free
from the uſual ſymptoms of enthuſiaſm,
heat and vehemence in devotion, auſterity
in inſtitutions, and a wild particularity in
the deſcriptions of a future ſtate ; free alſo
from the depravities of his age and country;
without ſuperſtition amongſt the moſt ſu-
perſtitious of men, yet not decrying po-
ſitive diſtinctions or external obſervances,
but ſoberly recalling them to the principle
of their eſtabliſhment, and to their place in
the ſcale of human duties ; without ſophiſ-
try or trifling, amidſt teachers remarkable
for nothing ſo much, as frivolous ſubtleties
and quibbling expoſitions ; candid and liberal in his judgement of the reſt of mankind, although belonging to a people, who
affected a ſeparate claim to divine favour,
and, in conſequence of that opinion, prone
to uncharitableneſs, partiality, and reſtric-
tion : when we find, in his religion, no
ſcheme of building up a hierarchy, or of
miniſtring to the views of human governments : in a word, when we compare Chriſtianity,

tianity, as it came from its author, either with other religions, or with itself in other hands, the moſt reluctant underſtanding will be induced to acknowledge the probity, I think alſo, the good ſenſe of thoſe, to whom it owes its origin ; and that ſome regard is due to the teſtimony of ſuch men, when they declare their knowledge that the reli- gion proceeded from God ; and when they appeal, for the truth of their aſſertion, to miracles which they wrought, or which they ſaw.

Perhaps the qualities which we obſerve in the religion, may be thought to prove ſomething more. They would have been extraordinary, had the religion come from any perſon ; from the perſon, from whom it did come, they are exceedingly ſo. What was Jeſus in external appearance ? a Jewiſh peaſant, the ſon of a carpenter, living with his father and mother in a remote province of Paleſtine, until the time that he pro- duced himſelf in his public character. He had no maſter to inſtruct or prompt him.

He

He had read no books, but the works of
Mofes and the prophets. He had vifited no
polifhed cities. He had received no leffons
from Socrates or Plato ; nothing to form in
him a tafte or judgement, different from
that of the reft of his countrymen, and of
perfons of the fame rank of life with himfelf. Suppofing it to be true, which it is
not, that all his points of morality might be
picked out of Greek and Roman writings,
they were writings which *he* had never feen.
Suppofing them to be no more, than what
fome or other had taught in various times
and places, he could not collect them together.

Who were his coadjutors in the undertaking, the perfons **into** whofe hands the
religion came after **his** death ? a few fifhermen upon the lake of Tiberias, perfons juft
as uneducated, and for the purpofe of framing rules of morality, as unpromifing as
himfelf. Suppofe the miffion to be real, all
this is accounted for ; the unfuitablenefs of
the authors to the production, of the characters

racters to the undertaking, no longer fur-
prifes us; but, without *reality*, it is very
difficult to explain, how fuch a fyftem
fhould proceed from fuch perfons. Chrift
was not like any other carpenter; the apoftles were not like any other fifhermen.

But the fubject is not exhaufted by thefe
obfervations. That portion of it, which is
moft reducible to points of argument, has
been ftated, and, I truft, truly. There are,
however, fome topics, of a more diffufe nature, which yet deferve to be propofed to
the reader's attention.

The *character of Chrift* is a part of the
morality of the gofpel: one ftrong obfervation upon which is, that, neither as reprefented by his followers, nor as attacked by
his enemies, is he charged with any perfonal
vice. This remark is as old as Origen :—
" Though innumerable lies and calumnies
had been forged againft the venerable Jefus,
none had dared to charge him with an in-
temper-

temperance*." Not a reflection upon his moral character, not an imputation or suspicion of any offence against purity and chastity, appears for five hundred years after his birth. This faultlessness is more peculiar than we are apt to imagine. Some stain pollutes the morals or the morality of almost every other teacher, and of every other lawgiver†. Zeno the stoic, and Diogenes the cynic, fell into the foulest impurities; of which also Socrates himself was more than suspected. Solon forbad unnatural crimes to slaves. Lycurgus tolerated theft as a part of education. Plato recommended a community of women. Aristotle maintained the general right of making war upon Barbarians. The elder Cato was remarkable for the ill usage of his slaves. The younger gave up the person of his wife. One loose principle is found in almost all the Pagan moralists; is distinctly, however, perceived in the writings of Plato, Xenophon, Cicero,

* Or. Ep. Celf. l. 3. num. 36. ed. Bened.
† See many instances collected by Grotius de Ver. in the notes to his second book, p. 116. Pocock's edition.

Seneca,

Seneca, Epictetus, and that is, the allowing,
and even the recommending to their difciples, a compliance with the religion, and
with the religious rites, of every country
into which they came. In fpeaking of the
founders of new inftitutions, we cannot
forget Mahomet. His licentious tranfgreffions of his own licentious rules; his abufe
of the character which he affumed, and of
the power which he had acquired, for the
purpofes of perfonal and privileged indulgence; his avowed claim of a fpecial per-
miffion from heaven of unlimited fenfuality,
is known to every reader, as it is confeffed
by every writer, of the Moflem ftory.

Secondly, in the hiftories which are left
us of Jefus Chrift, although very fhort, and
although dealing in narrative, and not in
obfervation or panegyric, we perceive, befide the abfence of every appearance of vice,
traces of devotion, humility, benignity, mildnefs, patience, prudence. I fpeak of *traces*
of thefe qualities, becaufe the qualities themfelves are to be collected from incidents;
inafmuch

inafmuch as the terms are never ufed of Chrift in the gofpels, nor is any formal character of him drawn in any part of the New Teftament.

Thus we fee the *devoutnefs* of his mind, in his frequent retirement to folitary prayer*; in his habitual giving of thanks†; in his reference of the beauties and operations of nature to the bounty of providence ‡; in his earneft addreffes to his Father, more particularly that fhort but folemn one before the raifing of Lazarus from the dead §; and in the deep piety of his behaviour in the garden, on the laft evening of his life‖: his *humility*, in his conftant reproof of contentions for fuperiority¶: the *benignity* and affectionatenefs of his temper, in his kindnefs to children **, in the tears which he fhed

---

* Mat. xiv. 23. ix. 28. xxvi. 36.

† Mat. xi. 25. Mark viii. 6. John vi. 23. Luke xxii. 17.

‡ Mat. vi. 26. 28.

§ John xi. 41.

‖ Mat. xxvi. 36—47.

¶ Mark ix. 33.   ** Mark x. 16.

over

over his falling country *, and upon the
death of his friend†; in his noticing of the
widow's mite‡; in his parables of the good
Samaritan, of the ungrateful fervant, and of
the pharifee and publican, of which parables
no one but a man of humanity could have
been the author: the *mildnefs* and lenity of
his character is difcovered, in his rebuke of
the forward zeal of his difciples at the Samaritan village §; in his expoftulation with
Pilate‖; in his prayer for his enemies at
the moment of his fuffering ¶, which,
though it has been fince very properly and
frequently imitated, was then, I apprehend,
new. His *prudence* is difcerned, where prudence is moft wanted, in his conduct upon
trying occafions, and in anfwers to artful
queftions. Of thefe the following are examples:—His withdrawing, in various inftances, from the firft fymptoms of tumult**,
and with the exprefs care, as appears from

* Luke xix. 41. † John xi. 35. ‡ Mark xii. 42.
§ Luke ix. 55. ‖ John xix. 11. ¶ Luke xxiii. 34.
** Mat. xiv. 22. Luke v. 15, 16. John v. 13. vi. 15.

St.

St. Matthew*, of carrying on his miniſtry in quietneſs; his declining of every ſpecies of interference with the civil affairs of the country, which diſpoſition is manifeſted by his behaviour in the caſe of the woman caught in adultery †, and in his repulſe of the application which was made to him, to interpoſe his deciſion about a diſputed inheritance ‡: his judicious, yet, as it ſhould ſeem, unprepared anſwers, will be confeſſed in the caſe of the Roman tribute §; in the difficulty concerning the interfering relations of a future ſtate, as propoſed to him in the inſtance of a woman who had married ſeven brethren ||; and, more eſpecially, in his reply to thoſe who demanded from him an explanation of the authority by which he acted, which reply conſiſted, in propounding a queſtion to them, ſituated between the very difficulties, into which they were inſidiouſly endeavouring to draw *him* ¶.

Our Saviour's leſſons, beſide what has al-

---

* Mat. xii. 19.   † John viii. 1.   ‡ Luke xii. 14.
§ Mat. xxii. 19. || Ib. 28.   ¶ xxi. 23 et ſeq.

ready

ready been remarked in them, touch, and that oftentimes by very affecting reprefentations, upon fome of the moft interefting topics of human duty, and of human meditation; upon the principles, by which the decifions of the laft day will be regulated*; upon the fuperior, or rather the fupreme, importance of religion †; upon penitence, by the moft prefling calls, and the moft encouraging invitations ‡; upon felf-denial §, watchfulnefs ||, placability ¶, confidence in God **, the value of fpiritual, that is, of mental worfhip † †, the neceffity of moral obedience, and the directing of that obedience to the fpirit and principle of the law, inftead of feeking for evafions in a technical conftruction of its terms ‡‡.

* Mat. xxv. 31 et feq.
† Mark viii. 35.   Mat. vi. 31—33.   Luke xii. 16. 21—4, 5.
‡ Luke xv.
§ Mat. v. 29.
|| Mark xiii. 37.   Mat. xxiv. 42.—xxv. 13.
¶ Luke xvii. 4.   Mat. xviii. 33.
** Mat. v. 25—30.
†† John iv. 23, 24.   ‡‡ Mat. v. 11.

If we extend our argument to other parts
of the New Teftament, we may offer, as
amongft the beft and fhorteft rules of life,
or, which is the fame thing, defcriptions of
virtue, that have ever been delivered, the
following paffages:

" Pure religion, and undefiled, before
God and the Father, is this; to vifit the
fatherlefs and widows in their affliction,
and to keep himfelf unfpotted from the
world*."

" Now the end of the commandment is,
charity, out of a pure heart, and a good confcience, and faith unfeigned †."

" For the grace of God that bringeth falvation, hath appeared to all men, teaching
us, that, denying ungodlinefs and worldly
lufts, we fhould live foberly, righteoufly,
and godly, in this prefent world‡."

Enumerations of virtues and vices, and

thofe fufficiently accurate, and unqueftionably juft, are given by St. Paul to his converts in three feveral epiftles*.

The relative duties of hufbands and wives,
of parents and children, of mafters and fervants, of Chriftian teachers and their flocks,
of governors and their fubjects, are fet forth
by the fame writer†, not indeed with the
copioufnefs, the detail, or the diftinctnefs, of
a moralift, who fhould, in thefe days, fit
down to write chapters upon the fubject, but
with the leading rules and principles in
each; and, above all, with truth, and with
authority.

Laftly, the whole volume of the New
Teftament is replete with *piety*; with, what
were almoft unknown to heathen moralifts,
devotional virtues, the moft profound veneration of the Deity, an habitual fenfe of his
bounty and protection, a firm confidence in

---

* Gal. v. 19. Col. iii. 12. 1 Cor. xiii.
† Eph. v. 33. vi. 1. vi. 5. 2 Cor. vi. 6, 7. Rom. xiii.

the

the final refult of his councils and difpenfa-
tions, a difpofition to refort, upon all occafions, to his mercy, for the fupply of human
wants, for affiftance in danger, for relief
from pain, for the pardon of fin.

CHAP.

CHAP. III.

The candour of the writers of the New Testament.

I MAKE this candour to confist, in their putting down many paffages, and noticing many circumftances, which no writer whatever was likely to have forged; and which no writer would have chofen to appear in his book, who had been careful to prefent the ftory in the moft unexceptionable form, or who had thought himfelf at liberty to carve and mould the particulars of that ftory, according to his choice, or according to his judgement of the effect.

A ftrong and well-known example of the fairnefs of the evangelifts, offers itfelf in their account of Chrift's refurrection, namely, in their unanimoufly ftating, that, after he was rifen, he appeared to his difciples alone. I do not mean, that they have ufed

the

the exclufive word *alone*; but that all the inftances which they have recorded of his appearance, are inftances of appearance to his difciples; that their reafonings upon it, and allufions to it, are confined to this fuppofition; and that, by one of them, Peter is made to fay, " Him God raifed up the third day, and fhewed him openly, not to all the people, but to witneffes chofen before of God, even to us, who did eat and drink with him after he rofe from the dead*." The commoneft underftanding muft have perceived, that the hiftory of the refurrection would have come with more advantage, if they had related that Jefus appeared, after he was rifen, to his foes as well as his friends, to the fcribes and pharifees, the Jewifh council, and the Roman governor; or even if they had afferted the public appearance of Chrift in general unqualified terms, without noticing, as they have done, the prefence of his difciples upon each occafion, and noticing it in fuch a manner as to lead their

---

* Acts x. 40, 41.

readers to suppose that none but disciples
were present. They *could* have represented
it one way as well as the other. And if their
point had been, to have the religion believed,
whether true or false; if they had fabricated
the story ab initio, or if they had been dif-
posed, either to have delivered their testimony
as witnesses, or to have worked up their materials and information as historians, in such a
manner as to render their narrative as spe-
cious and unobjectionable as they could; in
a word, if they had thought of any thing
but of the truth of the case, as they understood and believed it; they would, in their
account of Christ's several appearances after
his resurrection, at least have omitted this
restriction. At this distance of time, the
account as we have it, is perhaps more credible than it would have been the other way;
because this manifestation of the historian's
candour, is of more advantage to their testimony, than the difference in the circumstances of the account would have been to
the nature of the evidence. But this is an
effect which the evangelists would not fore-

see;

fee; and I think that it was by no means the cafe at the time when the books were compofed.

Mr. Gibbon has argued for the genuine-nefs of the Koran, from the confeffions which it contains, to the apparent difad-vantage of the Mahometan caufe *. The fame defence vindicates the genuinenefs of our gofpels, and without prejudice to the caufe at all.

There are fome other inftances in which the evangelifts honeftly relate what, they muft have perceived, would make againft them.

Of this kind is John the Baptift's meffage, preferved by St. Matthew and St. Luke, (xi. 2. vii. 18.) " Now when John had heard, in the prifon, the works of Chrift, he fent two of his difciples, and faid unto him, Art thou he that fhould come, or look we

* Vol. ix. c. 50. note 96.

for another? To confefs, ftill more to ftate, that John the Baptift had his doubts concerning the character of Jefus, could not but afford a handle to cavil and objection. But truth, like honefty, neglects appearances. The fame obfervation, perhaps, holds concerning the apoftacy of Judas *.

* I had once placed amongft thefe examples of fair conceffion, the remarkable words of St. Matthew, in his account of Chrift's appearance upon the Galilean mountain : " and when they faw him, they worfhipped him, *but fome doubted* *." I have fince, however, been convinced, by what is obferved concerning this paffage † in Dr. Townfend's difcourfe upon the refurrection, that the tranfaction, as related by St. Matthew, was really this : " Chrift appeared firft *at a diftance*; the greater part of the company, the moment they faw him, worfhipped, but fome, as yet, *i. e.* upon this firft diftant view of his perfon, doubted ; whereupon Chrift *came up* ‡ to them, and fpake to them," &c. : that the doubt, therefore, was a doubt only at firft, for a moment, and upon his being feen at a diftance, and was afterwards difpelled by his nearer approach, and by his entering into converfation with them.

* xxviii. 17.　　　　† Page 177.

‡ St. Matthew's words are, Και προσιλθων ὁ Ιησας ιλαλησεν αυτοις. This intimates, that, when he firft appeared, it was at a diftance, at leaft from many of the fpectators. (Ib. p. 197.)

John

John vi. 66. " From that time many of his difciples went back, and walked no more with him." Was it the part of a writer, who dealt in fuppreffion and difguife, to put down *this* anecdote?

Or this, which Matthew has preferved, (xiii. 58.) " He did not many mighty works there, becaufe of their unbelief."

Again, in the fame evangelift (v. 17, 18.) " Think not that I am come to deftroy the law or the prophets ; I am not come to deftroy, but to fulfil; for, verily, I fay unto you, till heaven and earth pafs, one jot, or one tittle, fhall in no wife pafs from the law, till all be fulfilled." At the time the gofpels were written, the apparent tendency of Chrift's miffion was to diminifh the authority of the Mofaic code, and it was fo confidered by the Jews themfelves. It is very improbable, therefore, that, without the conftraint of truth, Matthew fhould have afcribed a faying to Chrift, which *primo intuitu*, militated with the judgement

of

of the age in which his gofpel was written.
Marcion thought this text fo objectionable,
that he altered the words, fo as to invert the
fenfe *.

Once more, Acts xxv. 19. " They
brought none accufation againft him, of
fuch things, as I fuppofed, but had certain
queftions againft him of their own fuperftition, and of one Jefus which was dead,
whom Paul affirmed to be alive." Nothing
could be more in the character of a Roman
governor than thefe words. But that is not
precifely the point I am concerned with.
A mere panegyrift, or a difhoneft narrator,
would not have reprefented his caufe, or
have made a great magiftrate reprefent it,
in this manner, *i. e.* in terms not a little
difparaging, and befpeaking on his part,
much unconcern and indifference about the
matter. The fame obfervation may be repeated of the fpeech which is afcribed to
Gallio (Acts viii. 14.) " If it be a queftion

* Lard. vol. xv. p. 422.

of words, and names, and of your law,
look ye to it, for I will be no judge of fuch
matters."

Laftly, where do we difcern a ftronger
mark of candour, or lefs difpofition to extol
and magnify, than in the conclufion of the
fame hiftory? in which the evangelift, after
relating that Paul, upon his firft arrival at
Rome, preached to the Jews from morning
until evening, adds, " And fome believed
the things which were fpoken, and fome
believed not."

The following, I think, are paffages,
which were very unlikely to have prefented
themfelves to the mind of a forger or a
fabulift.

Matt. xxi. 21. " Jefus anfwered and
faid unto them, Verily I fay unto you, if ye
have faith and doubt not, ye fhall not only
do this, which is done unto the fig-tree, but
alfo, if ye fhall fay unto this mountain, be
thou removed, and be thou caft into the
fea,

sea, it shall be done; all things whatsoever
ye shall ask in prayer, believing, it shall be
done *." It appears to me very improbable,
that these words should have been put into
Christ's mouth, if he had not actually
spoken them. The term " faith," as here
used, is perhaps rightly interpreted of confidence in that internal notice, by which
the apostles were admonished of their power
to perform any particular miracle. And
this exposition renders the sense of the text
more easy. But the words, undoubtedly,
in their obvious construction, carry with
them a difficulty, which no writer would
have brought upon himself officiously.

Luke ix. 59. " And he said unto another, follow me ; but he said, Lord, suffer
me, first, to go and bury my father. Jesus
said unto him, let the dead bury their dead,
but go thou and preach the kingdom of
God †." This answer, though very ex-

* See also xvii. 20. Luke xvii. 6.
† See also Mat. viii. 21.

preſſive of the tranſcendent importance of religious concerns, was apparently harſh and repulſive; and ſuch as would not have been made for Chriſt, if he had not really uſed it. At leaſt, ſome other inſtance would have been choſen.

The following paſſage, I, for the ſame reaſon, think impoſſible to have been the production of artifice, or of a cold forgery: —" But I ſay unto you, that whoſoever is angry with his brother, without a cauſe, ſhall be in danger of the judgement; and whoſoever ſhall ſay to his brother, Raca, ſhall be in danger of the council; but whoſoever ſhall ſay, thou fool, ſhall be in danger of hell-fire (Gehennæ)." Mat. v. 22. It is emphatic, cogent, and well calculated for the purpoſe of impreſſion; but is inconſiſtent with the ſuppoſition of art or warineſs on the part of the relator.

The ſhort reply of our Lord to Mary Magdalen after his reſurrection (John xx. 16, 17.) " Touch me not, for I am not

yet

yet afcended unto my Father," in my opinion, muft have been founded in a reference or allufion to fome prior converfation, for the want of knowing which, his meaning is hidden from us. This very obfcurity, however, is a proof of genuinenefs. No one would have forged fuch an anfwer.

John vi. The whole of the converfation, recorded in this chapter, is, in the higheft degree, unlikely to be fabricated, efpecially the part of our Saviour's reply between the fiftieth and the fifty-eighth verfe. I need only put down the firft fentence, "I am the living bread which came down from heaven, if any man eat of this bread, he fhall live for ever; and the bread that I will give him is my flefh, which I will give for the life of the world." Without calling in queftion the expofitions that have been given of this paffage, we may be permitted to fay, that it labours under an obfcurity, in which it is impoffible to believe that any one, who made fpeeches for the perfons of his narrative, would have voluntarily involved

volved them. That this difcourfe was obfcure even at the time, is confeffed by the
writer who has preferved it, when he tells
us at the conclufion, that many of our
Lord's difciples, when they had heard this,
faid, " This is a hard faying, who can
bear it ?"

Chrift's taking of a young child, and
placing it in the midft of his contentious
difciples (Mat. xviii. 2.), though as decifive a proof, as any could be, of the benignity of his temper, and very expreffive of
the character of the religion which he wifhed to inculcate, was not by any means an
obvious thought. Nor am I acquainted
with any thing in any ancient writing
which refembles it.

The account of the inftitution of the
Eucharift bears ftrong internal marks of
genuinenefs. If it had been feigned, it
would have been more full. It would have
come nearer to the actual mode of cele-
brating the rite, as that mode obtained very
early

early in Chriftian churches ; and it would have been more formal than it is. In the forged piece, called the apoftolic conftitutions, the apoftles are made to enjoin many parts of the ritual, which was in ufe in the fecond and third centuries, with as much particularity, as a modern rubric could have done. Whereas, in the hiftory of the Lord's fupper, as we read it in St. Matthew's gofpel, there is not fo much as the command to repeat it. This, furely, looks like undefignednefs. I think alfo that the difficulty, arifing from the concifenefs of Chrift's expreffion, " This is my body," would have been avoided in a made-up ftory. I allow that the explication of thefe words, given by Proteftants, is fatisfactory ; but it is deduced from a diligent comparifon of the words in queftion, with forms of expreffion ufed in fcripture, and efpecially by Chrift, upon other occafions. No writer would, arbitrarily and unneceffarily, have thus caft in his reader's way a difficulty, which, to fay the leaft, it required refearch and erudition to clear up.

Now it ought to be obferved, that the argument which is built upon thefe examples, extends both to the authenticity of the books, and to the truth of the narrative: for it is improbable, that the forger of a hiftory in the name of another fhould have inferted fuch paffages into it: and it is improbable alfo, that the perfons whofe names the books bear, fhould have fabricated fuch paffages; or even have allowed them a place in their work, if they had not believed them to exprefs the truth.

The following obfervation, therefore, of Dr. Lardner, the moft candid of all advocates, and the moft cautious of all enquirers, feems to be well founded :—" Chriftians are induced to believe the writers of the gofpel, by obferving the evidences of piety and probity that appear in their writings, in which there is no deceit or artifice, or cunning, or defign." " No remarks," as Dr. Beattie hath properly faid, " are thrown in to anticipate objections; nothing of that caution, which never fails to diftinguifh the
                                      teftimony

teſtimony of thoſe, who are confcious of impoſture; no endeavour to reconcile the reader's mind to what may be extraordinary in the narrative."

I beg leave to cite alſo another author *, who has well expreſſed the reflection, which the examples now brought forward were intended to ſuggeſt. " It doth not appear that ever it came into the mind of theſe writers, to confider how this or the other action would appear to mankind, or what objections might be raiſed upon them. But, without at all attending to this, they lay the facts before you, at no pains to think whether they would appear credible or not. If the reader will not believe their teſtimony, there is no help for it: they tell the truth, and attend to nothing elſe. Surely this looks like fincerity, and that they publiſhed nothing to the world but what they believed themſelves."

* Duchal, p. 97, 98.

As

As no improper fupplement to this chapter, I crave a place here for obferving the extreme *naturalnefs* of fome of the things related in the New Teftament.

Mark ix. 24. Jefus faid unto him, " If thou canft believe, all things are poffible to him that believeth. And ftraightway the father of the child cried out, and faid with tears, Lord, I believe, help thou mine unbelief." The ftruggle in the father's heart, between folicitude for the prefervation of his child, and a kind of involuntary diftruft of Chrift's power to heal him, is here expreffed with an air of reality, which could hardly be counterfeited.

Again, (Mat. **xxi.** 9.) the eagernefs of the people to introduce Chrift into Jerufalem, and their demand, a fhort time afterwards, of his crucifixion, when he did not turn out what they expected him to be, fo far from affording matter of objection, reprefents popular favour, in exact agreement
with

with nature and with experience, as the flux and reflux of a wave.

The rulers and Pharifees rejecting Chrift, whilft many of the common people received him, was the effect, which, in the then ftate of Jewifh prejudices, I fhould have expected. And the reafon with which they, who rejected Chrift's miffion, kept themfelves in countenance, and with which alfo they anfwered the arguments of thofe who favoured it, is precifely the reafon, which fuch men ufually give:—" Have any of the Scribes or Pharifees believed on him?" John vii. 48.

In our Lord's converfation at the well, (John iv. 29.) Chrift had furprifed the Samaritan woman, with an allufion to a fingle particular in her domeftic fituation, " Thou haft had five hufbands, and he, whom thou now haft, is not thy hufband." The woman, foon after this, ran back to the city, and called out to her neighbours, " Come, fee a man which told me *all things* that ever

H 3 I did,"

I did." This exaggeration appears to me very natural; efpecially in the hurried ftate of fpirits into which the woman may be fuppofed to have been thrown.

The lawyer's fubtlety in running a diftinction upon the word neighbour, in the precept " Thou fhalt love thy neighbour as thyfelf," was no lefs natural than our Saviour's anfwer was decifive and fatisfactory. (Luke x. 29.) The lawyer of the New Teftament, it muft be obferved, was a Jewifh divine.

The behaviour of Gallio, Acts xviii. 12 —17, and of Feftus, xxv. 18, 19, have been obferved upon already.

The confiftency of St. Paul's character throughout the whole of his hiftory (viz. the warmth and activity of his zeal, firft againft, and then for Chriftianity) carries with it very much of the appearance of truth.

There

There are also some *proprieties*, as they may be called, observable in the gospels, that is, circumstances separately suiting with the situation, character, and intention of their respective authors.

St. Matthew, who was an inhabitant of Galilee, and did not join Christ's society until some time after Christ had come into Galilee to preach, has given us very little of his history prior to that period. St. John, who had been converted before, and who wrote to supply omissions in the other gospels, relates some remarkable particulars, which had taken place before Christ left Judea to go into Galilee *.

St. Matthew (xv. 1.) has recorded the cavil of the Pharisees against the disciples of Jesus, for eating " with unclean hands." St. Mark has also (vii. 1.) recorded the same transaction (taken probably from St. Matthew), but with this addition, " For the

* Hartley's Obf. vol. ii. p. 103.

Pharisees,

Pharifees, and all the Jews, except they wafh their hands often, eat not, holding the tradition of the elders; and when they come from the market, except they wafh they eat not; and many other things there be which they have received to hold, as the wafhing of cups and pots, brazen veffels, and of tables." Now St. Matthew was not only a Jew himfelf, but it is evident, from the whole ftructure of his gofpel, efpecially from his numerous references to the Old Teftament, that he wrote for Jewifh readers. The above explanation therefore in him would have been unnatural, as not being wanted by the readers whom he addreffed. But in Mark, who, whatever ufe he might make of Matthew's gofpel, intended his own narrative for a general circulation, and who himfelf travelled to diftant countries in the fervice of the religion, it was properly added.

CHAP.

CHAP. IV.

Identity of Chrift's character.

THE argument expreffed by this title I
apply principally to the comparifon of the
three firft gofpels with that of St. John. It
is known to every reader of fcripture, that
the paffages of Chrift's hiftory preferved by
St. John, are, except his paffion and refurrection, for the moft part different from thofe
which are delivered by the other evangelifts.
And I think the ancient account of this difference to be the true one, viz. that St. John
wrote *after* the reft, and to fupply what he
thought omiffions in their narratives, of
which the principal were our Saviour's con-
ferences with the Jews of Jerufalem, and his
difcourfes to his apoftles at his laft fupper.
But what I obferve in the comparifon of
thefe feveral accounts is, that, although actions and difcourfes are afcribed to Chrift by

St.

St. John, in general different from what are given to him by the other evangelists, yet, under this diversity, there is a similitude of *manner*, which indicates that the actions and discourses proceeded from the same person. I should have laid little stress upon a repetition of actions substantially alike, or of discourses containing many of the same expressions, because that is a species of resemblance, which would either belong to a true history, or might easily be imitated in a false one. Nor do I deny, that a dramatic writer is able to sustain propriety and distinction of character, through a great variety of separate incidents and situations. But the evangelists were not dramatic writers; nor possessed the talents of dramatic writers; nor will it, I believe, be suspected, that they *studied* uniformity of character, or ever thought of any such thing, in the person who was the subject of their histories. Such uniformity, if it exist, is on their part casual; and if there be, as I contend there is, a perceptible resemblance of *manner*, in passages, and between discourses, which are in them-

selves

felves extremely diftinct, and are delivered by hiftorians writing without any imitation of, or reference to one another, it affords a juft prefumption, that thefe are, what they profefs to be, the actions and the difcourfes of the fame real perfon; that the evangelifts wrote from fact, and not from imagination.

The article in which I find this agreement moft ftrong, is in our Saviour's mode of teaching, and in that particular property of it, which confifts in his drawing of his doctrine from the occafion; or, which is nearly the fame thing, raifing reflections from the objects and incidents before him, or turning a particular difcourfe then paffing into an opportunity of general inftruction.

It will be my bufinefs to point out this *manner* in the three firft evangelifts; and then to enquire, whether it do not appear alfo, in feveral examples of Chrift's difcourfes, preferved by St. John.

The reader will obferve in the following quotation,

quotation, that the italic letter contains the reflection, the common letter the incident or occasion from which it springs.

Mat. xii. 49, 50. " Then they said unto him, Behold thy mother and thy brethren stand without, desiring to speak with thee. But he answered, and said unto him that told him, Who is my mother? and who are my brethren? And he stretched forth his hands towards his disciples, and said, Behold my mother and my brethren; *for whosoever shall do the will of my Father which is in heaven, the same is my brother, and sister, and mother.*

Mat. xvi. 5. " And when his disciples were come to the other side, they had forgotten to take bread; then Jesus said unto them, *Take heed, and beware of the leaven of the Pharisees, and of the Sadducees.* And they reasoned among themselves, saying, It is because we have taken no bread.---How is it that ye do not understand, that I spake it not to you concerning bread, that ye should beware of the leaven of the Pharisees, and of

the

the Sadducees? Then underſtood they *how
that he bade them not beware of the leaven of
bread, but of the* DOCTRINE *of the Phariſees
and of the Sadducees.*"

Mat. xv. 1, 2. 10, 11. 17—20. " Then
came to Jeſus Scribes and Phariſees, which
were of Jeruſalem, ſaying, Why do thy diſciples tranſgreſs the traditions of the elders?
for they waſh not their hands when they
eat bread.——And he called the multitude,
and ſaid unto them, Hear and underſtand,
*not that which goeth into the mouth defileth a
man, but that which cometh out of the mouth,
this defileth a man.*——Then anſwered Peter,
and ſaid unto him, Declare unto us this parable. And Jeſus ſaid, Are ye alſo yet without underſtanding? Do ye not yet underſtand, that whatſoever entereth in at the
mouth, goeth into the belly, and is caſt out
into the draught? but thoſe things which
proceed out of the mouth come forth from
the heart, and **they** defile the man; *for out
of the heart proceed evil thoughts, murders,
adulteries, fornications, thefts, falſe witneſs,*
                                    blaſphemies;

blasphemies; these are the things which defile a man, BUT TO EAT WITH UNWASHEN HANDS DEFILETH NOT A MAN." Our Saviour, upon this occasion, expatiates rather more at large than usual, and his discourse also is more divided, but the concluding sentence brings back the whole train of thought to the incident in the first verse, viz. the objurgatory question of the Pharisees, and renders it evident that the whole sprung from that circumstance.

Mark x. 13, 14, 15. "And they brought young children to him, that he should touch them, and his disciples rebuked those that brought them.; but when Jesus saw it, he was much displeased, and said unto them, Suffer the little children to come unto me, and forbid them not, *for of such is the kingdom of God: verily I say unto you, whosoever shall not receive the kingdom of God as a little child, he shall not enter therein.*"

Mark i. 16, 17. "Now as he walked by the sea of Galilee, he saw Simon and Andrew

Andrew his brother cafting a net into the fea, for they were fifhers; and Jefus faid unto them, *Come ye after me, and I will make you fifhers of men.*"

Luke xi. 27. " And it came to pafs as he fpake thefe things, a certain woman of the company lift up her voice and faid unto him, Bleffed is the womb that bare thee, and the paps which thou haft fucked; but he faid, *Yea, rather bleffed are they, that hear the word of God, and keep it.*"

Luke xiii. 1—5. " There were prefent at that feafon fome that told him of the Galileans, whofe blood Pilate had mingled with their facrifices; and Jefus anfwering, faid unto them, *Suppofe ye that thefe Galileans were finners above all the Galileans, becaufe they fuffered fuch things? I tell you nay, but except ye repent, ye fhall all likewife perifh.*"

Luke xiv. 15. " And when one of them, that fat at meat with him, heard thefe things, he faid unto him, Bleffed is he that fhall eat

3

bread

bread in the kingdom of God. Then faid he unto him, *A certain man made a great fupper, and bade many,*" &c. The parable is rather too long for infertion, but affords a ftriking inftance of Chrift's *manner* of raifing a difcourfe from the occafion. Obferve alfo in the fame chapter, two other examples of advice, drawn from the circumftances of the entertainment, and the behaviour of the guefts.

We will now fee, how this *manner* difcovers itfelf in *St. John's* hiftory of Chrift.

John vi. 26. " And when they had found him on the other fide of the fea, they faid unto him, Rabbi, when cameft thou hither? Jefus anfwered them, and faid, Verily I fay unto you, ye feek me not becaufe ye faw the miracles, but becaufe ye did eat of the loaves and were filled. *Labour not for the meat which perifheth, but for that meat which endureth unto everlafting life, which the Son of man fhall give unto you.*"

John

John iv. 12. "Art thou greater than our father Abraham, who gave us the well, and drank thereof himself, and his children, and his cattle? Jesus answered and said unto her (the woman of Samaria), Whosoever drinketh of this water shall thirst again, but *whosoever drinketh of the water that I shall give him, shall never thirst; but the water that I shall give him, shall be in him a well of water, springing up into everlasting life.*"

John iv. 31. "In the mean while, his disciples prayed him, saying, Master, eat; but he said unto them, I have meat to eat that ye know not of. Therefore said the disciples one to another, Hath any man brought him aught to eat? Jesus saith unto them, *My meat is, to do the will of him that sent me, and to finish his work.*"

John ix. 1—5. "And as Jesus passed by, he saw a man which was blind from his birth: and his disciples asked him, saying, Who did sin, this man or his parents, that he was born blind? Jesus answered, Neither

Vol. II.   I   hath

hath this man finned, nor his parents, but that the works of God fhould be made manifeft in him. *I muft work the works of him that fent me, while it is day; the night cometh, when no man can work. As long as I am in the world, I am the light of the world.*"

John ix. 35—40. " Jefus heard that they had caft him (the blind man above mentioned) out; and when he had found him, he faid unto him, Doft thou believe on the Son of God? And he anfwered and faid, Who is he, Lord, that I might believe on him? And Jefus faid unto him, Thou haft both feen him, and it is he that talketh with thee. And he faid, Lord, I believe; and he worfhipped him. And Jefus faid, *For judgement I am come into this world, that they which fee not might fee, and that they which fee might be made blind.*"

All that the reader has now to do, is to compare the feries of examples taken from St. John, with the feries of examples taken from the other evangelifts, and to judge

8   whether

whether there be not a vifible agreement of *manner* between them. In the above quoted paffages, the occafion is ftated, as well as the reflection. They feem therefore the moft proper for the purpofe of our argument. A large, however, and curious collection has been made by different writers*, of inftances, in which it is extremely probable, that Chrift fpoke in allufion to fome object, or fome occafion then before him, though the mention of the occafion, or of the object, be omitted in the hiftory. I only obferve that thefe inftances are common to St. John's gofpel with the other three.

I conclude this article by remarking, that nothing of this *manner* is perceptible in the fpeeches recorded in the Acts, or in any other but thofe which are attributed to Chrift, and that, in truth, it was a very un-likely manner for a forger or fabulift to at-tempt; and a manner very difficult for any

* Newton on Daniel, p. 148, note *a*. Jortin Dif. p. 213. Bifhop Law's Life of Chrift.

writer

writer to execute, if he had to supply all the materials, both the incidents, and the obfervations upon them, out of his own head. A forger or a fabulift would have made for Chrift, difcourfes exhorting to virtue and diffuading from vice in general terms. It would never have entered into the thoughts of either, to have crowded together fuch a number of allufions, to time, place, and other little circumftances, as occur, for inftance, in the fermon on the mount, and which nothing but the actual prefence of the objects could have fuggefted *.

II. There appears to me to exift an affinity between the hiftory of Chrift's placing a little child in the midft of his difciples, as related by the three firft evangelifts †, and the hiftory of Chrift's wafhing his difciples' feet, as given by St. John ‡. In the ftories

---

* See Bifhop Law's Life of Chrift.
† Mat. xviii. 1. Mark ix. 33. Luke ix. 46.
‡ xiii. 3.

them-

themfelves there is no refemblance. But the
affinity, which I would point out, confifts
in thefe two articles : firft, that both ftories
denote the emulation which prevailed a-
mongft Chrift's difciples, and his own care
and defire to correct it. The moral of both
is the fame. Secondly, that both ftories are
fpecimens of the fame manner of teaching,
viz. by action ; a mode of emblematic inftruction extremely peculiar, and, in thefe
paffages, afcribed, we fee, to our Saviour,
by the three firft evangelifts and by St.
John, in inftances totally unlike, and without the fmalleft fufpicion of their borrowing
from each other.

III. A fingularity in Chrift's language,
which runs through all the evangelifts, and
which is found in thofe difcourfes of St.
John, that have nothing fimilar to them in
the other gofpels, is the appellation of " the
fon of man ;" and it is in all the evangelifts found under the peculiar circumftance
of being applied by Chrift to himfelf, but

of

of never being ufed of him, or towards him, by any other perfon. It occurs feventeen times in Matthew's gofpel, twelve times in Mark's, twenty-one times in Luke's, and eleven times in John's, and always with this reftriction.

IV. A point of agreement in the conduct of Chrift, as reprefented by his different hiftorians, is that of his withdrawing him-felf out of the way, whenever the beha-viour of the multitude indicated a difpofition to tumult.

Mat. xiv. 22. "And ftraightway Jefus conftrained his difciples to get into a fhip, and to go before him unto the other fide, while he fent the multitude away. And when he had fent the multitude away, he went up into a mountain apart to pray."

Luke v. 15, 16. "But fo much the more went there a fame abroad of him, and great multitudes came together to hear, and to to be healed by him of their infirmities: and he withdrew himself into the wilderness and prayed."

With these quotations compare the following from St. John.

Chap. v. 13. " And he that was healed wift not who it was, for Jesus had conveyed himself away, a multitude being in that place."

Chap. vi. 15. " When Jesus therefore perceived that they would come and take him by force to make him a king, he departed again into a mountain by himself alone."

In this laft inftance St. John gives the motive of Chrift's conduct, which is left unexplained by the other evangelifts, who have related the conduct itfelf.

V. Another, and a more fingular circumftance in Chrift's miniftry, was the referve,

which,

which, for some time, and upon some occasions at leaft, he ufed in declaring his own
character, and his leaving it to be collected
from his works rather than his profeffions.
Juft reafons for this referve have been affigned *. But it is not what one would
have expected. We meet with it in Matthew's gofpel (xvi. 20), " Then charged he
his difciples that they fhould tell no man
that he was Jefus the Chrift." Again, and
upon a different occafion, in Mark's (iii. 4);
" And unclean fpirits, when they faw him,
fell down before him, and cried, faying,
Thou art the Son of God ; and he ftraitly
charged them that they fhould not make
him known." Another inftance fimilar to
this laft is recorded by St. Luke (iv. 41),
What we thus find in the three evangelifts,
appears alfo in a paffage of St. John (x. 24.
35). " Then came the Jews round about
him, and faid unto him, How long doft thou
make us to doubt ? If thou be the Chrift,
tell us plainly." The occafion here was dif-

* See Locke's Reafonablenefs of Chriftianity.

ferent

ferent from any of the reft; and it was indirect. We only difcover Chrift's conduct
through the upbraidings of his adverfaries.
But all this ftrengthens the argument. I had
rather at any time furprife a coincidence in
fome oblique allufion, than read it in broad
affertions.

VI. In our Lord's commerce with his
difciples, one very obfervable particular is
the difficulty which they found in underftanding him, when he fpoke to them of
the future part of his hiftory, efpecially of
what related to his paffion or refurrection.
This difficulty produced, as was natural, a
wifh in them to afk for further explanation ;
from which, however, they appear to have
been fometimes kept back, by the fear of
giving offence. All thefe circumftances are
diftinctly noticed by Mark and Luke, upon
the occafion of his informing them (probably for the firft time) that the fon of man
fhould be delivered into the hands of men.
" They underftood not," the evangelifts tell
us, " this faying, and it was hid from them,
that

that they perceived it not ; and they feared to ask him of that saying" (Luke ix. 45. Mark ix. 32). In St. John's gospel we have, upon a different occasion, and in a different instance, the same difficulty of apprehension, the same curiosity, and the same restraint:—" A little while, and ye shall not see me, and again a little while, and ye shall see me, because I go to the Father. Then said some of his disciples among themselves, What is this that he saith unto us? A little while and ye shall not see me, and again a little while and ye shall see me, and because I go to the Father? They said, therefore, What is this that he saith, a little while? We cannot tell what he saith. Now Jesus knew that they were desirous to ask him, and said unto them," &c. John xvi. 16 et seq.

VII. The meekness of Christ during his last sufferings, which is conspicuous in the narratives of the three first evangelists, is preserved in that of St. John under separate examples. The answer given by him, in

St.

St. John *, when the high priest afked him of his difciples and his doctrine, " I fpake openly to the world, I ever taught in the fynagogue, and in the temple, whither the Jews always refort, and in fecret have I faid nothing; why afkeft thou me? Afk them which heard me, what I have faid unto them;" is very much of a piece with his reply to the armed party which feized him, as we read it in St. Mark's gofpel, and in St. Luke's †: " Are ye come out as againft a thief with fwords and with ftaves to take me? I was daily with you in the temple teaching, and ye took me not." In both anfwers we difcern the fame tranquillity, the fame reference to his public teaching. His mild expoftulation with Pilate upon two feveral occafions, as related by St. John ‡, is delivered with the fame unruffled temper, as that which conducted him through the laft fcene of his life, as defcribed by his other evangelifts. His an-

* xviii. 20.
† Mark xiv. 48. Luke xxii. 52.
‡ xviii. 34. ix. 11.

fwer,

fwer, in St. John's gofpel, to the officer
who ftruck him with the palm of his hand,
" If I have fpoken evil, bear witnefs of the
evil, but if well, why fmiteft thou me * ?"
was fuch an anfwer, as might have been
looked for from the perfon, who, as he proceeded to the place of execution, bid his
companions (as we are told by St. Luke †)
weep not for him, but for themfelves, their
pofterity, and their country; and who,
whilft he was fufpended upon the crofs,
prayed for his murderers, " for they know
not (faid he) what they do." The urgency
alfo of his judges and his profecutors to ex-
tort from him a defence to the accufation,
and his unwillingnefs to make any (which
was a peculiar circumftance) appears in St.
John's account, as well as in that of the
other evangelifts ‡.

There are moreover two other correfpon-
dencies between St. John's hiftory of the

* xxviii. 23.   † xxiii. 28.
‡ See John xix. 9. Mat. xxvii. 14. Luke xxiii. 9.

tranf-

tranſaction and theirs, of a kind ſomewhat
different from thoſe which we have been
now mentioning.

The three firſt evangeliſts record what
is called our Saviour's agony, *i. e.* his devotion in the garden, immediately before he
was apprehended ; in which narrative they
all make him pray, " that the cup might
paſs from him." This is the particular me-
taphor which they all aſcribe to him. St.
Matthew adds, " O my Father, if this cup
may not paſs away from me, except I drink
it, thy will be done*." Now St. John
does not give the ſcene in the garden ; but
when Jeſus was ſeized, and ſome reſiſtance
was attempted to be made by Peter, Jeſus,
according to his account, checked the attempt with this reply : " Put up thy ſword
into the ſheath ; the cup which my Father
hath given me, ſhall I not drink it † ?"
This is ſomething more than conſiſtency :
it is coincidence : becauſe it is extremely

* xxvi. 42.   † xviii. 11.

natural,

natural, that Jefus, who, before he was apprehended, had been praying his Father,
that " that cup might pafs from him," yet
with fuch a pious retractation of his requeft,
as to have added, " If this cup may not
pafs from me, thy will be done ;" it was
natural, I fay, for the fame perfon, when he
actually was apprehended, to exprefs the re-
fignation to which he had already made up
his thoughts, and to exprefs it in the form
of fpeech which he had before ufed, " The
cup which my Father hath given me, fhall
I not drink it ?" This is a coincidence between writers, in whofe narratives there is
no imitation, but great diverfity.

A fecond fimilar correfpondency is the
following : Matthew and Mark make the
charge, upon which our Lord was condemned, to be a threat of deftroying the
temple ; " We heard him fay, I will deftroy
this temple, made with hands, and, within
three days, I will build another made without hands * ;" but they neither of them in-

* Mark xiv. 5.

form

form us, upon what circumstance this ca-
lumny was founded. St. John, in the early
part of his history *, supplies us with this
information; for he relates, that, upon our
Lord's first journey to Jerusalem, when the
Jews asked him, " What sign shewest thou
unto us, seeing that thou doest these things?
He answered, Destroy this temple, and in
three days I will raise it up." This agreement could hardly arise from any thing but
the truth of the case. From any care or
design in St. John, to make his narrative
tally with the narratives of the other evangelists, it certainly did not arise, for no such
design appears, but the absence of it.

A strong, and more general instance of
agreement, is the following. The three first
evangelists have related the appointment of
the twelve apostles †; and have given a catalogue of their names in form. John,
without ever mentioning the appointment,
or giving the catalogue, supposes, through-

* ii. 19.
† Mat. x. 1. Mark iii. 14. Luke vi. 12.

out.

out his whole narrative, Chrift to be accompanied by a felect party of difciples; the
number of thefe to be twelve *; and whenever he happens to notice any one as of
that number †, it is one included in the catalogue of the other evangelifts; and the
names principally occurring in the courfe
of *his* hiftory of Chrift, are the names extant in their lift. This laft agreement, which
is of confiderable moment, runs through
every gofpel, and through every chapter of
each.

All this befpeaks reality.

* vi. 7. † xx. 24. vi. 71.

CHAP.

CHAP. V.

Originality of our Saviour's character.

THE Jews, whether right or wrong, had underſtood their prophecies to foretell the advent of a perſon, who, by ſome ſupernatural aſſiſtance, ſhould advance their nation to independence, and to a ſupreme degree of ſplendour and proſperity. This was the reigning opinion and expectation of the times.

Now, had Jeſus been an enthuſiaſt, it is probable that his enthuſiaſm would have fallen in with the popular deluſion, and that, whilſt he gave himſelf out to be the perſon intended by theſe predictions, he would have aſſumed the character, to which they were univerſally ſuppoſed to relate.

Had he been an impoſtor, it was his buſineſs to have flattered the prevailing hopes,
becauſe theſe hopes were to be the inſtruments of his attraction and ſucceſs.

But, what is better than conjectures, is
the fact, that all the pretended Meſſiahs
actually did ſo. We learn from Joſephus
that there were many of theſe. Some of
them, it is probable, might be impoſtors,
who thought that an advantage was to be
taken of the ſtate of public opinion. Others,
perhaps, were enthuſiaſts, whoſe imagination had been drawn to this particular object, by the language and ſentiments which
prevailed around them. But, whether impoſtors or enthuſiaſts, they concurred in
producing themſelves in the character
which their countrymen looked for, that
is to ſay, as the reſtorers and deliverers of
the nation, in that ſenſe in which reſtora-
tion and deliverance were expected by the
Jews.

Why

Why therefore Jesus, if he was, like them, either an enthusiast or impostor, did not pursue the same conduct as they did, in framing his character and pretensions, it will be found difficult to explain. A mission, the operation and benefit of which was to take place in another life, was a thing unthought of as the subject of these prophecies. That Jesus, coming to them as their Messiah, should come under a character totally different from that in which they expected him; should deviate from the general persuasion, and deviate into pretensions absolutely singular and original; appears to be inconsistent with the imputation of enthusiasm or imposture, both which, by their nature, I should expect, would, and both which, throughout the experience which this very subject furnishes, in fact *have*, followed the opinions that obtained at the time.

If it be said, that Jesus, having tried the other plan, turned at length to this; I an-

swer,

ſwer, that the thing is ſaid without evidence; againſt evidence; that it was competent to the reſt to have done the ſame,
yet that nothing of this ſort was thought of
by any.

CHAP.

CHAP. VI.

ONE argument, which has been much relied upon (but not more than its juft weight
deferves), is the conformity of the facts, occafionally mentioned or referred to in fcripture, with the ftate of things in thofe times,
as reprefented by foreign and independent
accounts. Which conformity proves, that
the writers of the New Teftament poffeffed
a fpecies of local knowledge, which could
only belong to an inhabitant of that country, and to one living in that age. This
argument, if well made out by examples,
is very little fhort of proving the abfolute
genuinenefs of the writings. It carries them
up to the age of the reputed authors, to an
age, in which it muft have been difficult to
impofe upon the Chriftian public, forgeries
in the names of thofe authors, and in which
there is no evidence that any forgeries were
attempted. It proves at leaft, that the books,

whoever

whoever were the authors of them, were compofed by perfons living in the time and country in which thefe things were tranf-acted ; and confequently capable, by their fituation, of being well informed of the facts which they relate. And the argument is ftronger, when applied to the New Tefta-ment, than it is in the cafe of almoft any other writings, by reafon of the mixed na-ture of the allufions which this book con-tains. The fcene of action is not confined to a fingle country, but difplayed in the greateft cities of the Roman empire. Allu-fions are made to the manners and prin-ciples of the Greeks, the Romans, and the Jews. This variety renders a forgery pro-portionably more difficult, efpecially to wri-ters of a pofterior age. A Greek or Roman Chriftian, who lived in the fecond or third century, would have been wanting in Jewifh literature ; a Jewifh convert in thofe ages would have been equally deficient in the knowledge of Greece and Rome *.

* Michaelis's Introduction to the New Teftament (Marfh's tranflation), c. ii. fec. xi.

This, however, is an argument which depends entirely upon an induction of particulars; and as, confequently, it carries with it little force, without a view of the inftances upon which it is built, I have to requeft the reader's attention to a detail of examples, diftinctly and articulately propofed. In collecting thefe examples, I have done no more than epitomize the firft volume of the firft part of Dr. Lardner's credibility of the gofpel hiftory. And I have brought the argument within its prefent compafs, firft, by paffing over fome of his fections in which the accordancy appeared to me lefs certain, or upon fubjects not fufficiently appropriate or circumftantial; fecondly, by contracting every fection into the feweft words poffible, contenting myfelf for the moft part with a mere *appofition* of paffages; and, thirdly, by omitting many difquifitions, which, though learned and accurate, are not abfolutely neceffary to the underftanding or verification of the argument.

The writer, principally made ufe of in

the

the enquiry, is Jofephus. Jofephus was
born at Jerufalem four years after Chrift's
afcenfion. He wrote his hiftory of the
Jewifh war fome time after the deftruction
of Jerufalem, which happened in the year
of our Lord feventy, that is thirty-feven
years after the afcenfion; and his hiftory of
the Jews he finifhed in the year ninety-
three, that is, fixty years after the afcenfion.

At the head of each article, I have referred, by figures included in brackets, to
the page of Dr. Lardner's volume, where
the fection, from which the abridgement is
made, begins. The edition ufed is that of
1741.

I. (p. 14.) Mat. xi. 22. " When he
(Jofeph) heard, that Archelaus did reign
in Judea, in the room of his father Herod,
he was afraid to go thither; notwithftanding, being warned of God in a dream, he
turned afide into the parts of Galilee."

In this paffage it is afferted, that Archelaus

laus fucceeded Herod in Judea; and it is implied, that his power did *not* extend to Galilee. Now we learn from Jofephus, that Herod the Great, whofe dominion included all the land of Ifrael, appointed Archelaus his fucceffor in *Judea*, and affigned the *reft* of his dominions to other fons; and that this difpofition was ratified, as to the main parts of it, by the Roman emperor[*].

St. Matthew fays, that Archelaus *reigned*, was *king* in Judea. Agreeably to this, we are informed by Jofephus, not only that Herod appointed Archelaus his fucceffor in Judea, but that he alfo appointed him with the title of king; and the Greek verb (βασιλευει), which the evangelift ufes to denote the government and rank of Archelaus, is ufed likewife by Jofephus[†].

The cruelty of Archelaus's character, which is not obfcurely intimated by the

---

[*] Ant. lib. 17, c. 8, fec. 1.
[†] De Bell, lib. 1, c. 33, fec. 7.

evan-

evangelift, agrees with divers particulars in his hiftory, preferved by Jofephus. " In the tenth year of his government, the chief of the Jews and Samaritans, not being able to endure his cruelty and tyranny, prefented complaints againft him to Cefar*."

II. (p. 19.) Luke iii. 1. " In the fifteenth year of the reign of Tiberius Cefar—Herod being tetrarch of Galilee, and his brother Philip tetrarch of Iturea and of the region of Trachonitis—the word of God came unto John."

By the will of Herod the Great, and the decree of Auguftus thereupon, his two fons were appointed, one (Herod Antipas) te-trarch of Galilee and Peræa, and the other (Philip) tetrarch of Trachonitis and the neighbouring countries†. We have there-fore thefe two perfons in the fituations in which St. Luke places them ; and alfo, that they were in thefe fituations in the *fifteenth*

---

* Ant. lib. 17, c. 13, fec. 1.

† Ant. lib. 17, c. 8, fec. 1.

year

year of Tiberius, in other words, that they continued in poffeffion of their territories and titles until that time, and afterwards, appears from a paffage of Jofephus, which relates of Herod, " that he was *removed* by Caligula, the fucceffor of Tiberius *; and of Philip, that he died in the *twentieth* year of Tiberius, when he had governed Trachonitis and Batanea and Gaulanitis thirty-feven years †.

III. (p. 20.) Mark v. 17 ‡. " Herod had fent forth, and laid hold upon John, and bound him in prifon, for Herodias' fake, his brother Philip's wife ; for he had married her."

With this compare Jof. Ant. l. 18. c. 6. fec. 1. " He (Herod the tetrarch) made a vifit to Herod his brother --- Here, falling in love with Herodias, the wife of the faid

---

* Ant. lib. 18, c. 8, fec. 2.

† Ant. lib. 18, c. 5, fec. 6.

‡ See alfo Mat. xiv. 1—13. Luke iii. 19.

Herod,

Herod, he ventured to make her proposals of marriage*."

Again, Mark vi. 22. " And when the *daughter of the said Herodias* came in and danced——"

With this also compare Jos. Ant. l. 18. c. 6. sec. 4. " Herodias was married to Herod, son of Herod the Great. *They had a daughter*, whose name was Salome ; after

---

* The affinity of the two accounts is unquestionable; but there is a difference in the name of Herodias's first husband, which, in the evangelist, is Philip, in Josephus, Herod. The difficulty, however, will not appear considerable, when we recollect how common it was, in those times, for the same person to bear two names: " Simon, which is called Peter ; Lebbeus, whose sirname is Thaddeus ; Thomas, which is called Didymus ; Simeon, who was called Niger ; Saul, who was also called Paul." The solution is rendered likewise easier in the present case, by the consideration, that Herod the Great had children by seven or eight wives; that Josephus mentions three of his sons under the name of Herod; that it is nevertheless highly probable, that the brothers bore some additional name, by which they were distinguished from one another. Lard. Vol. II. p. 897.

whose

whofe birth, Herodias, in utter violation of
the laws of her country, left her hufband
then living, and married Herod the tetrarch
of Galilee, her hufband's brother by the father's fide."

IV. (p. 29.) Acts xii. 1. " Now, about
that time, *Herod the king* ftretched forth his
hands, to vex certain of the church." In
the conclufion of the fame chapter, Herod's
death is reprefented to have taken place, foon
after this perfecution. The accuracy of our
hiftorian, or, rather, the unmeditated coincidence, which truth of it's own accord produces, is in this inftance remarkable. There
was no portion of time, for thirty years before, nor *ever* afterwards, in which there
was a *king* at Jerufalem, a perfon exercifing
that authority in Judea, or to whom that
title could be applied, except the three laft
years of this Herod's life, within which period, the tranfaction recorded in the Acts is
ftated to have taken place. This prince
was the grandfon of Herod the Great. In
the Acts he appears under his family name
of

of Herod; by Jofephus he is called Agrippa. For proof that he was a *king*, properly fo called, we have the teftimony of Jofephus in full and direct terms :—" Sending for him to his palace, Caligula put a crown upon his head, and appointed him king of the te-trarchie of Philip, intending alfo to give him the tetrarchie of Lyfanias*." And that Judea was at laft, but not until the laft, included in his dominions, appears by a fubfequent paffage of the fame Jofephus, wherein he tells us, that Claudius, by a decree, con-firmed to Agrippa the dominion which Caligula had given him, *adding alfo Judea and Samaria, in the utmoft extent, as poffeffed by his grandfather Herod* †.

V. (P. 32.) Acts xii. 19, 23. "And he (Herod) went down from Judea to Cefarea, and there abode.----And upon a fet day, Herod, arrayed in royal apparel, fat upon his throne, and made an oration unto them; and the people gave a fhout, faying, It is the voice of a god, and not of a man ; and im-

* Aat. xviii. c. vii. fec. 10. † Ib. xix. c. v. fec. 1.

mediately

mediately the angel of the Lord fmote him, becaufe he gave not God the glory, and he was eaten of worms, and gave up the ghoft."

Jof. Ant. lib. xix. c. 8. fec. 2. " He went to the city Cefarea. Here he celebrated fhowes in honour of Cefar. On the fecond day of the fhowes, early in the morning, he came into the theatre, dreffed in a robe of filver, of moft curious workmanfhip. The rays of the rifing fun, reflected from fo fplendid garb, gave him a majeftic and awful appearance. They called him a god, and intreated him to be propitious to them, fay-ing, Hitherto we have refpected you as a man, but now we acknowledge you to be more than mortal. The king neither re-proved thefe perfons, nor rejected the im-pious flattery.—Immediately after this he was feized with pains in his bowels, ex-tremely violent at the very firft.---He was carried therefore with all hafte to his palace. Thefe pains continually tormenting him, he expired in five days time."

The

The reader will perceive the accordancy of thefe accounts in various particulars. The place (Cefarea), the fet day, the gorgeous drefs, the acclamations of the affembly, the peculiar turn of the flattery, the reception of it, the fudden and critical incurfion of the difeafe, are circumftances noticed in both narratives. The worms mentioned by St. Luke are not remarked by Jofephus, but the appearance of thefe is a fymptom, not unufually, I believe, attending the difeafe, which Jofephus defcribes, viz. violent affee-tions of the bowels.

VI. (p. 41.) Acts xxiv. 24. "And after certain days, when Felix came with his wife Drufilla, which was a Jewefs, he fent for Paul."

Jof. Ant. lib. xx. c. 6. fec. 1, 2. "Agrippa gave his fifter Drufilla in marriage to Azizus, king of the Emefenes, when he had con-fented to be circumcifed—But this marriage of Drufilla with Azizus was diffolved in a fhort time after, in this manner:—When *Felix was procurator of Judea*, having had a fight
of

of her, he was mightily taken with her—She was induced to tranfgrefs the laws of her country, and marry Felix."

Here the public ftation of Felix, the name of his wife, and the fingular circumftance of her religion, all appear in perfect conformity with the evangelift.

VII. (p. 46.) "And after certain days, King Agrippa and Bernice came to Cefarea to falute Feftus." By this paffage we are in effect told, that Agrippa was a king, but not of Judea; for he came to falute Feftus, who at this time adminiftered the government of that country at Cefarea.

Now how does the hiftory of the age correfpond with this account? The Agrippa here fpoken of, was the fon of Herod Agrippa mentioned in the laft article; but that he did not fucceed to his father's kingdom, nor ever recovered Judea, which had been a part of it, we learn by the information of Jofephus, who relates of him, that, when

VOL. II.   L.   his

his father was dead, Claudius intended, at firft, to have put him immediately in pof-feffion of his father's dominions; but that, Agrippa being then but feventeen years of age, the emperor was perfuaded to alter his mind, and appointed Cufpius Fadus prefect of Judea and the whole kingdom*; which Fadus was fucceeded by Tiberius Alexander, Cumanus, Felix, Feftus†. But that, though difappointed of his father's kingdom, in which was included Judea, he was never-thelefs rightly ftyled *King* Agrippa; and that he was in poffeffion of confiderable territories bordering upon Judea, we gather from the fame authority; for after feveral fucceffive donations of country, " Claudius, at the fame time that he fent Felix to be procura-tor of Judea, promoted Agrippa from Chal-cis to a greater *kingdom*, giving to him the tetrarchie which had been Philip's; and he added moreover the *kingdom* of Lyfanias, and the province that had belonged to Varus‡."

* Ant. xix. c. 9. ad fin.
† Ib. xx. De Bell. lib. ii.
‡ De Bell. lib. ii. c. 12. ad fin.

St.

St. Paul addresses this person as a Jew: "King Agrippa, believeft thou the prophets? I know that thou believeft." As the fon of Herod Agrippa, who is defcribed by Jofephus to have been a zealous Jew, it is reafonable to fuppofe that he maintained the fame profeffion. But what is more material to remark, becaufe it is more clofe and circumftantial, is, that St. Luke, fpeaking of the father, (xii. 1. 3.) calls him Herod the king, and gives an example of the exercife of his authority at Jerufalem; fpeaking of the fon, (xxv. 13.) he calls him king, but not of Judea; which diftinction agrees correctly with the hiftory.

VIII. (p. 51.) Acts xiii. 7. "And when they had gone through the ifle (Cyprus) to Paphos, they found a certain forcerer, a falfe prophet, a Jew, whofe name was Barjefus, which was with the deputy of the country, Sergius Paulus, a prudent man."

The word, which is here tranflated deputy, fignifies *Proconful*, and upon this word

our

our obfervation is founded. The provinces
of the Roman empire were of two kinds;
thofe belonging to the emperor, in which
the governor was called Propretor; and thofe
belonging to the fenate, in which the governor was called Proconful. And this was
a regular diftinction. Now it appears from
Dio Caffius*, that the province of Cyprus,
which in the original diftribution was affigned to the emperor, had been transferred to
the fenate, in exchange for fome others; and
that, after this exchange, the appropriate
title of the Roman governor was Proconful.

Ib. xviii. 12. (p. 55.) " And when Gallio was deputy *(Proconful)* of Achaia."

The propriety of the title " Proconful"
is in this paffage ftill more critical. For the
province of Achaia, after paffing from the
fenate to the emperor, had been reftored
again by the emperor Claudius to the fenate
(and confequently its government had be-

---

* Lib. liv. ad A. U. 732.

come *proconfular*) only fix or feven years
before the time in which this tranfaction is
laid to have taken place*. And what con-
fines with ftrictnefs the appellation to the
time is, that Achaia under the following
reign ceafed to be a Roman province at all.

IX. (p. 152.) It appears, as well from
the general conftitution of a Roman province, as from what Jofephus delivers concerning the ftate of Judea in particular †,
that the power of life and death refided exclufively in the Roman governor; but that
the Jews, neverthelefs, had magiftrates and
a council, invefted with a fubordinate and
municipal authority. This œconomy is difcerned in every part of the gofpel narrative
of our Saviour's crucifixion.

X. (p. 203.) Acts ix. 31. "Then had
the churches reft throughout all Judea and
Galilee and Samaria."

---

* Suet. in Claud. c. xxv. Dio, lib. lxi.
† Ant. lib. xx. c. 8. fec. 5. c. i. fec. 2.

This

This *reſt* ſynchroniſes with the attempt of Caligula to place his ſtatue in the Temple of Jeruſalem; the threat of which outrage produced amongſt the Jews a conſternation, that, for a ſeaſon, diverted their attention from every other object *.

XI. (p. 218.) Acts xxi. 31. " And they took Paul, and drew him out of the temple; and forthwith the doors were ſhut. And as they went abouᵗ to kill him, tidings came to the chief captain of the *band*, that all Jeruſalem was in an uprore. Then the chief captain came near, and took him, and commanded him to be bound with two chains, and demanded who he was, and what he had done; and ſome cried one thing, and ſome another, among the multitude; and, when he could not know the certainty for the tumult, he commanded him to be carried into the *caſtle*. And when he came upon the *ſtaiᵣs*, ſo it was, that he was borne of the ſoldiers for the violence of the people."

* Joſ. de Bell. lib. xi. c. 10. ſec, 1. 3, 4.

In

In this quotation, we have the band of Roman foldiers at Jerufalem, their office (to fupprefs tumults), the caftle, the ftairs, both, as it fhould feem, adjoining to the temple. Let us enquire whether we can find thefe particulars in any other record of that age and place.

Jof. de Bell. lib. v. c. 5. fec. 8. " Antonia was fituated at the angle of the weftern and northern porticoes of the outer temple. It was built upon a rock fifty cubits high, fteep on all fides.—On that fide, where it joined to the porticoes of the temple, there were *ftairs* reaching to each portico, by which the *guard* defcended ; for there was always lodged here *a Roman legion*, and pofting themfelves in their armour in feveral places in the porticoes, they kept a watch on the people on the feaft days *to prevent all diforders* ; for, as the temple was a guard to the city, fo was Antonia to the temple."

XII. (p. 224.) Acts iv. 1. " And as they fpake unto the people, the priefts, and

L 4 *the*

the captain of the temple, and the Sadducees, came upon them." Here we have a public officer, under the title of captain of the temple, and he probably a Jew, as he accompanied the priefts and Sadducees in apprehending the apoftles.

Jof. de Bell. lib. ii. c. 17. fec. 2. " And at the *temple* Eleazar, the fon of Ananias the high prieft, a young man of a bold and refolute difpofition, then *captain*, perfuaded thofe who performed the facred miniftrations, not to receive the gift or facrifice of any ftranger."

XIII. (p. 225.) Acts xxv. 12. " Then Feftus, when he had conferred with the *council*, anfwered, Haft thou appealed unto Cefar? unto Cefar fhalt thou go." That it was ufual for the Roman prefidents to have a council, confifting of their friends, and other chief Romans in the province, appears exprefsly in the following paffage of Cicero's oration againft Verres :——" Illud negare poffes, aut nunc negabis, te, concilio tuo dimiffo,

miſſo, viris primariis, qui in conſilio C. Sa-
cerdotis fuerant, tibique eſſe volebant, re-
motis, de re judicatâ judicâſſe?"

XIV. (p. 235.) Acts xvi. 13. " And (at
Philippi) on the ſabbath, we went out of
the city by a river ſide, where prayer was
wont to be made," or where a proſeucha,
oratory, or place of prayer, was allowed.
The particularity to be remarked, is the
ſituation of the place where prayer was wont
to be made, viz. by a *river ſide.*

Philo, deſcribing the conduct of the Jews
of Alexandria upon a certain public occaſion, relates of them, that, " early in the
morning, flocking out of the gates of the
city, they go to the *neighbouring ſhores* (for
the *proſeuchæ* were deſtroyed), and, ſtand-
ing in a moſt pure place, they lift up their
voices with one accord *."

Joſephus gives us a decree of the city of

* Philo in Flacc. p. 382.

Halicar-

Halicarnaffus, permitting the Jews to build
oratories, a part of which decree runs thus.
—" We ordain that the Jews, who are willing, men and women, do obferve the fabbaths, and perform facred rites according to
the Jewifh laws, and *build oratories by the
fea-fide **."

Tertullian, among other Jewifh rites and
cuftoms, fuch as feafts, fabbaths, fafts, and
unleavened bread, mentions orationes *lito-
rales*, that is, prayers by the river fide †.

XV. (p. 255.) Acts xxvi. 5. " After
the moft *ftraiteft* fect of our religion, I lived
a Pharifee."

Jof. de Bell. l. i. c. 5. fec. 2. " The
Pharifees were reckoned the moft religious
of any of the Jews, and to be the moft
exact and fkilful in explaining the laws."

In the original there is an agreement,

* Jof. Ant lib. xiv. c. 10. fec. 24.
† Tertull. ad Nat. lib. i. c. 13.

not

not only in the fenfe but in the expreffion,
it being the fame Greek adjective, which is
rendered " ftrait" in the Acts, and " exact"
in Jofephus.

XVI. (p. 255.) Mark viii. 3, 4. " The
Pharifees and all the Jews, except they wafh,
eat not, holding the tradition of the elders;
and many other things there be which they
have received to hold."

Jof. Ant. lib. xiii. c. 10. fec. 6. " The
Pharifees have delivered to the people many
inftitutions, as received from the fathers,
which are not written in the law of Mofes."

XVII. (p. 259.) Acts xxiii. 8. " For
the Sadducees fay, that there is no refurrection, neither angel, nor fpirit, but the Pharifees confefs both."

Jof. de Bell. lib. ii. c. 8. fec. 14. " They
(the Pharifees) believe every foul to be im-
mortal, but that the foul of the good only
paffes into another body, and the foul of
the

the wicked is punished with eternal punishment." On the other hand, Ant. lib. xviii.
c. 1. fec. 4. " It is the opinion of the Sadducees that fouls perifh with the bodies."

XVIII. (p. 268.) Acts v. 17. " Then
the High Priest rofe up, and all they that
were with him, which is the fect of the
Sadducees, and were filled with indigna-
tion." St. Luke here intimates that the
High Priest was a Sadducee, which is a
character one would not have expected to
meet with in that station. This circumstance, remarkable as it is, was not however
without examples.

Jof. Ant. lib. xiii. c. 10. fec. 6, 7. " John
Hyrcanus, High Priest of the Jews, forfook
the Pharifees upon a difguft, and joined
himfelf to the party of the Sadducees."
This High Priest died one hundred and
feven years before the Chriftian æra.

Again, (Ant. lib. xx. c. 8. fec. 1.) " This
Ananus the younger, who, as we have faid
just

juſt now, had received the high prieſthood, was fierce and haughty in his behaviour, and above all men bold and daring; and, moreover, *was of the ſect of the Sadducees.*" This High Prieſt lived little more than twenty years after the tranſaction in the Acts.

XIX. (p. 282.) Luke ix. 51. "And it came to paſs, when the time was come, that he ſhould be received up, he ſteadfaſtly ſet his face to go to Jeruſalem, and ſent meſſengers before his face. And they went, and entered into a village of the Samaritans to make ready for him, and they did not receive him, becauſe his face was as though he would go to Jeruſalem."

Joſ. Ant. lib. xx. c. 5. ſec. 1. "It was the cuſtom of the Galileans, who went up to the holy city at the feaſts, to travel through the country of Samaria. As they were in their journey, ſome inhabitants of the village called Ginæa, which lies on the borders of Samaria and the great plain,

falling

falling upon them, killed a great many of them."

XX. (p. 278.) John iv. 20. "Our fathers," said the Samaritan woman, "worshipped in *this mountain*, and ye say, that Jerusalem is the place where men ought to worship."

Jos. Ant. lib. xviii. c. 5. sec. 1. "Commanding them to meet him at *Mount Gerizim*, which is by them (the Samaritans) esteemed the most sacred of all mountains."

XXI. (p. 312.) Mat. xxvi. 3. "Then assembled together the chief priests, and the elders of the people, unto the palace of the High Priest, *who was called Caiaphas*." That Caiaphas was High Priest, and High Priest throughout the presidentship of Pontius Pilate, and consequently at this time, appears from the following account:—He was made High Priest by Valerius Gratus, *predecessor* of Pontius Pilate, and was removed from his office by Vitellius, presi-

4   dent

dent of Syria, *after* Pilate was sent away out of the province of Judea. Josephus relates the *advancement* of Caiaphas to the High Priesthood in this manner: " Gratus gave the High Priesthood to Simon, the son of Camithus. He having enjoyed this honour not above a year, was succeeded by Joseph, *who is also called Caiaphas* *. After this Gratus went away for Rome, having been eleven years in Judea; and *Pontius Pi-late came thither as his successor.*" Of the *removal* of Caiaphas from his office, Josephus likewise afterward informs us; and connects it with a circumstance, which fixes the time to a date, subsequent to the determination of Pilate's government. " Vitellius (he tells us) ordered *Pilate to repair to Rome*; and *after that* went up himself to Jerusalem, and then gave directions concerning several matters. And, having done these things, he took away the priesthood from *the High Priest* Joseph, who is called *Caiaphas* †."

* Ant lib. xviii. c. 2. sec. 2.
† Id. ib. c. 5. sec. 3.

XXII.

XXII. (Michaelis, c. xi. fec. 11.) Acts
xxiii. 4. " And they that stood by said,
Revilest thou God's High Priest ? Then said
Paul, I wist not, brethren, that he was the
High Priest." Now, upon enquiry into
the history of the age, it turns out, that
Ananias, of whom this is spoken, was, in
truth, *not* the High Priest, though he was
fitting in judgement in that assumed capacity. The cafe was, that he had formerly
held the office, and had been depofed ; that
the perfon who fucceeded him had been
murdered ; that another was not yet appointed to the station ; and that, during the
vacancy, he had, of his own authority,
taken upon himfelf the difcharge of the office *. This fingular fituation of the high
priefthood took place during the interval
between the death of Jonathan, who was
murdered by order of Felix, and the acceffion of Ifmael, who was invefted with the
high priefthood by Agrippa ; and precifely
in this interval it happened, that St. Paul

* Jof. Ant. l. xx. c. v. fec. 2. c. vi. fec. 2. c. ix. fec. 2.

was

was apprehended, and brought before the Jewish council.

XXIII. (p. 323.) Mat. xxvi. 59. " Now the *chief priests* and elders, and all the council, fought falfe witnefs againft him."

Jof. Ant. lib. xviii. c. 15. fec. 3, 4. " Then might be feen the *high priests themfelves* with afhes on their heads, and their breafts naked."

The agreement here confifts in fpeaking of the high priefts, or chief priefts (for the name in the original is the fame), in the *plural number*, when in ftrictnefs there was only *one* High Prieft: which may be confidered as a proof, that the evangelifts were habituated to the manner of fpeaking then in ufe, becaufe they retain it, when it is neither accurate nor juft. For the fake of brevity I have put down from Jofephus, only a fingle example of the application of this title in the plural number; but it **is his** ufual ftyle.

Ib. (p. 871.) Luke iii. 1. " Now in the fifteenth year of the reign of Tiberius Cefar, Pontius Pilate being governor of Judea, and Herod being tetrarch of Galilee, *Annas and Caiaphas being the High Prieſts*, the word of God came unto John." There is a paſſage in Joſephus very nearly parallel to this, and which may at leaſt ſerve to vindicate the evangeliſt from objection, with reſpect to his giving the title of High Prieſt ſpecifically to two perſons at the ſame time : " Quadratus ſent two others of the moſt powerful men of the Jews, as alſo the *High Prieſts Jonathan and Ananias* *." That Annas was a perſon in an eminent ſtation, and poſſeſſed an authority co-ordinate with, or next to that of the High Prieſt properly ſo called, may be inferred from St. John's goſpel, which, in the hiſtory of Chriſt's crucifixion, relates that " the ſoldiers led him away to Annas firſt †." And this might be noticed

---

* De Bell. lib. xi. c. 12. ſec. 6.

† xviii. 13.

as an example of undesigned coincidence
in the two evangelists.

Again, (p. 870.) Acts iv. 6. Annas is
called the High Priest, though Caiaphas
was in the office of the High Priesthood.
In like manner in Josephus *, " Joseph the
son of Gorion, and the High Priest Ananus, were chosen to be supreme governors
of all things in the city." Yet Ananus,
though here called the High Priest Ananus,
was not then in the office of the High
Priesthood. The truth is, there is an indeterminateness in the use of this title in the
gospel; sometimes it is applied exclusively
to the person, who held the office at the
time; sometimes to one or two more, who
probably shared with him some of the
powers or functions of the office; and,
sometimes, to such of the priests as were
eminent by their station or character †: and
there is the very same indeterminateness in
Josephus.

* De Bell. ii. c. 20. sec. 3.
† Mark xiv. 53.

M 2 XXIV.

XXIV. (p. 347.) John xix. 19, 20.
" And Pilate wrote a title, and put it on
the crofs." That fuch was the cuftom of
the Romans upon thefe occafions, appears
from paffages of Suetonius and Dio Caffius:
" Patrem familias—canibus objecit, cum hoc
titulo, impie locutus parmularius." Suet. Do-
mit. cap. x. And in Dio Caffius we have
the following : " Having led him through
the midft of the court or affembly, *with a*
writing fignifying the caufe of his death, and
afterwards crucifying him." Book liv.

Ib. " And it was written in Hebrew,
Greek, and Latin." That it was alfo ufual,
about this time, in Jerufalem, to fet up ad-
vertifements in *different* languages, is gathered from the account which Jofephus gives,
of an expoftulatory meffage from Titus to
the Jews, when the city was almoft in his
hands ; in which he fays, Did ye not erect
pillars with infcriptions on them, *in the*
Greek and in our language, " Let no one pafs
beyond thefe bounds ?"

XXV.

XXV. (p. 352.) Mat. xxvii. 26. " When he had *fcourged* Jefus, he delivered him to be crucified."

The following paffages occur in Jofephus:

" Being *beaten*, they were crucified oppofite to the citadel *."

" Whom, having *firft fcourged with whips*, he crucified †."

" He was burnt alive, *having been firft beaten* ‡."

To which may be added one from Livy, Lib. xi. c. 5. " Productique omnes, *virgifque cæfi*, ac fecuri percuffi."

A modern example may illuftrate the ufe we make of this inftance. The preceding

* Page 1247, 24 edit. Hudf.
† P. 1080, 45 edit
‡ P. 1327, 43 edit.

of

of a capital execution by the corporal punishment of the sufferer, is a practice unknown
in England, but retained, in some instances
at least, as appears by the late execution of
a regicide, in Sweden. This circumstance,
therefore, in the account of an English execution purporting to come from an English
writer, would not only bring a suspicion
upon the truth of the account, but would,
in a considerable degree, impeach its pretensions, of having been written by the author
whose name it bore. Whereas the same
circumstance, in the account of a Swedish
execution, would verify the account, and
support the authenticity of the book in which
it was found ; or, at least, would prove that
the author, whoever he was, possessed the
information and the knowledge which he
ought to possess.

XXVI. (p. 353.) John xix. 16. " And
they took Jesus, and led him away, and he,
bearing his cross, went forth."

Plutarch. De iis qui sero puniuntur, p. 554.
A. Paris,

A. Paris, 1624. "Every kind of wicked-nefs produces its own particular torment, juft as every malefactor, when he is brought forth to execution, *carries his own crofs.*"

XXVII. John xix. 32. "Then came the foldiers, and *brake the legs* of the firft, and of the other, which was crucified with him."

Conftantine abolifhed the punifhment of the crofs; in commending which edict, a heathen writer notices this very circum-ftance of *breaking the legs*: "Eo pius, ut etiam vetus veterrimumque fupplicium, pa-tibulum, et *cruribus fuffringendis*, primus removerit." Aur. Vict. Cef. cap. xli.

XXVIII. (p. 457.) Acts iii. 1. "Now Peter and John went up together into the temple, at the hour of prayer, being the *ninth* hour."

Jof. Ant. lib. xv. c. 7. fec. 8. "Twice every day, in the morning, and at the *ninth*
M 4   hour,

hour, the priests perform their duty at the altar."

XXIX. (p. 462.) Acts xv. 21. "For Moses, of old time, hath, in every city, them that preach him, *being read in the fynagogues every fabbath day.*"

Jof. contra Ap. l. ii. "He (Moses) gave us the law, the moft excellent of all inftitutions; nor did he appoint that it fhould be heard, once only, or twice, or often, but that, laying afide all other works, we fhould meet together *every week* to hear it *read*, and gain a perfect underftanding of it."

XXX. (p. 465.) Acts xxi. 23. "We have four men, which have a *vow* on them; them take, and purify thyfelf with them, that they may *fhave their heads.*"

Jof. de Bell. l. xi. c. 15. "It is cuftomary for thofe who have been afflicted with fome diftemper, or have laboured under any other difficulties, to make a *vow* thirty days
before

before they offer facrifices, to abftain from wine, and *fhave the hair of their heads.*"

Ib. v. 24. " Them take, and purify thy-felf with them, and *be at charges with them, that they may fhave their heads.*"

Jof. Ant. l. xix. c. 6. " He (Herod Agrippa) coming to Jerufalem, offered up facrifices of thankfgiving, and omitted no-thing that was prefcribed by the law. For which reafon *he alfo ordered a good number of Nazarites to be fhaved.*" We here find that it was an act of piety amongft the Jews, to defray, for thofe who were under the Naza-ritic vow, the expences which attended its completion; and that the phrafe was, " that they might be fhaved." The cuftom and the expreffion are both remarkable, and both in clofe conformity with the fcripture ac-count.

XXXI. (p. 474.) 2 Cor. xi. 24. " Of the Jews five times received I forty ftripes, *fave one.*"

Jof.

Jof. Ant. iv. c. 8. fec. 21. "He that acts contrary hereto, let him receive forty ftripes, *wanting one*, from the public officer."

The coincidence here is fingular, becaufe the law *allowed* forty ftripes:—" Forty ftripes he may give him, and not exceed." Deut. xxv. 3. It proves that the author of the epiftle to the Corinthians was guided not by books, but by facts; becaufe his ftatement agrees with the actual cuftom, even when that cuftom deviated from the written law, and from what he muft have learnt by confulting the Jewifh code, as fet forth in the Old Teftament.

XXXII. (p. 490.) Luke iii. 12. "Then came alfo *publicans* to be baptized." From this quotation, as well as from the hiftory of Levi or Matthew (Luke v. 29.), and of Zaccheus (Luke xix. 2.), it appears, that the publicans or tax-gatherers were, frequently at leaft, if not always, Jews: which, as the country was then under a Roman government, and the taxes were paid to the
Romans,

Romans, was a circumstance not to be expected. That it was the truth however of the case, appears from a short passage of Josephus.

De Bell. lib. ii. c. 14. sec. 45. " But Florus not restraining these practices by his authority, the chief men of the Jews, *among whom was John the publican*, not knowing well what course to take, wait upon Florus, and give him eight talents of silver to stop the building."

XXXIII. (p. 496.) Acts xxii. 25. "And, as they bound him with thongs, Paul said unto the centurion that stood by, Is it lawful for you *to scourge a man that is a Roman*, and uncondemned ?"

" Facinus est vinciri civem Romanum : scelus verberari. Cic. in Verr.

" Cædebatur virgis, in medio foro Messanæ, civis Romanus, Judices, cum interea, nullus gemitus, nulla vox alia, istius miseri,
inter

inter dolorem crepitumque plagarum, audie-
batur, nifi hæc, *Civis Romanus fum.*"

XXXIV. (p. 513.) Acts xxii. 27. " Then
the chief captain came, and faid unto him
(Paul), Tell me, Art thou a Roman ? He
faid, Yea." The circumftance here to be
noticed is, that a *few* was a Roman citizen.

Jof. Ant. lib. xiv. c. 10. fec. 13. " Lucius
Lentulus, the conful, declared, I have dif-
miffed from the fervice, *the Jewifh Roman
citizens*, who obferve the rites of the Jewifh
religion at Ephefus."

Ib. v. 27. " And the chief captain anfwered, With *a great fum obtained I this
freedom.*"

Dio Caffius, lib. lx. " This privilege,
which had been *bought formerly at a great
price*, became fo cheap, that it was commonly faid, a man might be made a Roman
citizen for a few pieces of broken glafs."

XXXV.

XXXV. (p. 521.) Acts xxviii. 16. "And when we came to Rome, the centurion delivered the prisoners to the captain of the guard, but Paul was suffered to dwell by himself, with *a soldier that kept him.*"

With which join v. 20. "For the hope of Israel I am bound with *this chain.*"

" Quemadmodum eadem *catena*, et custodiam et *militem* copulat, sic ista, quæ tam dissimilia sunt, pariter incedunt." Seneca, ep. v.

" Proconsul æstimare solet, utrum in carcerem recipienda sit persona, an *militi tradenda.*" Ulpian. l. i. sec. De custod. et exhib. reor.

In the confinement of Agrippa by the order of Tiberius, Antonia managed, that the centurion who presided over the guards, and the *soldier to whom Agrippa was to be bound*, might be men of mild character. Jos. Ant. lib. xviii. c. 7. sec. 5. After the accession fion of Caligula, Agrippa alfo, like Paul, was suffered to dwell, yet as a prifoner, in his own houfe.

XXXVI. (p. 531.) Acts xxvii. 1. "And when it was determined that we fhould fail into Italy, they delivered Paul, *and certain other prifoners*, unto one named Julius." Since not only Paul, but certain other *prifoners*, were fent by the fame fhip into Italy, the text muft be confidered, as carrying with it an intimation, that the fending of perfons from Judea to be tried at Rome, was an ordinary practice. That in truth it was fo, is made out by a variety of examples which the writings of Jofephus furnifh; and amongft others by the following, which comes near both to the time and the fubject of the inftance in the Acts. "Felix, for fome flight offence, *bound and fent to Rome* feveral priefts of his acquaintance, and very good and honeft men, to anfwer for them-felves to Cefar." Jof. in Vit. fec. 3.

XXXVII. (p. 539.) Acts xi. 27. "And, in

in thefe days, came prophets from Jerufalem unto Antioch; and there ftood up one of them, named Agabus, and fignified by the fpirit that there fhould be a great dearth throughout all the world (or all the country), *which came to pafs in the days of Claudius Cefar."*

Jof. Ant. l. xx. c. 4. fec. 2. " In their time (i. e. about the fifth or fixth year of Claudius) a great dearth happened in Judea."

XXXVIII. (p. 555.) Acts xviii. 1, 2. " Becaufe that Claudius had commanded all Jews to depart from Rome."

Suet. Claud. c. xxv. " Judæos, impulfore Chrefto affiduè tumultuantes, Româ expulit."

XXXIX. (p. 664.) Acts v. 37. " After this man rofe up Judas of Galilee, in the days of the taxing, and drew away much people after him."

Jof. de Bell. l. vii. " He (viz. the perfon,

son, who, in another place, is called by Jofephus, Judas the Galilean, or Judas of Galilee) perfuaded not a few not to enroll themfelves, when Cyrenius the cenfor was fent into Judea."

XL. (p. 942.) Acts xxi. 38. " Art not thou that Egyptian, which, before thefe days, madeft an uprore, and leddeft out into the wildernefs four thoufand men, that were murderers?"

Jof. de Bell. l. ii. c. 13. fec. 5. " But the Egyptian falfe prophet brought a yet heavier difafter upon the Jews; for this impoftor, coming into the country, and gaining the reputation of a prophet, gathered together thirty thoufand men, who were deceived by him. Having brought them round out of the wildernefs, up to the mount of olives, he intended from thence to make his attack upon Jerufalem; but Felix coming fuddenly upon him with the Roman foldiers, prevented the attack.—A great number, or (as it fhould rather be rendered) the greateft

part

part of thofe that were with him, were either
flain, or taken prifoners."

In thefe two paffages, the defignation of
the impoftor, an " Egyptian," without his
proper name; "the wildernefs;" his efcape,
though his followers were deftroyed; the
time of the tranfaction, in the prefidentfhip
of Felix, which could not be any long time
before the words in Luke are fuppofed to
have been fpoken; are circumftances of
clofe correfpondency. There is one, and
only one, point of difagreement, and that is,
in the number of his followers, which in
the Acts are called four thoufand, and by
Jofephus thirty thoufand: but, befide that
the names of numbers, more than any other
words, are liable to the errors of tranfcribers,
we are, in the prefent inftance, under the
lefs concern to reconcile the evangelift with
Jofephus, as Jofephus is not, in this point,
confiftent with himfelf. For whereas, in
the paffage here quoted, he calls the number
thirty thoufand, and tells us that the greateft part, or a great number (according as

his words are rendered) of thofe that were
with him, were deftroyed; in his Antiquities,
he reprefents four hundred to have been
killed upon this occafion, and two hundred
taken prifoners*: which certainly was not
the " greateft part," nor " a great part,"
nor " a great number," out of thirty thoufand. It is probable alfo, that Lyfias and
Jofephus fpoke of the expedition in its different ftages: Lyfias, of thofe who followed
the Egyptian out of Jerufalem ; Jofephus, of
all who were collected about him afterwards,
from different quarters.

XLI. (Lardner's Jewifh and Heathen
Teftimonies, vol. iii. p. 21.) Acts xvii. 22.
" Then Paul ftood in the midft of Mars-hill,
and faid, Ye men of Athens, I perceive that
in all things ye are too fuperftitious, for, as
I paffed by and beheld your devotions, *I
found an altar with this infcription, TO THE
UNKNOWN GOD.* Whom therefore ye
ignorantly worfhip, him declare I unto
you."

---

* Lib. xx. c. 7. fec. 6.

Diogenes

Diogenes Laertius, who wrote about the year 210, in his history of Epimenides, who is supposed to have flourished nearly six hundred years before Christ, relates of him the following story: that, being invited to Athens for the purpose, he delivered the city from a pestilence in this manner—
" Taking several sheep, some black, others white, he had them up to the Areopagus, and then let them go where they would, and gave orders to those who followed them, wherever any of them should lie down, to sacrifice it to the god to whom it belonged; and so the plague ceased. Hence," says the historian, " it has come to pass, *that, to this present time, may be found in the boroughs of the Athenians* ANONYMOUS *altars*; a memorial of the expiation then made *."
These altars, it may be presumed, were called *anonymous*, because there was not the name of any particular deity inscribed upon them.

Pausanias, who wrote before the end of

* In Epimenide, l. i. segm. 110.

the

the fecond century, in his defcription of
Athens, having mentioned an altar of Jupiter
Olympius, adds, " *And nigh unto it is an
altar of unknown gods**." And, in another
place, fpeaks " *of altars of gods called un-
known†.*"

Philoftratus, who wrote in the beginning
of the third century, records it as an obfervation of Apollonius Tyanæus, " That it was
wife to fpeak well of all the gods, *efpecially
at Athens, where altars of unknown demons
were erected‡.*"

The *author of the dialogue Philopatris*, by
many fuppofed to have been Lucian, who
wrote about the year 170, by others fome anonymous heathen writer of the fourth century,
makes Critias fwear *by the unknown god of
Athens;* and, near the end of the dialogue,
has thefe words, " But let us find out *the
unknown god at Athens*, and, ftretching our

---

* Pauf. l. v. p. 412.
† Ib. l. i. p. 4.
‡ Philof. Apoll. Tyan. l. vi. c. 3.

hands

hands to heaven, offer to him our praises and thankſgivings *."

This is a very curious, and a very important coincidence. It appears beyond controverſy, that altars with this inſcription were exiſting at Athens, at the time when St. Paul is alledged to have been there. It ſeems alſo, which is very worthy of obſervation, that this inſcription was *peculiar* to the Athenians. There is no evidence that there were altars inſcribed " to the unknown God" in any other country. Suppoſing the hiſtory of St. Paul to have been a fable, how is it poſſible, that ſuch a writer as the author of the Acts of the Apoſtles was, ſhould hit upon a circumſtance ſo extraordinary, and introduce it by an alluſion ſo ſuitable to St. Paul's office and character?

———————

The examples here collected, will be ſufficient, I hope, to ſatisfy us, that the writers

* Lucian. in Philop. tom. ii. Græv. p. 767. 780.

of

of the Chriſtian hiſtory knew ſomething of
what they were writing about. The argument is alſo ſtrengthened by the following
conſiderations:

I. That theſe agreements appear, not only
in articles of public hiſtory, but, ſometimes,
in minute, recondite, and very peculiar circumſtances, in which, of all others, a forger
is moſt likely to have been found tripping.

II. That the deſtruction of Jeruſalem,
which took place forty years after the commencement of the Chriſtian inſtitution, produced ſuch a change in the ſtate of the
country, and the condition of the Jews, that
a writer who was unacquainted with the
circumſtances of the nation *before* that event,
would find it difficult to avoid miſtakes, in
endeavouring to give detailed accounts of
tranſactions connected with thoſe circumſtances, foraſmuch as he could no longer
have a living exemplar to copy from.

III. That there appears, in the writers of
the

the New Teſtament, a knowledge of the affairs of thoſe times, which we do not find in authors of later ages. In particular, many of the Chriſtian writers of the ſecond and third centuries, and of the following ages, had falſe notions concerning the ſtate of Judea, between the nativity of Jeſus and the deſtruction of Jeruſalem *. Therefore *they* could not have compoſed our hiſtories.

Amidſt ſo many conformities, we are not to wonder that we meet with ſome difficulties. The principal of theſe I will put down, together with the ſolutions which they have received. But in doing this I muſt be contented with a brevity, better ſuited to the limits of my volume, than to the nature of a controverſial argument. For the hiſtorical proofs of my aſſertions, and for the Greek criticiſms upon which ſome of them are founded, I refer the reader to the ſecond volume of the firſt part of Dr. Lardner's large work.

* Lard. part i. vol. ii. p. 960.

I. The

I. The taxing, during which Jefus was born, was " firft made," as we read, according to our tranflation, in St. Luke, " whilft Cyrenius was governor of Syria *." Now it turns out, that Cyrenius was not governor of Syria until twelve, or, at the fooneft, ten years after the birth of Chrift; and that a taxing, cenfus, or affeffment, was made in Judea in the beginning of his government. The charge, therefore, brought againft the evangelift is, that, intending to refer to this taxing, he has mifplaced the date of it, by an error of ten or twelve years.

The anfwer to the accufation is found in his ufing the word " firft "—" And this taxing was *firft* made ;" for, according to the miftake imputed to the evangelift, this word could have no fignification whatever: it could have had no place in his narrative; becaufe, let it relate to what it will, taxing, cenfus, enrollment, or affeffment, it imports that the writer had more than one of thefe

* Chap. ii. ver. 2.

in

in contemplation. It acquits him therefore of the charge, it is inconfiftent with the fuppofition, of his knowing only of the taxing in the beginning of Cyrenius's government. And if the evangelift knew, which this word proves that he did, of fome other taxing befide that, it is too much, for the fake of convicting him of a miftake, to lay it down as certain, that he intended to refer to *that*.

The fentence in St. Luke may be conftrued thus: " This was the firft affeffment (or enrollment) of Cyrenius, governor of Syria *;" the words " governor of Syria" being ufed after the name of Cyrenius as his

* If the word which we render " firft" be rendered " before," which it has been ftrongly contended that the Greek idiom allows of, the whole difficulty vanifhes, for then the paffage would be—" Now this taxing was made before Cyrenius was governor of Syria;" which correfponds with the chronology. But I rather choofe to argue, that, however the word " firft" be rendered, to give it a meaning at all, it militates with the objection. In this I think there can be no miftake.

addition

addition or title. And this title, belonging to him at the time of writing the account, was naturally enough fubjoined to his name, though acquired after the tranfaction which the account defcribes. A modern writer, who was not very exact in the choice of his expreffions, in relating the affairs of the Eaft-Indies, might eafily fay, that fuch a thing was done by *Governor* Haftings, though, in truth, the thing had been done by him before his advancement to the fta-tion from which he received the name of governor. And this, as we contend, is pre-cifely the inaccuracy which has produced the difficulty in St. Luke.

At any rate, it appears from the form of the expreffion, that he had two taxings or enrollments in contemplation. And if Cy-renius had been fent upon this bufinefs into Judea, before he became governor of Syria (againft which fuppofition there is no proof, but rather external evidence of an enroll-ment going on about this time under fome

6

perfon

perſon or other *), then the cenſus on all
hands acknowledged to have been made by
him in the beginning of his government,
would form a ſecond, ſo as to occaſion the
other to be called the *firſt*.

II. Another chronological objection ariſes
upon a date aſſigned in the beginning of
the third chapter of St. Luke †. " Now in
the fifteenth year of the reign of Tiberius
Cæſar—Jeſus *began to be about thirty* years
of age ;" for ſuppoſing Jeſus to have been
born, as St. Matthew, and St. Luke alſo
himſelf, relates, in the time of Herod, he
muſt, according to the dates given in Joſephus, and by the Roman hiſtorians, have

---

* Joſephus (Ant. xvii. c. 2. ſec. 6.) has this remarkable paſſage—" When therefore the whole Jewiſh nation took an oath to be faithful to Ceſar, and the inte-
reſts of the king." This tranſaction correſponds in the
courſe of the hiſtory with the time of Chriſt's birth.
What is called a cenſus, and which we render taxing,
was delivering upon oath an account of their property.
This might be accompanied with an oath of fidelity, or
might be miſtaken by Joſephus for it.

† Lard. part i. vol. ii. p. 768.

been

been at leaſt thirty-one years of age in the fifteenth year of Tiberius. If he was born, as St. Matthew's narrative intimates, one or two years before Herod's death, he would have been thirty-two, or thirty-three years old, at that time.

This is the difficulty: the ſolution turns upon an alteration in the conſtruction of the Greek. St. Luke's words in the original are allowed, by the general opinion of learned men, to ſignify, not " that Jeſus began to be about thirty years of age," but " that he was about thirty years of age when he began his miniſtry." This conſtruction being admitted, the adverb " about" gives us all the latitude we want, and more; eſpecially when applied, as it is in the preſent inſtance, to a decimal number, for ſuch numbers, even without this qualifying addition, are often uſed in a laxer ſenſe than is here con-tended for *.

III. Acts

* Livy, ſpeaking of the peace, which the conduct of Romulus had procured to the ſtate, during the *whole* reign

III. Acts v. 36. " For before these days rose up Theudas, boasting himself to be somebody; to whom a number of men, about four hundred, joined themselves: who was slain; and all, as many as obeyed him, were scattered and brought to nought.".

Josephus has preserved the account of an impostor, of the name of Theudas, who created some disturbances, and was slain; but, according to the date assigned to this man's appearance (in which, however, it is very possible that Josephus may have been mistaken *), it must have been, at the least, seven years, after Gamaliel's speech,

reign of his successor † (Numa), has these words— " Ab illo enim profectis viribus datis tantum valuit, ut, in *quadraginta* deinde annos, tutam pacem haberet:" yet, afterwards, in the same chapter, " Romulus (he says) septem et triginta regnavit annos, Numa tres et quadraginta."

* Michaelis's Introduction to the New Testament (Marsh's translation), vol. i. p. 61.

† Liv. Hist. c. i. sec. 16.

of which this text is a part, was delivered.
It has been replied to the objection *, that
there might be two impostors of this name:
and it has been observed, in order to give a
general probability to the solution, that the
same thing appears to have happened in
other instances of the same kind. It is
proved from Josephus, that there were not
fewer than four persons, of the name of
Simon, within forty years, and not fewer
than three, of the name of Judas, within
ten years, who were all leaders of insurrec-
tions: and it is likewise recorded by this
historian, that, upon the death of Herod
the Great, (which agrees very well with the
time of the commotion referred to by Gamaliel, and with his manner of stating that
time " before these days") there were innumerable disturbances in Judea †. Archbi-
shop Usher was of opinion, that one of the
three Judas's above mentioned was Gamaliel's Theudas ‡; and that, with a less varia-

* Lardner, part i. vol. ii. p. 922.
† Ant. l. xvii. c. 12. sec. 4.
‡ Annals, p. 797.

tion

tion of the name than we actually find in
the gospels, where one of the twelve apoftles is called by Luke, Judas; and by Mark,
Thaddeus *. Origen, however he came at
his information, appears to have believed,
that there was an impoftor of the name of
Theudas before the nativity of Chrift †.

IV. Matt. xxiii. 34. " Wherefore, behold, I fend unto you prophets, and wife
men, and fcribes: and fome of them ye
fhall kill and crucify ; and fome of them
fhall ye fcourge in your fynagogues, and
perfecute them from city to city : that
upon you may come all the righteous blood
fhed upon the earth, from the blood of
righteous Abel unto the blood of *Zacharias,
fon of Barachias, whom ye flew between the
temple and the altar."*

There is a Zacharias, whofe death is related in the fecond book of Chronicles, in

a manner which perfectly supports our Saviour's allusion *. But this Zacharias was the son of *Jehoiada*.

There is also Zacharias the prophet; who was the son of Barachiah, and is so described in the superscription of his prophecy, but of whose death we have no account.

I have little doubt, but that the first Zacharias was the person spoken of by our Saviour; and that the name of the father has been since added, or changed, by some one, who took it from the title of the prophecy, which happened to be better known to him than the history in the Chronicles.

* " And the Spirit of God came upon Zechariah, the son of Jehoiada the priest, which stood above the people, and said unto them, Thus saith God, Why transgress ye the commandments of the Lord, that ye cannot prosper? Because ye have forsaken the Lord, he hath also forsaken you. And they conspired against him, *and stoned him with stones, at the commandment of the king, in the court of the house of the Lord.*" 2 Chron. xxiv. 20, 21.

There

There is likewife a Zacharias, the fon of Baruch, related by Jofephus to have been flain in the temple a few years before the deftruction of Jerufalem. It has been infinuated, that the words put into our Saviour's mouth, contain a reference to this tranfaction, and were compofed by fome writer, who either confounded the time of the tranfaction with our Saviour's age, or inadvertently overlooked the anachronifm.

Now fuppofe it to have been fo; fuppofe thefe words to have been fuggefted by the tranfaction related in Jofephus, and to have been falfely afcribed to Chrift; and obferve what extraordinary coincidences (accidentally, as it muft in that cafe have been) attend the forger's miftake.

Firft, That we have a Zacharias in the book of Chronicles, whofe death, and the manner of it, correfponds with the allufion.

Secondly, that although the name of this perfon's father be erroneoufly put down in the gofpel, yet we have a way of accounting for the error, by fhewing another Zacharias in the Jewifh fcriptures, much better known than the former, whofe patronymic was actually that which appears in the text.

Every one, who thinks upon the fubject, will find thefe to be circumftances, which could not have met together in a miftake, which did not proceed from the circumftances themfelves.

I have noticed, I think, all the difficulties of this kind. They are few; fome of them admit of a clear, others of a probable folution. The reader will compare them with the number, the variety, the clofenefs, and the fatisfactorinefs, of the inftances which are to be fet againft them; and he will remember the fcantinefs, in many cafes, of our intelligence, and that difficulties always attend imperfect information.

CHAP.

CHAP. VII.

Undesigned Coincidences.

BETWEEN the letters which bear the name of St. Paul in our collection, and his history in the Acts of the Apostles, there exist many notes of correspondency. The simple perusal of the writings is sufficient to prove, that neither the history was taken from the letters, nor the letters from the history. And the *undesignedness* of the agreements (which undesignedness is gathered from their latency, their minuteness, their obliquity, the suitableness of the circumstances in which they consist, to the places in which those circumstances occur, and the circuitous references by which they are traced out) demonstrates that they have not been produced by meditation, or by any fraudulent contrivance. But coincidences, from which these causes are excluded, and

which

which are too clofe and numerous to be accounted for by accidental concurrences of
fiction, muft neceffarily have truth for their
foundation.

This argument appeared to my mind of
fo much value (efpecially for its affuming
nothing befide the exiftence of the books),
that I have purfued it through St. Paul's
thirteen epiftles, in a work publifhed by me
four years ago under the title of Horæ Pau-
linæ. I am fenfible how feebly any argument, which depends upon an induction of
particulars, is reprefented without examples.
On which account, I wifhed to have abridg-
ed my own volume, in the manner in which
I have treated Dr. Lardner's in the preceding chapter. But, upon making the attempt, I did not find it in my power to
render the articles intelligible by fewer
words than I have there ufed. I muft be
content, therefore, to refer the reader to the
work itfelf. And I would particularly in-
vite his attention to the obfervations which
are made in it upon the three firft epiftles.
I per-

I perfuade myfelf that he will find the proofs, both of agreement and undefignednefs, fupplied by thefe epiftles, fufficient to fupport the conclufion which is there maintained, in favour both of the genuinenefs of the writings, and the truth of the narrative.

It remains only, in this place, to point out how the argument *bears* upon the general queftion of the Chriftian hiftory.

Firft, St. Paul in thefe letters affirms, in unequivocal terms, his own performance of miracles, and, what ought particularly to be remembered, " *That miracles were the figns of an apoftle* *." If this teftimony come from St. Paul's own hand, it is invaluable. And that it does fo, the argument before us fixes in my mind a firm affurance.

Secondly, it fhows that the feries of action, reprefented in the epiftles of St. Paul, was real; which alone lays a foundation

* Rom. xv. 18, 19. 2 Cor. xii. 12.

for

for the propofition, which forms the fubject
of the firft part of our prefent work, viz.
that the original witneffes of the Chriftian
hiftory devoted themfelves to lives of toil,
fuffering, and danger, in confequence of
their belief of the truth of that hiftory, and
for the fake of communicating the knowledge of it to others.

Thirdly, it proves that Luke, or whoever
was the author of the Acts of the Apoftles
(for the argument does not depend upon
the name of the author, though I know no
reafon for queftioning it) was well acquainted with St. Paul's hiftory ; and that he probably was, what he profeffes himfelf to be,
a companion of St. Paul's travels : which, if
true, eftablifhes, in a confiderable degree,
the credit even of his gofpel, becaufe it
fhews, that the writer, from his time, fituation, and connections, poffeffed opportunities of informing himfelf truly concerning
the tranfactions which he relates. I have
little difficulty in applying to the Gofpel of
St. Luke what is proved concerning the

Acts

Acts of the Apostles, confidering them as two parts of the fame hiftory; for, though there are inftances of *fecond* parts being forgeries, I know none where the fecond part is genuine, and the firft not fo.

I will only obferve, as a fequel of the argument, though not noticed in my work, the remarkable fimilitude between the ftyle of St. John's gofpel, and of St. John's firft epiftle. The ftyle of St. John's is not at all the ftyle of St. Paul's epiftles, though both are very fingular; nor is it the ftyle of St. James's or of St. Peter's epiftle: but it bears a refemblance to the ftyle of the gofpel infcribed with St. John's name, fo far as that refemblance can be expected to appear, which is not in fimple narrative, fo much as in reflections, and in the reprefentation of difcourfes. Writings, fo circumftanced, prove themfelves, and one another, to be genuine. This correfpondency is the more valuable, as the epiftle itfelf afferts, in St. John's manner indeed, but in terms fufficiently explicit, the writer's perfonal know-

ledge

ledge of Chrift's hiſtory: " That which
was from the beginning, which we have
heard, which we have ſeen with our eyes,
which we have looked upon, and our hands
have handled, of the word of life, that
which we have ſeen and heard, declare we
unto you *." Who would not deſire, who
perceives not the value of an account, delivered by a writer ſo well informed as
this?

* C. i. v. 1. 3.

CHAP.

CHAP. VIII.

Of the History of the Resurrection.

THE history of the resurrection of Christ is a part of the evidence of Christianity; but I do not know, whether the proper strength of this passage of the Christian history, or wherein its peculiar value, as a head of evidence, consists, be generally understood. It is not that, as a miracle, the resurrection ought to be accounted a more decisive proof of supernatural agency than other miracles are; it is not that, as it stands in the Gospels, it is better attested than some others; it is not, for either of these reasons, that more weight belongs to it than to other miracles, but for the following, viz. That it is completely certain, that the apostles of Christ, and the first teachers of Christianity, asserted the fact. And this would have been certain, if the four gospels had been lost, or never written. Every piece of scripture re-

7   cognizes

cognizes the refurrection. Every epiftle of every apoftle, every author contemporary with the apoftles, of the age immediately fucceeding the apoftles, every writing from that age to the prefent, genuine or fpurious, on the fide of Chriftianity or againft it, concur in reprefenting the refurrection of Chrift as an article of his hiftory, received without doubt or difagreement by all who called themfelves Chriftians, as alledged from the beginning by the propagators of the inftitution, and alledged as the center of their teftimony. Nothing, I apprehend, which a man does not himfelf fee or hear, can be more certain to him than this point. I do not mean that nothing can be more certain than that Chrift rofe from the dead; but that nothing can be more certain, than that his apoftles, and the firft teachers of Chriftianity, gave out that he did fo. In the other parts of the gofpel narrative, a queftion may be made, whether the things, related of Chrift, be the very things which the apoftles and firft teachers of the religion delivered concerning him? And this queftion depends

a good

a good deal upon the evidence we poſſeſs of the genuineneſs, or rather perhaps, of the antiquity, credit, and reception of the books. Upon the ſubject of the reſurrection, no ſuch diſcuſſion is neceſſary, becauſe no ſuch doubt can be entertained. The only points, which can enter into our conſideration, are, whether the apoſtles knowingly publiſhed a falſehood, or whether they were themſelves deceived; whether either of theſe ſuppoſitions be poſſible. The firſt, I think, is pretty generally given up. The nature of the undertaking, and of the men; the extreme unlikelihood that ſuch men ſhould engage in ſuch a meaſure as a *ſcheme*; their perſonal toils and dangers and ſufferings in the cauſe; their appropriation of their whole time to the object; the warm and ſeemingly unaffected zeal and earneſtneſs with which they profeſs their ſincerity, exempt their memory from the ſuſpicion of impoſture. The ſolution more deſerving of notice, is that which would reſolve the conduct of the apoſtles into *enthuſiaſm*; which would claſs the evidence of Chriſt's reſurrection with

the

the numerous stories that are extant of the apparitions of dead men. There are circumstances in the narrative, as it is preserved in our histories, which destroy this comparison entirely. It was not one person, but many, who saw him; they saw him not only separately, but together, not only by night but by day, not at a distance but near, not once but several times; they not only saw him, but touched him, conversed with him, eat with him, examined his person to satisfy their doubts. These particulars are decisive; but they stand, I do admit, upon the credit of our records. I would answer, therefore, the insinuation of enthusiasm, by a circumstance which arises out of the nature of the thing; and the reality of which must be confessed by all, who allow, what I believe is not denied, that the resurrection of Christ, whether true or false, was asserted by his disciples from the beginning: and that circumstance is, the nonproduction of the dead body. It is related in the history, what indeed the story of the resurrection necessarily implies, that the corpse corpfe was miffing out of the fepulchre: it is related alfo in the hiftory, that the Jews reported that the followers of Chrift had ftolen it away *. And this account, though loaded with great improbabilities, fuch as the fituation of the difciples, their fears for their own fafety at the time, the unlikeli-hood of their expecting to fucceed, the dif-ficulty of actual fuccefs †, and the inevitable

---

* " And this faying," St. Matthew writes, " is commonly reported amongft the Jews until this day." (xxviii. 15.) The evangelift may be thought good au-thority as to this point, even by thofe who do not admit his evidence in every other point: and this point is fuf-ficient to prove that the body was miffing.

It has alfo been rightly, I think, obferved by Dr. Townfend (Dif. upon the Ref. p. 126.), that the ftory of the guards carried collufion upon the face of it :— " His difciples came by night, and ftole him away, while we flept." Men in their circumftances would not have made fuch an acknowledgement of their neg-ligence, without previous affurances of protection and impunity.

† " Efpecially at the full moon, the city full of peo-ple, many probably paffing the whole night, as Jefus and his difciples had done, in the open air, the fepulchre fo near the city as to be now inclofed within the walls." Prieftley on the Refur. p. 24.

confequence of detection and failure, was, nevertheless, the moft credible account that could be given of the matter. But it proceeds entirely upon the fuppofition of fraud, as all the old objections did. What account can be given of the *body*, upon the fuppofition of enthufiafm? It is impoffible our Lord's followers could believe that he was rifen from the dead, if his corpfe was lying before them. No enthufiafm ever reached to fuch a pitch of extravagancy as that: a fpirit may be an illufion, a body is a real thing; an object of fenfe, in which there can be no miftake. All accounts of fpectres leave the body in the grave. And, although the body of Chrift might be removed by *fraud*, and for the purpofes of fraud, yet, without any fuch intention, and by fincere but deluded men, which is the reprefentation of the apoftolic character we are now examining, no fuch attempt could be made. The prefence and the abfence of the dead body are alike inconfiftent with the hypothefis of enthufiafm: for if prefent, it muft have cured their enthufiafm at once; if abfent,

fent, fraud, not enthufiafm, muft have carried it away.

But further, if we admit upon the con-
current teftimony of all the hiftories, fo
much of the account as ftates that the religion of Jefus was fet up at Jerufalem, and
fet up with afferting, in the very place in
which he had been buried, and a few days
after he had been buried, his refurrection
out of the grave, it is evident that if his
body could have been found, the Jews would
have produced it, as the fhorteft and com-
pleteft anfwer poffible to the whole ftory.
The attempt of the apoftles could not have
furvived this refutation a moment. If we
alfo admit, upon the authority of St. Matthew, that the Jews were advertifed of the
expectation of Chrift's followers, and that
they had taken due precaution in confequence of this notice, and that the body was
in marked and public cuftody, the obfervation receives more force ftill. For, notwithftanding their precaution, and although thus
prepared and forewarned ; when the ftory
of

of the refurrection of Chrift came forth, as
it immediately did ; when it was publicly
afferted by his difciples, and made the
ground and bafis of their preaching in his
name, and collecting followers to his religion, the Jews had not the body to produce : but were obliged to meet the teftimony of the apoftles by an anfwer, not
containing indeed any impoffibility in itfelf,
but abfolutely inconfiftent with the fuppofition of their integrity ; that is, in other
words, inconfiftent with the fuppofition,
which would refolve their conduct into
enthufiafm.

CHAP.

CHAP. IX.

The Propagation of Christianity.

I N this argument, the first consideration is the fact; in what degree, within what time, and to what extent, Christianity actually was propagated.

The accounts of the matter, which can be collected from our books, are as follow: A *few days* after Christ's disappearance out of the world, we find an assembly of disciples at Jerusalem, to the number of " about one hundred and twenty*;" which hundred and twenty were, probably, a little association of believers, met together, not merely as believers in Christ, but as personally connected with the apostles, and with one another. Whatever was the number of be-

---

* Acts i. 5.

lievers then in Jerusalem, we have no reason to be surprised that so small a company should assemble; for there is no proof that the followers of Christ were yet formed into a society, that the society was reduced into any order, that it was at this time even understood, that a new religion (in the sense which that term conveys to us) was to be set up in the world, or how the professors of that religion were to be distinguished from the rest of mankind. The death of Christ had left, we may suppose, the generality of his disciples in great doubt, both as to what they were to do, and concerning what was to follow.

This meeting was held, as we have already said, a few days after Christ's ascension; for, ten days after that event was the day of pentecost, when, as our history relates *, upon a signal display of divine agency attending the persons of the apostles, there were added to the society " about

* Acts ii. 1

three

three thoufand fouls *." But here, it is not,
I think, to be taken, that thefe three
thoufand were all converted by this fingle
miracle; but rather that many, who were
before believers in Chrift, became now pro-
feffors of Chriftianity; that is to fay, when
they found that a religion was to be eftablifhed, a fociety formed and fet up in the
name of Chrift, governed by his laws,
avowing their belief in his miffion, united
amongft themfelves, and feparated from the
reft of the world, by vifible diftinctions, in
purfuance of their former conviction, and
by virtue of what they had heard and feen
and known of Chrift's hiftory, they publicly
became members of it.

We read in the fourth † chapter of the
Acts, that, foon after this, " the number of
the men," i. e. of the fociety openly profeffing their belief in Chrift, " was about five
thoufand." So that here is an increafe of
two thoufand within a very fhort time.
And it is probable that there were many,

* Acts ii. 41.   † Verfe 4.

P 2   both

both now and afterwards, who, although
they believed in Chrift, did not think it
neceffary to join themfelves to this fociety;
or who waited to fee what was likely to become of it. Gamaliel, whofe advice to the
Jewifh council is recorded Acts iv. 34, appears to have been of this defcription; perhaps Nicodemus, and perhaps alfo Jofeph
of Arimathea. This clafs of men, their
character and their rank, are likewife pointed out by St. John, in the twelfth chapter
of his gofpel: " Neverthelefs among the
chief rulers alfo many believed on him;
but becaufe of the Pharifees they did not
confefs him, left they fhould be put out of
the fynagogue: for they loved the praife of
men more than the praife of God." Perfons fuch as thefe, might admit the miracles
of Chrift, without being immediately convinced that they were under obligation to
make a public profeffion of Chriftianity, at
the rifk of all that was dear to them in life,
and even of life itfelf *.

Chriftianity,

---

* " Befide thofe who profeffed, and thofe who rejected and oppofed Chriftianity, there were, in all pro-

Chriſtianity, however, proceeded to increaſe in Jeruſalem by a progreſs equally
rapid with its firſt ſucceſs; for, in the next*
chapter of our hiſtory, we read that "believers were the more added to the Lord,
multitudes both of men and women." And

bability, multitudes between both, neither perfect Chriſtians, nor yet unbelievers. They had a favourable opinion of the goſpel, but worldly conſiderations made
them unwilling to own it. There were many circumſtances which inclined them to think that Chriſtianity
was a divine revelation, but there were many inconve-
niences which attended the open profeſſion of it; and
they could not find in themſelves courage enough to
bear them, to diſoblige their friends and family, to ruin
their fortunes, to loſe their reputation, their liberty and
their life, for the ſake of the new religion. Therefore
they were willing to hope, that if they endeavoured to
obſerve the great precepts of morality, which Chriſt
had repreſented as the principal part, the ſum and ſubſtance of religion; if they thought honourably of the
goſpel, if they offered no injury to the Chriſtians, if
they did them all the ſervices that they could *ſafely*
perform, they were willing to hope that God would
accept this, and that he would excuſe and forgive the
reſt." Jortin's Diſ. on the Chriſt. Rel. p. 91, ed. 4.

* Acts v. 14.

P 3

this

this enlargement of the new fociety appears
in the firſt verſe of the ſucceeding chapter,
wherein we are told, that, " when the number of the diſciples was *multiplied*, there aroſe
a murmuring of the Grecians againſt the
Hebrews becauſe their widows were neglected * ;" and, afterwards in the ſame
chapter, it is declared expreſsly, that " the
number of the diſciples multiplied in Jeruſalem greatly, and that a great company of
the prieſts were obedient to the faith."

This I call the firſt period in the propagation of Chriſtianity. It commences with
the aſcenſion of Chriſt ; and extends, as
may be collected from incidental notes of
time †, to ſomething more than one year
after that event. During which term the
preaching of Chriſtianity, ſo far as our do-
cuments inform us, was confined to the
ſingle city of Jeruſalem. And how did it
ſucceed there ? The firſt aſſembly which we

---

* Acts vi. 1.

† Vide Pearſon's Antiq. l. xviii. c. 7. Benſon's Hiſt.
of Chriſt. book i. p. 148.

meet

meet with of Chrift's difciples, and that a
few days after his removal from the world,
confifted of " one hundred and twenty."
About a week after this " three thoufand
were added" in one day ; and the number
of Chriftians, publicly baptized, and publicly affociating together, were very foon increafed to " five thoufand." " Multitudes
both of men and women continued to be
added :" " difciples multiplied greatly," and
" many of the Jewifh priefthood, as well as
others, became obedient to the faith ;" and
this within a fpace of lefs than two years
from the commencement of the inftitution.

By reafon of a perfecution raifed againft
the church at Jerufalem, the converts were
driven from that city, and difperfed throughout the regions of Judea and Samaria *.
Wherever they came, they brought their religion with them ; for our hiftorian informs
us †, that " they, that were fcattered abroad,
went every where preaching the word."

* Acts viii. 1.   † Verfe 4.

The

The effect of this preaching comes afterwards to be noticed, where the hiftorian is led, in the courfe of his narrative, to obferve, that *then* (*i. e.* about three years *poftterior to this) " the churches had reft throughout all Judea, and Galilee and Samaria, and were edified, and walking in the fear of the Lord, and in the comfort of the Holy Ghoft, were multiplied." This was the work of the fecond period, which comprifes about four years.

Hitherto the preaching of the gofpel had been confined to Jews, to Jewifh profelytes, and to Samaritans. And I cannot forbear from fetting down, in this place, an obfervation of Mr. Bryant's, which appears to me to be perfectly well founded :—" The Jews ftill remain, but how feldom is it that we can make a fingle profelyte ! There is reafon to think, that there were more converted by the apoftles in one day, than have

* Benfon, book i. p. 207.

since been won over in the last thousand years *."

It was not yet known to the apostles, that they were at liberty to propose the religion to mankind at large. That " mystery," as St. Paul calls it †, and as it then was, was revealed to Peter by an especial miracle. It appears to have been ‡ about seven years after Christ's ascension, that the gospel was preached to the Gentiles of Cesarea. A year after this, a great multitude of Gentiles were converted at Antioch in Syria. The expressions employed by the historian are these— " a great number believed, and turned to the Lord;" " much people was added unto the Lord;" " the apostles Barnabas and Paul taught much people §." Upon Herod's death, which happened in the next year ||, it is observed that " the word of God grew

* Bryant on the Truth of the Christian Religion, p. 112.
† Eph. iii. 3—6.   ‡ Benson, b. ii. p. 236.
§ Acts xi. 21. 24. 26. || Benson, b. ii. p. 289.

and

and multiplied *." Three years from this time, upon the preaching of Paul at Iconium, the metropolis of Lycaonia, " a great multitude both of Jews and Greeks believed † ;" and afterwards, in the courſe of this very progreſs, he is repreſented as " making many diſciples" at Derbe, a principal city in the ſame diſtrict. Three years ‡ after this, which brings us to ſixteen after the aſcenſion, the apoſtles wrote a public letter from Jeruſalem to the Gentile converts in Antioch, Syria, and Cilicia, with which letter Paul travelled through theſe countries, and found the churches " eſtabliſhed in the faith, and increaſing in number daily §." From Aſia the apoſtle proceeded into Greece, where, ſoon after his arrival in Macedonia, we find him at Theſſalonica; in which city " ſome of the Jews believed, and of the devout Greeks a great multitude ‖." We meet alſo here with an

* Acts xii. 24.   † Ib. xiv. 1.

‡ Benſon's Hiſt. Chriſt. b. iii. p. 50.

§ Acts xvi. 5.   ‖ Ib. xvii. 4.

accidental

accidental hint of the general progrefs of
the Chriftian miffion, in the exclamation of
the tumultuous Jews of Theffalonica, " that
they, who had turned the world upfide
down, were come thither alfo *." At Berea,
the next city at which St. Paul arrives, the
hiftorian, who was prefent, informs us that
" *many* of the Jews believed †." The next
year and half of St. Paul's miniftry was
fpent at Corinth. Of his fuccefs in that city
we receive the following intimations: " that
many of the Corinthians believed and were
baptized," and " that it was revealed to the
apoftle by Chrift, that he had *much* people
in that city ‡." Within lefs than a year after his departure from Corinth, and twenty-
five § years after the afcenfion, St. Paul
fixed his ftation at Ephefus, for the fpace of
two years ‖ and fomething more. The effect
of his miniftry in that city and neighbour-
hood, drew from the hiftorian a reflection,
" how mightily grew the word of God and

* Acts v. 6. † Ib. xvii. 12. ‡ Ib. xviii. 8—10.
§ Benfon, b. iii. p. 160. ‖ Acts xix. 10.

pre-

prevailed *.". And at the conclusion of this
period, we find Demetrius at the head of a
party, who were alarmed by the progress of
the religion, complaining, that " not only at
Ephefus, but also throughout all Asia, (*i. e.*
the province of Lydia, and the country adjoining to Ephefus) this Paul hath perfuaded
and turned away much people †." Befide
thefe accounts, there occurs, incidentally,
mention of converts at Rome, Alexandria,
Athens, Cyprus, Cyrene, Macedonia, Philippi.

This is the third period in the propagation of Chriftianity, fetting off in the feventh
year after the afcenfion, and ending at the
twenty-eighth. Now, lay thefe three pe-
riods together, and obferve how the progrefs of the religion by thefe accounts is
reprefented. The inftitution, which properly *began* only after its author's removal
from the world, before the end of thirty
years had fpread itfelf through Judea, Ga-

---

* Acts xix. 20.   † Ib. v. 26.

lilee, and Samaria, almoſt all the numerous
diſtricts of the Leſſer Aſia, through Greece,
and the iſlands of the Ægean Sea, the ſea
coaſt of Africa, and had extended itſelf to
Rome, and into Italy. At Antioch in Syria,
at Joppa, Epheſus, Corinth, Theſſalonica,
Berea, Iconium, Derbe, Antioch in Piſidia,
at Lydda, Saron, the number of converts is
intimated by the expreſſions " a great number," great multitudes," " much people."
Converts are mentioned, without any deſignation of their number *, at Tyre, Ceſa-
rea, Troas, Athens, Philippi, Lyſtra, Da-

---

* Conſidering the extreme conciſeneſs of many parts
of the hiſtory, the ſilence about the numbers of converts
is no proof of their paucity ; for at Philippi, no mention whatever is made of the number, yet St. Paul addreſſed an epiſtle to that church. The churches of
Galatia, and the affairs of thoſe churches, were conſiderable enough to be the ſubject of another letter, and
of much of St. Paul's ſolicitude, yet no account is pre-
ſerved in the hiſtory of his ſucceſs, or even of his preaching in that country, except the ſlight notice which theſe
words convey :—" when they had gone throughout
Phrygia, and the region of Galatia, they eſſayed to go
into Bythinia." Acts xvi. 6.

4   maſcus.

mafcus. During all this time, Jerufalem
continued not only the centre of the miffion,
but a principal feat of the religion ; for when
St. Paul returned thither, at the conclufion
of the period of which we are now confidering the accounts, the other apoftles pointed out to him, as a reafon for his compliance
with their advice, " how many thoufands
(myriads, ten thoufands) there were in that
city who believed *."

Upon this abftract, and the writing from
which it is drawn, the following obfervations feem material to be made :

I. That the account comes from a perfon,
who was himfelf concerned in a portion of
what he relates, and was contemporary with
the whole of it ; who vifited Jerufalem, and
frequented the fociety of thofe who had acted, and were acting, the chief parts in the
tranfaction. I lay down this point pofitive-

* Acts xxi. 20.

ly ;

ly; for had the ancient atteftations to this valuable record been lefs fatisfactory than they are, the unaffectednefs and fimplicity with which the author notices his prefence upon certain occafions, and the entire ab-fence of art and defign from thefe notices, would have been fufficient to perfuade my mind, that, whoever he was, he actually lived in the times, and occupied the fitua-tion, in which he reprefents himfelf to be. When I fay " whoever he was," I do not mean to caft a doubt upon the name, to which antiquity hath afcribed the Acts of the Apo-ftles (for there is no caufe, that I am ac-quainted with, for queftioning it), but to ob-ferve, that in fuch a cafe as this, the time and fituation of the author, is of more im-portance than his name ; and that *thefe* ap-pear from the work itfelf, and in the moft unfufpicious form.

II. That this account is a very *incom-plete* account of the preaching and propaga-tion of Chriftianity ; I mean, that, if what we read in the hiftory be true, much more

than what the hiftory contains muft be true
alfo. For, although the narrative from
which our information is derived has been
intitled the Acts of the Apoftles, it is in fact
a hiftory of the twelve apoftles, only during
a fhort time of their continuing together at
Jerufalem ; and even of this period the account is very concife. The work afterwards
confifts of a few important paffages of Peter's miniftry, of the fpeech and death of
Stephen, of the preaching of Philip the dea-
con ; and the fequel of the volume, that is,
two thirds of the whole, is taken up with the
converfion, the travels, the difcourfes and
hiftory of the new apoftle Paul, in which
hiftory alfo large portions of time are often
paffed over with very fcanty notice.

III. That the account, fo far as it goes,
is for this very reafon more credible. Had
it been the author's defign to have *difplayed*
the early progrefs of Chriftianity, he would
undoubtedly have collected, or, at leaft, have
fet forth, accounts of the preaching of the
reft of the apoftles, who cannot, without extreme

treme improbability, be suppofed to have re-
mained filent and inactive, or not to have
met with a fhare of that fuccefs which attended their colleagues. To which may be
added, as an obfervation of the fame kind,

IV. That the intimations of the number
of converts, and of the fuccefs of the preaching of the apoftles, come out for the moft
part *incidentally*; are drawn from the hiftorian by the occafion; fuch as the murmuring
of the Grecian converts, the reft from perfecution, Herod's death, the fending of Barnabas to Antioch and Barnabas calling Paul
to his affiftance, Paul coming to a place and
finding there difciples, the clamour of the
Jews, the complaint of artificers interefted
in the fupport of the popular religion, the
reafon affigned to induce Paul to give fatisfaction to the Chriftians of Jerufalem.
Had it not been for thefe occafions, it
is probable that no notice whatever would
have been taken of the number of converts,
in feveral of the paffages in which that notice now appears. All this tends to remove

the fufpicion of a defign to exaggerate or deceive.

PARALLEL TESTIMONIES with the hiftory, are the letters which have come down
to us of St. Paul, and of the other apoftles.
Thofe of St. Paul are addreffed to the
churches of Corinth, Philippi, Theffalonica,
the church of Galatia, and, if the infcription
be right, of Ephefus, his miniftry at all
which places is recorded in the hiftory ; to
the church of Coloffe, or rather to the
churches of Coloffe and Laodicea jointly,
which he had not then vifited. They re-
cognize by reference the churches of Judea,
the churches of Afia, and " all the churches
of the Gentiles *." In the epiftle † to the
Romans, the author is led to deliver a remarkable declaration, concerning the extent
of his preaching, its efficacy, and the caufe
to which he afcribes it, " to make the Gentiles obedient by word and deed, through
mighty figns and wonders, by the power of

* 1 Theff. ii. 14.   † Rom. xv. 18, 19.

the Spirit of God; fo that from Jerufalem, and round about unto Illyricum, I have fully preached the gofpel of Chrift." In the epiftle to the Coloffians *, we find an oblique, but very ftrong fignification, of the then general ftate of the Chriftian miffion, at leaft as it appeared to St. Paul: " If ye continue in the faith, grounded and fettled, and be not moved away from the hope of the gofpel, which ye have heard, and *which was preached to every creature which is under heaven ;"* which gofpel, he had reminded them near the beginning † of his letter, " was prefent with them *as it was in all the world.*" The expreffions are hyperbolical ; but they are hyperboles which could only be ufed by a writer who entertained a ftrong fenfe of the fubject. The firft epiftle of Peter accofts the Chriftians difperfed throughout Pontus, Galatia, Cappadocia, Afia and Bithynia.

It comes next to be confidered, how far

* Col. i. 23.   † Ib. i. 6.

thefe

thefe accounts are confirmed, or followed up, by other evidence.

Tacitus, in delivering a relation, which has already been laid before the reader, of the fire which happened at Rome in the tenth year of Nero, which coincides with the thirtieth year after Chrift's afcenfion, afferts, that the emperor, in order to fupprefs the rumours of having been himfelf the author of the mifchief, procured the Chriftians to be accufed. Of which Chriftians, thus brought into his narrative, the following is fo much of the hiftorian's account, as belongs to our prefent purpofe : " They had their denomination from Chriftus, who, in the reign of Tiberius, was put to death as a criminal by the procurator Pontius Pilate. This pernicious fuperftition, though checked for a while, broke out again, and fpread not only over Judea, but reached the city alfo. At firft they only were apprehended, who confeffed themfelves of that fect ; afterwards *a vaft multitude* were difcovered by them." This teftimony to the early propagation of
Chriftianity

Chriftianity is extremely material. It is from an hiftorian of great reputation, living near the time; from a ftranger and an ene-my to the religion : and it joins immediately with the period through which the fcrip-ture accounts extend. It eftablifhes thefe points, that the religion began at Jerufalem, that it fpread throughout Judea, that it had reached Rome, and not only fo, but that it had there obtained a great number of con-verts. This was about fix years after the time that St. Paul wrote his epiftle to the Romans, and fomething more than two years after he arrived there himfelf. The converts to the religion were then fo nume-rous at Rome, that of thofe who were be-trayed by the information of the perfons firft perfecuted, a great multitude (multitudo in-gens) were difcovered and feized.

It feems probable, that the temporary check which Tacitus reprefents Chriftianity to have received (repreffa in præfens) refer-red to the perfecution at Jerufalem, which followed the death of Stephen (Acts viii.);

Q 3

and which, by difperfing the converts, caufed the inftitution, in fome meafure, to difappear. Its fecond eruption at the fame place, and within a fhort time, has much in it of the character of truth. It was the firmnefs and perfeverance of men who knew what they relied upon.

Next in order of time, and perhaps fuperior in importance, is the teftimony of Pliny the younger. Pliny was the Roman governor of Pontus and Bithynia, two confiderable diftricts in the northern part of Afia Minor. The fituation in which he found his province, led him to apply to the emperor (Trajan) for his direction as to the conduct he was to hold towards the Chriftians. The letter, in which this application is contained, was written not quite eighty years after Chrift's afcenfion. The prefident, in this letter, ftates the meafures he had already purfued, and then adds, as his reafon for reforting to the emperor's counfel and authority, the following words :—" Sufpending all judicial proceedings, I have recourfe to you

you for advice ; for it has appeared to me a
matter highly deferving confideration, efpecially upon account of the great number of
perfons who are in danger of fuffering : for
many of all ages, and of every rank, of both
fexes likewife, are accufed, and will be accufed. Nor has the contagion of this fuperftition feized cities only, but the leffer
towns alfo, and the open country. Neverthelefs it feemed to me that it may be reftrained and corrected. It is certain that the
temples, which were almoft forfaken, begin
to be more frequented ; and the facred folemnities, after a long intermiffion, are revived. Victims, likewife, are everywhere
(paffim) bought up ; whereas, for fome time,
there were few to purchafe them. Whence
it is eafy to imagine, what numbers of men
might be reclaimed, if pardon were granted
to thofe that fhall repent *."

It is obvious to obferve, that the paffage
of Pliny's letter, here quoted, proves, not

* C. Plin. Trajano Imp. lib. x. ep. xcvii.

Q 4   only

only that the Chriſtians in Pontus and Bithynia were now numerous, but that they
had ſubſiſted there for ſome conſiderable
time. " It is certain (he ſays) that the temples, which were almoſt forſaken (plainly
aſcribing this deſertion of the popular worſhip to the prevalency of Chriſtianity), begin to be more frequented ; and the ſacred
ſolemnities, after a *long* intermiſſion, are revived." There are alſo two clauſes in the
former part of the letter which indicate the
ſame thing ; one, in which he declares that
he had " never been preſent at any trials of
Chriſtians, and therefore knew not what was
the uſual ſubject of enquiry and puniſhment,
or how far either was wont to be urged :"
the ſecond clauſe is the following, " others
were named by an informer, who, at firſt,
confeſſed themſelves Chriſtians, and afterwards denied it ; the reſt ſaid, they had been
Chriſtians, ſome three years ago, ſome
longer, and ſome above twenty years." It
is alſo apparent that Pliny ſpeaks of the
Chriſtians as a deſcription of men well
known to the perſon to whom he writes.

His

His firſt ſentence concerning them is, " I
have never been preſent at the trials of Chriſtians." This mention of the name of Chriſtians, without any preparatory explanation,
ſhews that it was a term familiar both to the
writer of the letter, and the perſon to whom
it was addreſſed. Had it not been ſo, Pliny
would naturally have begun his letter by informing the emperor, that he had met with
a certain ſet of men in the province called
Chriſtians.

Here then is a very ſignal evidence of the
progreſs of the Chriſtian religion in a ſhort
ſpace. It was not fourſcore years after the
crucifixion of Jeſus when Pliny wrote this
letter; nor ſeventy years ſince the apoſtles
of Jeſus began to mention his name to the
Gentile world. Bithynia and Pontus were
at a great diſtance from Judea, the centre
from which the religion ſpread; yet in theſe
provinces Chriſtianity had long ſubſiſted,
and Chriſtians were now in ſuch numbers
as to lead the Roman governor to report to
the emperor, that they were found, not only

in

in cities, but in villages and in open countries; of all ages, of every rank and condition; that they abounded fo much as to
have produced a vifible defertion of the
temples, that beafts brought to market for
victims had few purchafers, that the facred
folemnities were much neglected; circumftances noted by Pliny, for the exprefs purpofe of fhewing to the emperor the effect
and prevalency of the new inftitution.

No evidence remains, by which it can be
proved that the Chriftians were more numerous in Pontus and Bithynia than in other
parts of the Roman empire; nor has any
reafon been offered to fhew why they fhould
be fo. Chriftianity did not begin in thefe
countries, nor near them. I do not know,
therefore, that we ought to confine the defcription in Pliny's letter to the ftate of
Chriftianity in thofe provinces, even if no
other account of the fame fubject had come
down to us; but, certainly, this letter may
fairly be applied in aid and confirmation of
the reprefentations given of the general ftate

of

of Chriftianity in the world, by Chriftian writers of that and the next fucceeding age.

Juftin Martyr, who wrote about thirty years after Pliny, and one hundred and fix after the afcenfion, has thefe remarkable words : " There is not a nation, either of Greek or Barbarian, or of any other name, even of thofe who wander in tribes, and live in tents, amongft whom prayers and thankfgivings are not offered to the Father and Creator of the univerfe by the name of the crucified Jefus *." Tertullian, who comes about fifty years after Juftin, appeals to the governors of the Roman empire in thefe terms : " We were but of yefterday, and we have filled your cities, iflands, towns and boroughs, the camp, the fenate, and the fo-rum. They (the heathen adverfaries of Chriftianity) lament, that every fex, age and condition, and perfons of every rank alfo, are converts to that name †." I do allow that thefe expreffions are loofe, and

* Dial. cum Tryph.   † Tertull. Apol. c. 37.

may be called declamatory. But even de-
clamation hath its bounds: this public boaſt-
ing upon a ſubject, which muſt be known
to every reader, was not only uſeleſs but unnatural, unleſs the truth of the caſe, in a conſiderable degree, correſponded with the deſcription; at leaſt unleſs it had been both
true and notorious, that great multitudes of
Chriſtians, of all ranks and orders, were to
be found in moſt parts of the Roman empire. The ſame Tertullian, in another paſſage, by way of ſetting forth the extenſive
diffuſion of Chriſtianity, enumerates as belonging to Chriſt, beſide many other countries, the " Moors and Gætulians of Africa,
the borders of Spain, ſeveral nations of
France, and parts of Britain inacceſſible to
the Romans, the Sarmatians, Daci, Germans,
and Scythians * :" and, which is more material than the extent of the inſtitution, the
number of Chriſtians in the ſeveral countries
in which it prevailed, is thus expreſſed by
him: " Although ſo great a multitude, that in

* Ad Jud. c. 7.

almoſt

almoſt every city we form the greater part, we paſs our time modeſtly and in ſilence*." Clement Alexandrinus, who preceded Tertullian by a few years, introduces a compariſon between the ſucceſs of Chriſtianity, and that of the moſt celebrated philoſophical inſtitutions. " The philoſophers were confined to Greece, and to their particular retainers; but the doctrine of the Maſter of Chriſtianity did not remain in Judea, as philoſophy did in Greece, but is ſpread throughout the whole world, in every nation and village and city, both of Greeks and Barbarians, converting both whole houſes and ſeparate individuals, having already brought over to the truth not a few of the philoſophers themſelves. If the Greek philoſophy be prohibited, it immediately vaniſhes; whereas, from the firſt preaching of *our* doctrine, kings and tyrants, governors and preſidents, with their whole train, and with the populace on their ſide, have endeavoured with their whole might to exterminate it,

* Ad Scap. c. 3.

yet

yet doth it flourish more and more *." Origen, who follows Tertullian at the distance
of only thirty years, delivers nearly the same
account : " In every part of the world (says
he), throughout all Greece, and in all other
nations, there are innumerable and immense
multitudes, who, having left the laws of their
country, and those whom they esteemed
gods, have given themselves up to the law
of Moses, and the religion of Christ; and
this, not without the bitterest resentment
from the idolaters, by whom they were frequently put to torture, and sometimes to
death : and it is wonderful to observe, how,
in so short a time, the religion has increased,
amidst punishment and death, and every
kind of torture †." In another passage Origen draws the following candid comparison
between the state of Christianity in his time,
and the condition of its more primitive
ages :—" By the good providence of God
the Christian religion has so flourished and
increased continually, that it is now preached

* Clem. Al. Strom. lib. vi. ad fin.
† Or. in Celf. lib. i.

freely

freely without moleftation, although there
were a thoufand obftacles to the fpreading
of the doctrine of Jefus in the world. But
as it was the will of God that the Gentiles
fhould have the benefit of it, all the councils of men againft the Chriftians were de-
feated ; and by how much the more emperors and governors of provinces, and the
people every where, ftrove to deprefs them,
fo much the more have they increafed and
prevailed exceedingly *."

It is well known, that within lefs than
eighty years after this, the Roman empire
became Chriftian under Conftantine ; and
it is probable that Conftantine declared himfelf on the fide of the Chriftians, becaufe
they were the powerful party: for Arnobius,
who wrote immediately before Conftantine's
acceffion, fpeaks of the whole world as filled with Chrift's doctrine, of its diffufion
throughout all countries, of an innumerable
body of Chriftians in diftant provinces, of

* Or. con. Celf. lib. vii.

the

the strange revolution of opinion, of men of the greatest genius, orators, grammarians, rhetoricians, lawyers, physicians, having come over to the institution, and that also in the face of threats, executions, and tortures *." And not more than twenty years after Conftantine's entire poffeffion of the empire, Julius Firmicus Maternus calls upon the emperors Conftantius and Conftans to extirpate the relics of the ancient religion; the reduced and fallen condition of which is defcribed by our author in the following words:—" Licet adhuc in quibufdam regionibus idololatriæ morientia palpitent membra, tamen in eo res eft, ut a Chriftianis omnibus terris peftiferum hoc malum funditùs amputetur;" and in another place, " modicum tantum fupereft, ut legibus veftris---extincta idololatriæ pereat funefta contagio †." It will not be thought that we quote this

---

* Arnob. in Gentes, l. i. p. 27. 9. 24. 42. 44. ed. Lug. Bat. 1650.

† De Error. Profan. Relig. c. xxi. p. 172. quoted by Lardner, vol. viii. p. 262.

writer

writer in order to recommend his temper or
his judgement, but to shew the comparative
state of Christianity and of Heathenism at
this period. Fifty years afterwards, Jerome
represents the decline of Paganism in language which conveys the same idea of its
approaching extinction : " Solitudinem pa-
titur et in urbe gentilitas. Dii quondam
nationum, cum bubonibus et noctuis, in so-
lis culminibus remanserunt *." Jerome here
indulges a triumph, natural and allowable in
a zealous friend of the cause, but which
could only be suggested to his mind by the
consent and universality with which he saw
the religion received. " But now (says he)
the passion and resurrection of Christ are
celebrated in the discourses and writings of
all nations. I need not mention Jews,
Greeks and Latins. The Indians, Persians,
Goths and Egyptians, philosophise, and
firmly believe the immortality of the soul
and future recompences, which, before, the
greatest philosophers had denied, or doubted

* Jer. ad Lect. ep. 57.

of, or perplexed with their difputes. The fiercenefs of Thracians and Scythians is now foftened by the gentle found of the gofpel; and every where Chrift is all in all *." Were therefore the motives of Conftantine's converfion ever fo problematical, the eafy eftablifhment of Chriftianity, and the ruin of Heathenifm under him and his immediate fucceffors, is of itfelf a proof of the progrefs which Chriftianity had made in the preceding period. It may be added alfo, " that Maxentius, the rival of Conftantine, had fhewn himfelf friendly to the Chriftians. Therefore, of thofe who were contending for worldly power and empire, one actually favoured and flattered them, and another may be fufpected to have joined himfelf to them, partly from confideration of intereft: fo confiderable were they become, under external difadvantages of all forts †." This at leaft is certain, that throughout the whole tranfaction hitherto, the great

---

* Jer. ep. 8. ad Heliod.
† Lardner, vol. vii. p. 380.

5   feemed

feemed to follow, not to lead, the public opinion.

It may help to convey to us fome notion of the extent and progrefs of Chriftianity, or rather of the character and quality of many early Chriftians, of their learning and their labours, to notice the number of Chriftian *writers* who flourifhed in thefe ages. St. Jerome's catalogue contains *fixty-fix* writers within the three firft centuries, and the fix firft years of the fourth ; and *fifty-four* between that time and his own, viz. A. D. 392. Jerome introduces his catalogue with the following juft remonftrance : — " Let thofe who fay the church has had no philofophers, nor eloquent and learned men, obferve who and what they were, who founded, eftablifhed, and adorned it ; let them ceafe to accufe our faith of rufticity, and confefs their miftake*." Of thefe writers, feveral, as Juftin, Irenæus, Clement of Alexandria, Tertullian, Origen, Bardefanes,

---

* Jer. Prol. in lib. de fer. ecc.

Hippolitus,

Hippolitus, Eufebius, were voluminous writers. Chriftian writers abounded particularly
about the year 178. Alexander, bifhop of
Jerufalem, founded a library in that city
A. D. 212. Pamphilus, the friend of Origen, founded a library at Cefarea A. D. 294.
Public defences were alfo fet forth, by various advocates of the religion, in the courfe
of its three firft centuries. Within one hundred years after Chrift's afcenfion, Quadratus and Ariftides, whofe works, except fome
few fragments of the firft, are loft ; and
about twenty years afterwards, Juftin Martyr, whofe works remain, prefented apolo-
gies for the Chriftian religion to the Roman
emperors ; Quadratus and Ariftides to Adrian, Juftin to Antoninus Pius, and a fecond
to Marcus Antoninus. Melito bifhop of
Sardis, and Apollinaris bifhop of Hierapo-
lis, and Miltiades, men of great reputation,
did the fame to Marcus Antoninus twenty
years afterwards * : and ten years after this,

* Eufeb. Hift. lib. iv. c. 26. See alfo Lardner, vol. ii.
p. 666.

Apollonius,

Apollonius, who fuffered martyrdom under the emperor Commodus, compofed an apology for his faith, which he read in the fenate, and which was afterwards publifhed*. Fourteen years after the apology of Apollonius, Tertullian addreffed the work, which now remains under that name, to the governors of provinces in the Roman empire; and, about the fame time, Minucius Felix compofed a defence of the Chriftian religion, which is ftill extant; and, fhortly after the conclufion of this century, copious defences of Chriftianity were publifhed by Arnobius and Lactantius.

* Lard. vol. ii. p. 687.

SEC-

SECTION II.

Reflections upon the preceding Account.

IN viewing the progress of Christianity, our first attention is due to the number of converts at Jerusalem, immediately after its founder's death; because this success was a success at the *time*, and upon the *spot*, when and where the chief part of the history had been transacted.

We are, in the next place, called upon to attend to the early establishment of numerous Christian societies in Judea and Galilee, which countries had been the scene of Christ's miracles and ministry, and where the memory of what had passed, and the knowledge of what was alledged, must have yet been fresh and certain.

We are, thirdly, invited to recollect the
success

success of the apostles and of their companions, at the several places to which they came, both within and without Judea; because it was the credit given to original witnesses, appealing for the truth of their accounts to what themselves had seen and heard. The effect also of their preaching, strongly confirms the truth of what our history positively and circumstantially relates, that they were able to exhibit to their hearers supernatural attestations of their mission.

We are, lastly, to consider the *subsequent* growth and spread of the religion, of which we receive successive intimations, and satisfactory, though general and occasional, accounts, until its full and final establishment.

In all these several stages, the history is without a parallel; for it must be observed, that we have not now been tracing the progress, and describing the prevalency, of an opinion, founded upon philosophical or critical arguments, upon mere deductions of

reason,

reason, or the conftruction of ancient writings, (of which kind are the feveral theories which have, at different times, gained poffeffion of the public mind in various departments of fcience and literature ; and of one or other of which kind are the tenets alfo which divide the various fects of Chriftianity) : but that we fpeak of a fyftem, the very bafis and poftulatum of which was a fupernatural character afcribed to a particular perfon ; of a doctrine, the truth whereof depended entirely upon the truth of a matter of fact then recent. " To eftablifh a new religion, even amongft a few people, or in one fingle nation, is a thing in itfelf exceedingly difficult. To reform fome corruptions which may have fpread in a religion, or to make new regulations in it, is not perhaps fo hard, when the main and principal parts of that religion are preferved entire and unfhaken ; and yet this very often cannot be accomplifhed, without an extraordinary concurrence of circumftances, and may be attempted a thoufand times without fuccefs. But to introduce a new

faith,

faith, a new way of thinking and acting, and to perfuade many nations to quit the religion in which their anceftors had lived and died, which had been delivered down to them from time immemorial, to make them forfake and defpife the deities which they had been accuftomed to reverence and worfhip; this is a work of ftill greater difficulty *. The refiftance of education, worldly policy, and fuperftition, is almoft invincible."

If men, in thefe days, be Chriftians in confequence of their education, in fubmiffion to authority, or in compliance with fafhion, let us recollect that the very contrary of this, at the beginning, was the cafe. The firft race of Chriftians, as well as millions who fucceeded them, became fuch in formal oppofition to all thefe motives; to the whole power and ftrength of this influence. Every argument therefore, and every inftance, which fets forth the preju-

* Jortin's Dif. on the Chrift. Rel. p. 107. ed. iv.

dice

dice of education, and the almoſt irreſiſtible effects of that prejudice (and no perſons are more fond of expatiating upon this ſubject than deiſtical writers) in fact confirms the evidence of Chriſtianity.

But, in order to judge of the argument which is drawn from the early propagation of Chriſtianity, I know no fairer way of proceeding, than to compare what we have ſeen of the ſubject, with the ſucceſs of Chriſtian miſſions in modern ages. In the Eaſt-India miſſion, ſupported by the ſociety for promoting Chriſtian knowledge, we hear ſometimes of thirty, ſometimes of forty, being baptized in the courſe of a year, and theſe principally children. Of converts properly ſo called, that is, of adults voluntarily embracing Chriſtianity, the number is extremely ſmall. "Notwithſtanding the labour of miſſionaries for upwards of two hundred years, and the eſtabliſhments of different Chriſtian nations who ſupport them, there are not twelve thouſand Indian

dian Chriftians, and thofe almoft entirely outcafts *."

I lament, as much as any man, the little progrefs which Chriftianity has made in thefe countries, and the inconfiderable effect that has followed the labours of its miffionaries; but I fee in it a ftrong proof of the divine origin of the religion. What had the apoftles to affift them in propagating Chriftianity, which the miffionaries have not? If piety and zeal had been fufficient, I doubt not but that our miffionaries poffefs thefe qualities in a high degree, for nothing, except piety and zeal, could engage them in the undertaking. If fanctity of life and manners was the allurement, the conduct of thefe men is unblameable. If the advantage of education and learning be looked to, there is not one of the modern miffionaries, who is not, in this refpect, fuperior to all the apoftles; and that not only abfolutely, but, what

* Sketches relating to the hiftory, learning, and manners of the Hindoos, p. 48. quoted by Dr. Robertfon, Hift. Dif. concerning ancient India, p. 236.

is

is of more importance, *relatively*, in comparison, that is, with those amongst whom they exercise their office. If the intrinsic excellency of the religion, the perfection of its morality, the purity of its precepts, the eloquence or tenderness or sublimity of various parts of its writings, were the recommendations by which it made its way, these remain the same. If the character and circumstances, under which the preachers were introduced to the countries in which they taught, be accounted of importance, this advantage is all on the side of the modern missionaries. They come from a country and a people, to which the Indian world look up with sentiments of deference. The apostles came forth amongst the Gentiles under no other name than that of Jews, which was precisely the character they despised and derided. If it be disgraceful in India to become a Christian, it could not be much less so to be enrolled amongst those, " quos per flagitia invisos, vulgus Christianos appellabat." If the religion which they had to encounter be considered, the difference, I

apprehend,

apprehend, will not be great. The theology of both was nearly the fame, " what is fuppofed to be performed by the power of Jupiter, of Neptune, of Æolus, of Mars, of Venus, according to the mythology of the weft, is afcribed, in the eaft, to the agency of Agrio the god of fire, Varoon the god of oceans, Vayoo the god of wind, Cama the god of love *." The facred rites of the weftern polytheifm were gay, feftive, and licentious; the rites of the public religion in the eaft partake of the fame character, with a more avowed indecency. " In every function performed in the pagodas, as well as in every public proceffion, it is the office of thefe women (*i. e.* of women prepared by the Brahmins for the purpofe) to dance before the idol, and to fing hymns in his praife; and it is difficult to fay, whether they trefpafs moft againft decency by the geftures they exhibit, or by the verfes which they recite. The walls of the pa-

* Baghvat Geeta, p. 94, quoted by Dr. Robertfon, Ind. Dif. p. 306.

godas

godas were covered with paintings in a ftyle no lefs indelicate * †."

On both fides of the comparifon the popular religion had a ftrong eftablifhment. In ancient Greece and Rome it was ftrictly incorporated with the ftate. The magiftrate was the prieft. The higheft offices of government bore the moft diftinguifhed part in the celebration of the public rites. In India, a powerful and numerous caft poffefs exclufively the adminiftration of the eftablifhed worfhip; and are, of confequence, devoted to its fervice, and attached to its intereft. In both, the prevailing mythology was deftitute of any proper evidence, or rather, in both the origin of the tradition is run up into ages long anterior to the exift-

* Others of the deities of the Eaft are of an auftere and gloomy character, to be propitiated by victims, fometimes by human facrifices, and by voluntary torments of the moft excruciating kind.

† Voyage de Gentil. vol. i. p. 244—260. Preface to Code of Gentoo Laws, p. 57, quoted by Dr. Robertfon, p. 320.

ence

ence of credible hiſtory, or of written language. The Indian chronology computes æras by millions of years, and the life of man by thouſands *; and in theſe, or prior to theſe, is placed the hiſtory of their divinities. In both, the eſtabliſhed ſuperſtition held the ſame place in the public opinion; that is to ſay, in both it was credited by the bulk of the people †, but by the learned and philoſophic

---

* " The Suffec Jogue, or age of purity, is ſaid to have laſted three million two hundred thouſand years, and they hold that the life of man was extended in that age to one hundred thouſand years; but there is a difference amongſt the Indian writers of ſix millions of years in the computation of this æra." Ib.

† " How abſurd ſoever the articles of faith may be, which ſuperſtition has adopted, or how unhallowed the rites which it preſcribes, the former are received, in every age and country, with unheſitating aſſent, by the great body of the people, and the latter obſerved with ſcrupulous exactneſs. In our reaſonings concerning opinions and practices, which differ widely from our own, we are extremely apt to err. Having been inſtructed ourſelves in the principles of a religion, worthy in every reſpect of that divine wiſdom by which they were dictated, we frequently expreſs wonder at the credulity of nations, in embracing ſyſtems of belief which

appear

philofophic part of the community, either
derided, or regarded by them as only fit to
be upholden for the fake of its political
ufes ‡.

Or if it fhould be allowed, that the ancient heathens believed in their religion lefs

appear to us fo directly repugnant to right reafon ; and
fometimes fufpect, that tenets fo wild and extravagant
do not really gain credit with them. But experience
may fatisfy us, that neither our wonder nor fufpicions are
well founded. No article of the public religion was
called in queftion by thofe people of ancient Europe,
with whofe hiftory we are beft acquainted ; and no practice, which it enjoined, appeared improper to them.
On the other hand, every opinion that tended to diminifh the reverence of men for the gods of their country, or to alienate them from their worfhip, excited,
among the Greeks and Romans, that indignant zeal
which is natural to every people attached to their religion by a firm perfuafion of its truth." Ind. Dif.
p. 321.

‡ That the learned Brahmins of the Eaft are rational
theifts, and fecretly reject the eftablifhed theory, and
contemn the rites that were founded upon them, or rather confider them as contrivances to be fupported for
their political ufes, fee Dr. Robertfon's Ind. Dif.
p. 324—334.

generally

generally than the present Indians do, I am far from thinking that this circumstance would afford any facility to the work of the apostles, above that of the modern missionaries. To me it appears, and I think it material to be remarked, that a disbelief of the established religion of their country has no tendency to dispose men for the reception of another; but that, on the contrary, it generates a settled contempt of all religious pretensions whatever. General infidelity is the hardest soil which the propagators of a new religion can have to work upon. Could a Methodist or Moravian promise himself a better chance of success with a French esprit fort, who had been accustomed to laugh at the Popery of his country, than with a believing Mahometan or Hindoo? Or are our modern unbelievers in Christianity, for that reason, in danger of becoming Mahometans or Hindoos? It does not appear that the Jews, who had a body of historical evidence to offer for their religion, and who at that time undoubtedly entertained and held forth the expectation of a future state, derived any great advantage, as to the extension of their system, from the discredit into which the popular religion had fallen with many of their heathen neighbours.

We have particularly directed our observations to the state and progress of Christianity amongst the inhabitants of *India* ; but the history of the Christian mission in other countries, where the efficacy of the mission is left solely to the conviction wrought by the preaching of strangers, presents the same idea, as the Indian mission does, of the feebleness and inadequacy of human means. About twenty-five years ago, was published in England, a translation from the Dutch of a history of Greenland, and a relation of the mission, for above thirty years carried on in that country by the Unitas Fratrum, or Moravians. Every part of that relation confirms the opinion we have stated. Nothing could surpass, or hardly equal, the zeal and patience of the missionaries. Yet their historian, in the conclusion of his narrative, could find place for no reflections

more

more encouraging than the following : — " A person that had known the heathen, that had feen the little benefit from the great pains hitherto taken with them, and confidered that one after another had abandoned all hopes of the converfion of thofe infidels (and fome thought they would never be converted, till they faw miracles wrought as in the apoftles' days, and this the Greenlanders expected and demanded of their inftructors) : one that confidered this, I fay, would not much wonder at the paft unfruitfulnefs of thefe young beginners, as at their fteadfaft perfeverance in the midft of nothing but diftrefs, difficulties and impediments, internally and externally; and that they never defponded of the converfion of thofe poor creatures amidft all feeming impoffibilities *."

From the widely difproportionate effects, which attend the preaching of modern miffionaries of Chriftianity, compared with what followed the miniftry of Chrift and

* Hift. of Greenland, vol. ii. p. 376.

his

his apostles, under circumstances either alike, or not so unlike as to account for the difference, a conclusion is fairly drawn, in support of what our histories deliver concerning them, viz. that they possessed means of conviction, which we have not; that they had proofs to appeal to, which we want.

SECTION III.

Of the Religion of Mahomet.

THE only event in the history of the human species, which admits of comparison with the propagation of Christianity, is the success of Mahometanism. The Mahometan institution was rapid in its progress, was recent in its history, and was founded upon a supernatural or prophetic character assumed by its author. In these articles the resemblance with Christianity is confessed. But there are points of difference, which separate, we apprehend, the two cases entirely.

I. Mahomet did not found his pretensions upon miracles, properly so called; that is, upon proofs of supernatural agency, capable of being known and attested by others. Christians are warranted in this assertion by the evidence of the Koran, in which Ma-

S 3   homet

homet not only does not affect the power
of working miracles, but exprefsly difclaims
it. The following paffages of that book
furnifh direct proofs of the truth of what
we alledge: "The infidels fay, unlefs a
fign be fent down unto him from his lord,
we will not believe; thou art a preacher
only *." Again, "Nothing hindered us
from fending *thee* with miracles, except that
the former nations have charged them with
impofture †." And laftly, "They fay, unlefs
a fign be fent down unto him from his lord,
we will not believe; anfwer, figns are in
the power of God alone, and I am no more
than a public preacher. Is it not fufficient
for them, that we have fent down unto them
the book of the Koran to be read unto
them ‡ ?" Befide thefe acknowledgments,
I have obferved *thirteen* diftinct places, in
which Mahomet puts the objection (unlefs
a fign, &c.) into the mouth of the unbeliever, in not one of which does he alledge

---

* Sale's Koran, c. xiii. p. 201 ed. quarto.
† c. xvii. p. 232.   ‡ c. xxix. p. 328.

a miracle

a miracle in reply. His anſwer is, " that
God giveth the power of working miracles
when and to whom he pleaſeth * ;" " that
if he ſhould work miracles, they would not
believe † ;" " that they had before rejected
Moſes, and Jeſus and the Prophets, who
wrought miracles ‡ ;" " that the Koran
itſelf was a miracle §."

The only place in the Koran, in which it
can be pretended that a ſenſible miracle is
referred to (for I do not allow the ſecret vi-
ſitations of Gabriel, the night journey of
Mahomet to heaven, or the preſence in battle of inviſible hoſts of angels, to deſerve the
name of *ſenſible* miracles) is the beginning
of the fifty-fourth chapter. The words are
theſe—" The hour of judgement approach-
eth, *and the moon hath been ſplit in ſunder*,
but if the unbelievers ſee a ſign, they turn
aſide ſaying, this is a powerful charm."
The Mahometan expoſitors diſagree in their
interpretation of this paſſage ; ſome explain-

---

* Sale's Koran, c. v. x. xiii. twice.   † c. vi.

‡ c. iii. xxi. xxviii.   § c. xvi.

ing

ing it to be a mention of the splitting of the moon, as one of the future signs of the approach of the day of judgement; others referring it to a miraculous appearance which had then taken place *. It seems to me not improbable, that Mahomet may have taken advantage of some extraordinary halo, or other unusual appearance of the moon, which had happened about this time; and which supplied a foundation both for this passage, and for the story which in after times had been raised out of it.

After this more than silence; after these authentic *confessions* of the Koran, we are not to be moved with miraculous stories related of Mahomet by Abulfeda, who wrote his life about six hundred years after his death; or which are found in the legend of Al Jannabi, who came two hundred years later †.

On

---

* Vide Sale in loc.

† It does not, I think, appear, that these historians had any written accounts to appeal to more ancient than the Sonnah, which was a collection of traditions,

made

On the contrary, from comparing what Mahomet himself wrote and said, with what
was afterwards reported of him by his followers, the plain and fair conclusion is, that,
when the religion was established by con-
quest, then, and not till then, came out the
stories of his miracles.

Now this difference alone constitutes, in
my opinion, a bar to all reasoning from one
case to the other. The success of a religion
founded upon a miraculous history, shews
the credit which was given to the history;
and this credit, under the circumstances in
which it was given, *i. e.* by persons capable
of knowing the truth, and interested to enquire after it, is evidence of the reality of
the history, and, by consequence, of the
truth of the religion. Where a miraculous
history is not alledged, no part of this argu-

made by order of the Caliphs, two hundred years after
Mahomet's death. Mahomet died A. D. 632; Al.
Bochari, one of the six doctors who compiled the Sonnah, was born A. D. 809, died 869. Prideaux's Life
of Mahomet, p. 192. ed. 7th.

ment

ment can be implied. We admit that multitudes acknowledged the pretenfions of Mahomet; but thefe pretenfions being deftitute of miraculous evidence, we know that the grounds upon which they were acknowledged, could not be fecure grounds of perfuafion to his followers, nor their example any authority to us. Admit the whole of Mahomet's authentic hiftory, fo far as it was of a nature capable of being known or witneffed by others, to be true, (which is certainly to admit all that the reception of the religion can be brought to prove), and Mahomet might ftill be an impoftor, or enthufiaft, or an union of both. Admit to be true almoft any part of Chrift's hiftory, of that, I mean, which was public, and within the cognifance of his followers, and he muft have come from God. Where matter of fact is not in queftion, where miracles are not alledged, I do not fee that the progrefs of a religion is a better argument of its truth, than the prevalency of any fyftem of opinions in natural religion, morality, or phyfics, is a proof of the truth of thofe opinions.

nions. And we know that this fort of argument is inadmissible in any branch of philosophy whatever.

But it will be faid, if one religion could make it way without miracles, why might not another? To which I reply, firft, that this is not the queftion: the proper queftion is not, whether a religious inftitution could be fet up without miracles, but whether a religion, or a change of religion, founding itfelf in miracles, could fucceed without any reality to reft upon? I apprehend thefe two cafes to be very different; and I apprehend Mahomet's not taking this courfe to be one proof, amongft others, that the thing is difficult, if not impoffible, to be accomplifhed: certainly it was not from an unconfcioufnefs of the value and importance of miraculous evidence, for it is very obfervable, that in the fame volume, and fometimes in the fame chapters, in which Mahomet fo repeatedly difclaims the power of working miracles himfelf, he is inceffantly referring to the miracles of preceding prophets. One

would

would imagine, to hear fome men talk, or
to read fome books, that the fetting up of a
religion by dint of miraculous pretences was
a thing of every day's experience; whereas
I believe, that, except the Jewifh and Chriftian religion, there is no tolerably well au-
thenticated account of any fuch thing having been accomplifhed.

II. Secondly, the eftablifhment of Mahomet's religion was effected by caufes, which,
in no degree, appertained to the origin of
Chriftianity.

During the firft twelve years of his miffion, Mahomet had recourfe only to perfuafion. This is allowed. And there is fufficient reafon from the effect to believe, that
if he had confined himfelf to this mode of
propagating his religion, we of the prefent
day fhould never have heard either of him
or it. "Three years were filently employed in the converfion of *fourteen* profelytes.
For ten years the religion advanced with a
flow and painful progrefs within the walls

of

of Mecca. The number of profelytes in the feventh year of his miffion may be efti- mated by the abfence of *eighty-three* men and eighteen women, who retired to Æthio- pia *." Yet this progrefs, fuch as it was, appears to have been aided by fome very important advantages, which Mahomet found in his fituation, in his mode of con- ducting his defign, and in his doctrine.

1. Mahomet was the grandfon of the moft powerful and honourable family in Mecca; and although the early death of his father had not left him a patrimony fuitable to his birth, he had, long before the com- mencement of his miffion, repaired this de- ficiency by an opulent marriage. A perfon confiderable by his wealth, of high defcent, and nearly allied to the chiefs of his coun- try, taking upon himfelf the character of a religious teacher, would not fail of attract- ing attention and followers.

* Gibbon's Hift. vol. ix. p. 244 et feq. ed. Dub.

G

2. Ma-

2. Mahomet conducted his defign, in the outfet efpecially, with great art and prudence. He conducted it as a politician would conduct a plot. His firft application was to his own family. This gained him his wife's uncle, a confiderable perfon in Mecca, together with his coufin Ali, afterwards the celebrated Caliph, then a youth of great expectation, and even already diftinguifhed by his attachment, impetuofity and courage *. He next addreffed himfelf to Abu Becr, a man amongft the firft of the Koreifh in wealth and influence. The intereft and example of Abu Becr drew in five other principal perfons in Mecca, whofe folicitations prevailed upon five more of the

* Of which Mr. Gibbon has preferved the following fpecimen :—" When Mahomet called out in an affembly of his family, who among you will be my companion, and my vizir ? Ali, then only in the fourteenth year of his age, fuddenly replied, O prophet, I am the man ; whofoever rifes againft thee, I will dafh out his teeth, tear out his eyes, break his legs, rip up his belly. O prophet, I will be thy vizir over them." Vol. ix. p. 245.

fame

fame rank. This was the work of three years; during which time every thing was tranfacted in fecret. Upon the ftrength of thefe allies, and under the powerful protection of his family, who, however fome of them might difapprove his enterprife, or deride his pretenfions, would not fuffer the orphan of their houfe, the relict of their favourite brother, to be infulted, Mahomet now commenced his public preaching. And the advance which he made, during the nine or ten remaining years of his peaceable miniftry, was by no means greater than what, with thefe advantages, and with the additional and fingular circumftance of there being no *eftablifhed* religion at Mecca at that time to contend with, might reafonably have been expected. How foon his primitive adherents were let into the fecret of his views of empire, or in what ftage of his undertaking thefe views firft opened themfelves to his own mind, it is not now eafy to determine. The event however was, that thefe his firft profelytes all ultimately attained to

riches

riches and honours, to the command of armies, and the government of kingdoms *.

3. The Arabs deduced their defcent from Abraham through the line of Ifhmael. The inhabitants of Mecca, in common probably with the other Arabian tribes, acknowledged, as, I think, may clearly be collected from the Koran, one fupreme deity, but had affociated with him many objects of idolatrous worfhip. The great doctrine, with which Mahomet fet out, was the ftrict and exclufive unity of God. Abraham, he told them, their illuftrious anceftor; Ifhmael, the father of their nation; Mofes, the law-giver of the Jews; and Jefus, the author of Chriftianity, had all afferted the fame thing; that their followers had univerfally corrupted the truth, and that *he* was now commiffioned to reftore it to the world. Was it to be wondered at, that a doctrine fo fpecious, and authorifed by names, fome or other of which were holden in the higheft

* Gib. vol. ix. p. 244.

veneration

veneration by every defcription of his hearers, fhould, in the hands of a popular miffionary, prevail to the extent in which Mahomet fucceeded by his pacific miniftry?

4. Of the inftitution which Mahomet
joined with this fundamental doctrine, and
of the Koran in which that inftitution is delivered, we difcover, I think, two purpofes
that pervade the whole, viz. to make converts, and to make his converts foldiers.
The following particulars, amongft others,
may be confidered as pretty evident indica-
tions of thefe defigns :

1. When Mahomet began to preach, his
addrefs to the Jews, the Chriftians, and to
the Pagan Arabs, was, that the religion
which he taught, was no other than what
had been originally their own. " We believe in God, and that which hath been fent
down unto us, and that which hath been
fent down unto Abraham, and Ifmael and
Ifaac, and Jacob and the tribes, and that
which was delivered unto Mofes and Jefus,

and that which was delivered unto the Prophets from their Lord; we make no distinction between any of them *." " He hath ordained you the religion which he commanded Noah, and which we have revealed unto thee, O Mohammed, and which we commanded Abraham and Mofes and Jefus, faying, obferve this religion, and be not divided therein †." " He hath chofen you, and hath not impofed on you any difficulty in the religion which he hath given you, the religion of your father Abraham ‡."

2. The author of the Koran never ceafes from defcribing the future anguifh of unbelievers, their defpair, regret, penitence, and torment. It is the point which he labours above all others. And thefe defcriptions are conceived in terms, which will appear in no fmall degree impreffive, even to the modern reader of an Englifh tranflation.

* Sale's Koran, c. ii. p. 17.   † Ib. c. xlii. p. 393.
‡ Ib. c. xxii. p. 281.

Doubtlefs

Doubtless they would operate with much greater force upon the minds of those to whom they were immediately directed. The terror which they seem well calculated to inspire, would be to many tempers a powerful application.

3. On the other hand, his voluptuous paradise; his robes of silk, his palaces of marble, his rivers and shades, his groves and couches, his wines, his dainties; and, above all, his seventy-two virgins assigned to each of the faithful, of resplendent beauty and eternal youth; intoxicated the imaginations, and seized the passions, of his Eastern followers.

4. But Mahomet's highest heaven was reserved for those, who fought his battles, or expended their fortunes in his cause. "Those believers who sit still at home, not having any hurt, and those who employ their fortunes and their persons for the religion of God, shall not be held equal. God hath preferred those who employ their for-

tunes

tunes and their perfons in that caufe, to a
degree above thofe who fit at home. God
hath indeed promifed every one Paradife,
but God hath preferred thofe who *fight for
the faith*, before thofe who fit ftill, by adding unto them a great reward ; by degrees
of honour conferred upon them from him,
and by granting them forgivenefs and mercy *." Again, " Do ye reckon the giving
drink to the pilgrims, and the vifiting of
the holy temple, to be actions as meritorious
as thofe performed by him who believeth in
God and the laft day, and *fighteth for the
religion of God?* they fhall not be held equal
with God. ---They who have believed, and
fled their country, and employed their fubftance and their perfons in the defence of
God's true religion, fhall be in the higheft
degree of honour with God ; and thefe are
they who fhall be happy. The Lord fend-
eth them good tidings of mercy from him,
and good will, and of gardens wherein they
fhall enjoy lafting pleafures. They fhall

* Ib. c. iv. p. 73.

continue

continue therein for ever, for with God is a great reward *." And, once more, " Verily God hath purchaſed of the true believers their ſouls and their ſubſtance, promiſing them the enjoyment of Paradiſe, on condition that they *fight for the cauſe of God*, whether they ſlay or be ſlain, the promiſe for the ſame is aſſuredly due by the law and the goſpel and the Koran † ‡."

5. His doctrine of predeſtination was applicable, and was applied by him, to the ſame purpoſe of fortifying and of exalting the courage of his adherents. " If any thing of the matter had happened unto us,

---

* Ib. c. ix. p. 151.

† Ib. p. 164.

‡ " The ſword (ſaith Mahomet) is the key of heaven and of hell; a drop of blood ſhed in the cauſe of God, a night ſpent in arms, is of more avail than two months of faſting or prayer. Whoſoever falls in battle, his ſins are forgiven at the day of judgement; his wounds ſhall be reſplendent as vermilion, and odoriferous as muſk, and the loſs of his limbs ſhall be ſupplied by the wings of angels and cherubim." Gibb. vol ix. p. 256.

we

we had not been flain here. Anfwer, if ye
had been in your houfes, verily they would
have gone forth to fight, whofe flaughter
was decreed to the places where they
died *."

6. In warm regions, the appetite of the
fexes is ardent, the paffion for inebriating
liquors moderate. In compliance with this
diftinction, although Mahomet laid a re-
ftraint upon the drinking of wine, in the
ufe of women he allowed an almoft un-
bounded indulgence. Four wives, with the
liberty of changing them at pleafure †, together with the perfons of all his captives ‡,
was an irrefiftible bribe to an Arabian war-
rior. " God is minded," fays he, fpeaking
of this very fubject, " to make his religion
light unto you, for man was created weak."
How different this from the unaccommo-
dating purity of the Gofpel? How would
Mahomet have fucceeded with the Chrif-

* C. iii. p. 54. † C. iv. p. 63.
‡ Gibb. p. 255.

tian

tian lesson in his mouth, " Whosoever
looketh after a woman to lust after her, hath
committed adultery with her already in his
heart." It must be added, that Mahomet
did not venture upon the prohibition of
wine, till the fourth year of the Hegira, or
the seventeenth of his mission *, when his
military successes had completely established
his authority. The same observation holds
of the fast of the Ramadan †, and of the
most laborious part of his institution, the
pilgrimage to Mecca ‡.

What has hitherto been collected from
the records of the Mussulman history, relates to the twelve or thirteen years of Mahomet's peaceable preaching, which part
alone of his life and enterprise admits of
the smallest comparison with the origin of

* Mod. Un. Hist. vol. i. p. 126. † Ib. p. 112.

‡ This latter, however, already prevailed amongst the
Arabs, and had grown out of their excessive veneration
for the Caaba. Mahomet's law, in this respect, was
rather a compliance than an innovation §.

§ Sale's Prolim. p. 122.

T 4 Christianity.

Chriftianity. A new fcene is now unfolded.
The city of Medina, diftant about ten days
journey from Mecca, was at that time diftracted by the hereditary contentions of two
hoftile tribes. Thefe feuds were exafperated
by the mutual perfecutions of the Jews and
Chriftians, and of the different Chriftian
fects by which the city was inhabited *.
The religion of Mahomet prefented, in
fome meafure, a point of union or compro-
mife to thefe divided opinions. It embraced
the principles which were common to them
all. Each party faw in it an honourable
acknowledgement of the fundamental truth
of their own fyftem. To the Pagan Arab,
fomewhat imbued with the fentiments and
knowledge of his Jewifh or Chriftian fellow
citizen, it offered no offenfive, or very improbable theology. This recommendation
procured to Mahometanifm a more favourable reception at Medina, than its author
had been able, by twelve years painful en-
deavours, to obtain for it at Mecca. Yet,

* Mod. Un. Hift. vol. i. p. 100.

after

after all, the progrefs of the religion was
inconfiderable. His miffionary could only
collect a congregation of forty perfons *.
It was not a religious, but a political affo-
ciation, which ultimately introduced Mahomet into Medina. Haraffed, as it fhould
feem, and difgufted by the long continuance
of factions and difputes, the inhabitants of
that city faw in the admiffion of the Prophet's authority, a reft from the miferies
which they had fuffered, and a fuppreffion
of the violence and fury which they had
learnt to condemn. After an embaffy therefore, compofed of believers and unbelievers†,
and of perfons of both tribes, with whom a
treaty was concluded of ftrict alliance and
fupport, Mahomet made his public entry,
and was received as the Sovereign of Medina.

From this time, or foon after this time,
the impoftor changed his language and his
conduct. Having now a town at his com-

* Ib. p. 85.   † Ib. p. 85.

mand, where to arm his party, and to head
them with fecurity, he enters upon new
councils. He now pretends that a divine
commiffion is given to him to attack the
infidels, to deftroy idolatry, and to fet up
the true faith by the fword*. An early
victory over a very fuperior force, achieved
by conduct and bravery, eftablifhed the re-
nown of his arms, and of his perfonal cha-
racter†. Every year after this was marked
by battles or affaffinations. The nature and
activity of Mahomet's future exertions may
be eftimated from the computation, that, in
the nine following years of his life, he commanded his army in perfon in eight general engagements‡, and undertook, by himfelf or his lieutenants, fifty military enter-
prifes.

From this time we have nothing left to
account for, but that Mahomet fhould collect an army, that his army fhould conquer,
and that his religion fhould proceed together

* Ib. p. 88.   † Victory of Bedr, ib. p. 106.
‡ Un. Hift. vol. i. p. 255.

with his conquefts. The ordinary experience of human affairs, leaves us little to
wonder at, in any of thefe effects: and they
were likewife each affifted by peculiar faci-
lities. From all fides, the roving Arabs
crowded around the ftandard of religion and
plunder, of freedom and victory, of arms
and rapine. Befide the highly painted joys
of a carnal paradife, Mahomet rewarded
his followers in this world with a liberal divifion of the fpoils, and with the perfons of
their female captives*. The condition of
Arabia, occupied by fmall independent
tribes, expofed it to the impreffion, and
yielded to the progrefs of a firm and refolute army. After the reduction of his native peninfula, the weaknefs alfo of the Roman provinces on the North and the Weft,
as well as the diftracted ftate of the Perfian
empire on the Eaft, facilitated the fuccefsful
invafion of neighbouring countries. That
Mahomet's conquefts fhould carry his religion along with them, will excite little fur-

* Gibb. vol. ix. p. 255.

prife, when we know the conditions which he propofed to the vanquifhed. Death or converfion was the only choice offered to idolaters. " Strike off their heads; ftrike off all the ends of their fingers * : kill the idolaters, wherefoever ye fhall find them †." To the Jews and Chriftians was left the fomewhat milder alternative, of fubjection and tribute, if they perfifted in their own religion, or of an equal participation in the rights and liberties, the honours and privileges, of the faithful, if they embraced the religion of their conquerors. " Ye Chriftian dogs, you know your option ; the Koran, the tribute, or the fword ‡." The corrupt ftate of Chriftianity in the feventh century, and the contentions of its fects, unhappily fo fell in with mens care of their fafety, or their fortunes, as to induce many to forfake its profeffion. Add to all which, that Mahomet's victories not only operated by the natural effect of conqueft, but that they

* Sale's Coran, c. viii. p. 140. † Ib. c. ix. p. 149.
‡ Gibb. ib. p. 337.

were

were conftantly reprefented both to his friends and enemies, as divine declarations in his favour. Succefs was evidence. Pro-fperity carried with it, not only influence, but proof. "Ye have already," fays he, after the battle of Bedr, " had a miracle fhown you, in two armies which attacked each other ; one army fought for God's true re-ligion, but the other were infidels*." Again, " *Ye* flew not thofe who were flain at Bedr, but God flew them. --- If ye defire a deci-fion of the matter between us, now hath a decifion come unto you †."

Many more paffages might be collected out of the Koran to the fame effect. But they are unneceffary. The fuccefs of Ma-hometanifm during this, and indeed every future period of its hiftory, bears fo little refemblance to the early propagation of Chriftianity, that no inference whatever can juftly be drawn from it to the prejudice of the Chriftian argument. For what are we

---

* Sale's Kor. c. iii. p. 36.   † Ch. viii. p. 141.

comparing ?

comparing? A Galilean peasant, accompanied by a few fishermen, with a conqueror at the head of his army. We compare Jesus, without force, without power, without support, without one external circumstance of attraction or influence, prevailing against the prejudices, the learning, the hierarchy of his country, against the ancient religious opinions, the pompous religious rites, the philosophy, the wisdom, the authority of the Roman empire, in the most polished and enlightened period of its existence, with Mahomet making his way amongst Arabs; collecting followers in the midst of conquests and triumphs, in the darkest ages and countries of the world, and when success in arms not only operated by that command of men's wills and persons which attends prosperous undertakings, but was considered as a sure testimony of divine approbation. That multitudes, persuaded by this argument, should join the train of a victorious chief; that still greater multitudes should, without any argument, bow down before irresistible power, is a conduct in

which

which we cannot fee much to furprife us:
in which we can fee nothing that refembles
the caufes, by which the eftablifhment of
Chriftianity was effected.

The fuccefs therefore of Mahometanifm
ftands not in the way of this important conclufion, that the propagation of Chriftianity,
in the manner and under the circumftances
in which it was propagated, is an *unique* in
the hiftory of the fpecies. A Jewifh peafant
overthrew the religion of the world.

I have, neverthelefs, placed the prevalency of the religion amongft the auxiliary
arguments of its truth ; becaufe, whether it
had prevailed or not, or whether its prevalency can or cannot be accounted for, the
direct argument remains ftill. It is ftill true,
that a great number of men upon the fpot,
perfonally connected with the hiftory and
with the author of the religion, were induced by what they heard and faw and
knew, not only to change their former opinions, but to give up their time, and facrifice
their

their eafe, to traverfe feas and kingdoms
without reft and without wearinefs, to commit themfelves to extreme dangers, to undertake inceffant toils, to undergo grievous
fufferings, and all this, folely in confequence,
and in fupport, of their belief of facts, which,
if true, eftablifh the truth of the religion,
which, if falfe, they muft have known to
be fo.

PART III.

A BRIEF CONSIDERATION OF SOME POPULAR OBJECTIONS.

***

CHAP. I.

The Difcrepancies between the feveral Gofpels.

I KNOW not a more rafh or unphilofo-phical conduct of the underftanding, than to reject the fubftance of a ftory, by reafon of fome diverfity in the circumftances with which it is related. The ufual character of human teftimony is fubftantial truth under circumftantial variety. This is what the daily experience of courts of juftice teaches. When accounts of a tranfaction come from the mouths of different witneffes, it is fel-

dom that it is not poffible to pick out apparent or real inconfiftencies between them.
Thefe inconfiftencies are ftudioufly difplayed by an adverfe pleader, but oftentimes
with little impreffion upon the minds of the
judges. On the contrary, a clofe and minute agreement induces the fufpicion of
confederacy and fraud. When written hiftories touch upon the fame fcenes of action,
the comparifon almoft always affords ground
for a like reflection. Numerous, and fometimes important, variations prefent themfelves; not feldom alfo, abfolute and final
contradictions; yet neither one nor the other
are deemed fufficient to fhake the credibility
of the main fact. The embaffy of the Jews
to deprecate the execution of Claudian's order to place his ftatue in their temple, Philo
places in harveft, Jofephus in feed-time; both
contemporary writers. No reader is led by
this inconfiftency to doubt, whether fuch an
embaffy was fent, or whether fuch an order
was given. Our own hiftory fupplies examples of the fame kind. In the account of
the Marquis of Argyle's death in the reign

of

of Charles the Second, we have a very remarkable contradiction. Lord Clarendon relates that he was condemned to be hanged,
which was performed the fame day : on the
contrary, Burnet, Woodrow, Heath, Echard,
concur in ftating that he was beheaded ; and
that he was condemned upon the Saturday,
and executed upon the Monday *. Was
any reader of Englifh hiftory ever fceptic
enough to raife from hence a queftion, whether the Marquis of Argyle was executed, or
not ? Yet this ought to be left in uncertainty,
according to the principles upon which the
Chriftian hiftory has fometimes been attacked. Dr. Middleton contended, that the different hours of the day affigned to the crucifixion of Chrift, by John and by the other
evangelifts, did not admit of the reconcilement which learned men had propofed ; and
then concludes the difcuffion with this hard
remark : " We muft be forced, with feveral
of the critics, to leave the difficulty juft as

---

* See Biog. Britan.

we

we found it, chargeable with all the confequences of manifeft inconfiftency *." But
what are thefe confequences? by no means
the difcrediting of the hiftory as to the principal fact, by a repugnancy (even fuppofing
that repugnancy not to be refolvable into
different modes of computation) in the time
of the day in which it is faid to have taken
place.

A great deal of the difcrepancy, obfervable
in the Gofpels, arifes from *omiffion*; from a
fact or a paffage of Chrift's life being noticed
by one writer, which is unnoticed by another. Now omiffion is at all times a very
uncertain ground of objection. We perceive it, not only in the comparifon of different writers, but even in the fame writer,
when compared with himfelf. There are a
great many particulars, and fome of them of
importance, mentioned by Jofephus in his
Antiquities, which, as we fhould have fup-

* Middleton's Reflections anfwered by Benfon. Hift.
Chrif. vol. iii. p. 50.

pofed, ought to have been put down by him in their place in the Jewifh Wars *. Sueto- nius, Tacitus, Dio Caffius, have, all three, written of the reign of Tiberius, Each has mentioned many things omitted by the reft †, yet no objection is from thence taken to the refpective credit of their hiftories. We have in our own times, if there were not fome- thing indecorous in the comparifon, the life of an eminent perfon, written by three of his friends, in which there is very great variety in the incidents felected by them; fome ap- parent, and perhaps fome real contradictions; yet without any impeachment of the fub- ftantial truth of their accounts, of the authen- ticity of the books, of the competent informa- tion or general fidelity of the writers.

But thefe difcrepancies will be ftill more numerous, when men do not write hiftories, but *memoirs*; which is perhaps the true name, and proper defcription of our Gofpels: that is, when they do not undertake, or ever

---

* Lard. part i. vol. ii. p. 735, et feq.   † Ib. p. 743.

meant

meant to deliver, in order of time, a regular
and complete account of *all* the things of
importance, which the perfon, who is the
fubject of their hiftory, did or faid; but only,
out of many fimilar ones, to give fuch paffages, or fuch actions and difcourfes, as offered themfelves more immediately to their attention, came in the way of their enquiries,
occurred to their recollection, or were fuggefted by their *particular defign* at the time
of writing.

This particular defign may appear fometimes, but not always, nor often. Thus I
think that the particular defign, which St.
Matthew had in view whilft he was writing
the hiftory of the refurrection, was to atteft
the faithful performance of Chrift's promife
to his difciples to go before them into Galilee; becaufe he alone, except Mark, who
feems to have taken it from him, has recorded this promife, and he alone has confined
his narrative to that fingle appearance to the
difciples which fulfilled it. It was the pre-
concerted, the great and moft public mani-
feftation

feftation of our Lord's perfon. It was the
thing which dwelt upon St. Matthew's mind,
and he adapted his narrative to it. But,
that there is nothing in St. Matthew's language, which negatives other appearances,
or which imports that this his appearance to
his difciples in Galilee, in purfuance of his
promife, was his firft or only appearance, is
made pretty evident by St. Mark's Gofpel,
which ufes the fame terms concerning the
appearance in Galilee as St. Matthew ufes,
yet itfelf records two other appearances prior
to this; " Go your way, tell his difciples
and Peter, that he goeth before you into Galilee, then fhall ye fee him as he faid unto
you." (xvi. 7.) We might be apt to infer
from thefe words, that this was the *firft* time
they were to fee him : at leaft, we might infer it, with as much reafon as we draw the
inference from the fame words in Matthew :
yet the hiftorian himfelf did not perceive
that he was leading his readers to any fuch
conclufion; for, in the twelfth and two
following verfes of this chapter, he informs
us of two appearances, which, by comparing

the

the order of events, are fhewn to have been prior to the appearance in Galilee. " He appeared in another form unto two of them, as they walked, and went into the country; and went and told it unto the refidue, neither believed they them: afterwards he appeared unto the eleven, as they fat at meat, and upbraided them with their unbelief, becaufe they believed not them that had feen him after he was rifen."

Probably the fame obfervation, concerning the *particular defign* which guided the hiftorian, may be of ufe in comparing many other paffages of the Gofpels.

CHAP. II.

Erroneous Opinions imputed to the Apoſtles.

A Species of candour which is ſhewn towards every other book, is ſometimes refuſed to the Scriptures ; and that is, the placing of a diſtinction between judgment and teſtimony. We do not uſually queſtion the credit of a writer, by reaſon of any opinion he may have delivered upon ſubjects unconnected with his evidence; and even upon ſubjects connected with his account, or mixed with it in the ſame diſcourſe or writing, we naturally ſeparate facts from opinions, teſtimony from obſervation, narrative from argument.

To apply this equitable conſideration to the Chriſtian records, much controverſy, and much objection has been raiſed, concerning the

the quotations of the Old Teftament found
in the New ; fome of which quotations, it is
faid, are applied in a fenfe, and to events,
apparently different from that which they
bear, and from thofe to which they belong,
in the original. It is probable to my apprehenfion, that many of thofe quotations were
intended by the writers of the New Teftament as nothing more than *accommodations*.
They quoted paffages of their fcripture,
which fuited, and fell in with, the occafion
before them, without always undertaking to
affert, that the occafion was in the view of
the author of the words. Such accommodations of paffages from old authors, from
books efpecially, which are in every one's
hands, are common with writers of all countries ; but in none, perhaps, were more to
be expected, than in the writings of the Jews,
whofe literature was almoft entirely confined
to their fcriptures. Thofe prophecies which
are alledged with more folemnity, and which
are accompanied with a precife declaration,
that they originally refpected the event then
related, are, I think, truly alledged. But
were

were it otherwife; is the judgment of the writers of the New Teftament, in interpreting paffages of the Old, or fometimes, perhaps, in receiving eftablifhed interpretations, fo connected, either with their veracity, or with their means of information concerning what was paffing in their own times, as that a critical miftake, even were it clearly made out, fhould overthrow their hiftorical credit?—Does it diminifh it? Has it any thing to do with it?

Another error, imputed to the firft Chriftians, was the expected approach of the day of judgment. I would introduce this objection, by a remark, upon what appears to me a fomewhat fimilar example. Our Saviour, fpeaking to Peter of John, faid, "If I will that he tarry till I come, what is that to thee *." Thefe words, we find, had been fo mifconftrued, as that "a report" from thence "went abroad among the brethren, that that difciple fhould not die." Suppofe that this

* John xxi. 23.

had

had come down to us amongſt the prevailing opinions of the early Chriſtians, and that
the particular circumſtance, from which the
miſtake ſprung, had been loſt, (which hu-
manly ſpeaking was moſt likely to have been
the caſe) ſome, at this day, would have been
ready to regard and quote the error, as an
impeachment of the whole Chriſtian ſyſtem.
Yet with how little juſtice ſuch a concluſion
would have been drawn, or rather ſuch a
preſumption taken up, the information,
which we happen to poſſeſs, enables us now
to perceive. To thoſe who think that the
Scriptures lead us to believe, that the early
Chriſtians, and even the Apoſtles, expected
the approach of the day of judgment in their
own times, the ſame reflection will occur,
as that which we have made, with reſpect to
the more partial perhaps and temporary, but
ſtill no leſs ancient error, concerning the
duration of St. John's life. It was an error,
it may be likewiſe ſaid, which would effec-
tually hinder thoſe, who entertained it, from
acting the part of impoſtors.

The

The difficulty which attends the subject of the present chapter, is contained in this question; if we once admit the fallibility of the apostolic judgment, where are we to stop, or in what can we rely upon it? To which question, as arguing with unbelievers, and as arguing for the substantial truth of the Christian history, and for that alone, it is competent to the advocate of Christianity to reply, Give me the apostle's testimony, and I do not stand in need of their judgment; give me the facts, and I have complete security for every conclusion I want.

But, although I think that it is competent to the Christian apologist to return this answer; I do not think that it is the only answer which the objection is capable of receiving. The two following cautions, founded, I apprehend, in the most reasonable distinctions, will exclude all uncertainty upon this head, which can be attended with danger.

First, to separate what was the object of the apostolic mission, and declared by them

to

to be fo, from what was extraneous to it, or only incidentally connected with it. Of points clearly extraneous to the religion, nothing need be faid. Of points incidentally connected with it, fomething may be added. Demoniacal poffeffion is one of thefe points: concerning the reality of which, as this place will not admit the examination, or even the production of the arguments on either fide of the queftion, it would be arrogance in me to deliver any judgment. And it is unneceffary. For what I am concerned to obferve is, that even they who think that it was a general, but erroneous, opinion of thofe times; and that the writers of the New Teftament, in common with other Jewifh writers of that age, fell into the manner of fpeaking and of thinking upon the fubject, which then univerfally prevailed; need not be alarmed by the conceffion, as though they had any thing to fear from it, for the truth of Chriftianity. The doctrine was not what Chrift brought into the world. It appears in the Chriftian records, incidentally and accidentally, as being the fubfifting

opinion

opinion of the age and country in which his miniftry was exercifed. It was no part of the object of *his* revelation, to regulate mens opinions concerning the action of fpiritual fubftances upon animal bodies. At any rate it is unconnected with teftimony. If a dumb perfon was by a word reftored to the ufe of his fpeech, it fignifies little to what caufe the dumbnefs was afcribed; and the like of every other cure wrought upon thofe who are faid to have been poffeffed. The malady was real, the cure was real, whether the popular explication of the caufe was well founded, or not. The matter of fact, the change, fo far as it was an object of fenfe, or of teftimony, was in either cafe the fame.

Secondly, that, in reading the apoftolic writings, we diftinguifh between their doctrines and their arguments. Their doctrines came to them by revelation properly fo called; yet in propounding thefe doctrines in their writings or difcourfes, they were wont to illuftrate, fupport and enforce them,

by

by such analogies, arguments, and confiderations as their own thoughts fuggefled.
Thus the call of the Gentiles, that is, the
admiffion of the Gentiles to the Chriftian
profeffion without a previous fubjection to
the law of Mofes, was imparted to the Apoftles by revelation, and was attefted by the
miracles which attended the Chriftian miniftry amongft them. The Apoftles own
affurance of the matter refted upon this
foundation. Neverthelefs, St. Paul, when
treating of the fubject, offers a great variety
of topics in its proof and vindication. The
doctrine itfelf muft be received; but is it neceffary, in order to defend Chriftianity, to
defend the propriety of every comparifon,
or the validity of every argument, which
the apoftle has brought into the difcuffion?
The fame obfervation applies to fome other
inftances; and is, in my opinion, very well
founded. " When divine writers argue
upon any point, we are always bound to believe the conclufions that their reafonings
end in, as parts of divine revelation; but we
are not bound to be able to make out, or

4

even

even to affent to, all the premifes made ufe
of by them, in their whole extent, unlefs it
appear plainly, that they affirm the premifes
as exprefsly as they do the conclufions proved by them *."

* Burnet's Expof. art. 6.

CHAP. III.

The Connection of Christianity with the Jewish History.

UNDOUBTEDLY, our Saviour assumes the divine origin of the Mosaic institution: and, independently of his authority, I conceive it to be very difficult to assign any other cause for the commencement or existence of that institution; especially for the singular circumstance of the Jews adhering to the unity, when every other people slid into polytheism; for their being men in religion, children in every thing else; behind other nations in the arts of peace and war, superior to the most improved in their sentiments and doctrines relating to the deity *. Undoubtedly

---

* " In the doctrine, for example, of the unity, the eternity, the omnipotence, the omniscience, the omnipresence, the wisdom and the goodness of God; in their opinions concerning providence, and the creation, preservation,

doubtedly alſo, our Saviour recogniſes the
prophetic character of many of their ancient
writers. So far, therefore, we are bound as
Chriſtians to go. But to make Chriſtianity
anſwerable with its life, for the circumſtan-
tial truth of each ſeparate paſſage of the Old
Teſtament, the genuineneſs of every book,
the information, fidelity, and judgment of
every writer in it, is to bring, I will not ſay

vation, and government of the world." Campbell on
Mir. p. 207. To which we may add, in the acts of
their religion not being accompanied either with cruel-
ties or impurities ; in the religion itſelf being free from
a ſpecies of ſuperſtition, which prevailed univerſally in
the popular religions of the ancient world, and which is
to be found perhaps in all religions that have their origin in human artifice and credulity, viz. fanciful connections between certain appearances, and actions, and
the deſtiny of nations or individuals. Upon theſe conceits reſted the whole train of auguries and auſpices,
which formed ſo much even of the ſerious part of the
religions of Greece and Rome, and of the charms and
incantations which were practiſed in thoſe countries by
the common people. From every thing of this ſort
the religion of the Jews, and of the Jews alone, was
free. Vid. Prieſtley's Lectures on the Truth of the
Jewiſh and Chriſtian Revelation, 1794.

great,

great, but unneceffary difficulties, into the whole fyftem. Thefe books were univer- fally read and received by the Jews of our Saviour's time. He and his apoftles, in common with all other Jews, referred to them, alluded to them, ufed them. Yet, except where he exprefsly afcribes a divine authority to particular predictions, I do not know that we can ftrictly draw any conclufion from the books being fo ufed and applied, befide the proof, which it unquef- tionably is, of their notoriety and reception at that time. In this view our fcriptures af- ford a valuable teftimony to thofe of the Jews. But the nature of this teftimony ought to be underftood. It is furely very different from, what it is fometimes repre- fented to be, a fpecific ratification of each particular fact and opinion; and not only of each particular fact, but of the motives affigned for every action, together with the judgment of praife or difpraife beftowed upon them. St. James, in his epiftle *,

* v. 11.

fays, " Ye have heard of the patience of
Job, and have feen the end of the Lord."
Notwithftanding this text, the reality of
Job's hiftory, and even the exiftence of fuch
a perfon, has been always deemed a fair
fubject of enquiry and difcuffion amongft
Chriftian divines. St. James's authority is
confidered as good evidence of the exiftence
of the book of Job at that time, and of its
reception by the Jews, and of nothing more.
St. Paul, in his fecond epiftle to Timothy*,
has this fimilitude : " Now, as Jannes and
Jambres withftood Mofes, fo do thefe alfo
refift the truth." Thefe names are not found
in the Old Teftament. And it is uncertain,
whether St. Paul took them from fome apo-
cryphal writing then extant, or from tradition. But no one ever imagined, that St.
Paul is here afferting the authority of the
writing, if it was a written account which
he quoted, or making himfelf anfwerable
for the authenticity of the tradition ; much
lefs, that he fo involves himfelf with either

* iii. 8.

X 3

of

of thefe queftions, as that the credit of his
own hiftory and miffion fhould depend
upon the fact, whether " Jannes and Jambres withftood Mofes, or not." For what
reafon a more rigorous interpretation fhould
be put upon other references, it is difficult
to know. I do not mean, that other paffages
of the Jewifh hiftory ftand upon no better
evidence than the hiftory of Job, or of Jannes and Jambres (I think much otherwife) ;
but I mean, that a reference in the New
Teftament, to a paffage in the Old, does
not fo fix its authority, as to exclude all
enquiry into its credibility, or into the feparate reafons upon which that credibility is
founded ; and that it is an unwarrantable,
as well as unfafe rule to lay down concerning the Jewifh hiftory, what was never laid
down concerning any other, that either
every particular of it muft be true, or the
whole falfe.

I have thought it neceffary to ftate this
point explicitly, becaufe a fafhion revived by
Voltaire, and purfued by the difciples of his
fchool,

school, seems to have much prevailed of late, of attacking Christianity through the sides of Judaism. Some objections of this class are founded in misconstruction, some in exaggeration; but all proceed upon a supposition, which has not been made out by argument, viz. that the attestation, which the author and first teachers of Christianity gave to the divine mission of Moses and the prophets, extends to every point and portion of the Jewish history; and so extends, as to make Christianity responsible in its own credibility, for the circumstantial truth, I had almost said for the critical exactness, of every narrative contained in the Old Testament.

CHAP. IV.

Rejection of Christianity.

WE acknowledge that the Christian religion, although it converted great numbers, did not produce an univerfal, or even a general conviction in the minds of men, of the age and countries in which it appeared. And this want of a more complete and extenfive fuccefs, is called the *rejection* of the Chriftian hiftory and miracles; and has been thought by fome, to form a ftrong objection to the reality of the facts which the hiftory contains.

The matter of the objection divides itfelf into two parts, as it relates to the Jews, and as it relates to Heathen nations; becaufe the minds of thefe two defcriptions of men may have been, with refpect to Chriftianity, under the influence of very different caufes. The cafe of the Jews, inafmuch as

our

our Saviour's miniſtry was originally addreſſed to them, offers itſelf firſt to our conſideration.

Now, upon the ſubject of the truth of
the Chriſtian religion, with *us* there is but
one queſtion, viz. whether the miracles were
actually wrought? From acknowledging the
miracles we paſs inſtantaneouſly to the ac-
knowledgment of the whole. No doubt
lies between the premiſes and the concluſion. If we believe the works, or any one
of them, we believe in Jeſus. And this
order of reaſoning is become ſo univerſal
and familiar, that we do not readily apprehend how it could ever have been otherwiſe. Yet it appears to me perfectly certain, that the ſtate of thought, in the mind
of a Jew of our Saviour's age, was totally
different from this. After allowing the reality of the miracle, he had a great deal to
do to perſuade himſelf that Jeſus was the
Meſſiah. This is clearly intimated by various paſſages of the goſpel hiſtory. It appears that, in the apprehenſion of the writers
of

of the New Teftament, the miracles did
not irrefiftibly carry, even thofe who faw
them, to the conclufion intended to be
drawn from them ; or fo compel affent, as
to leave no room for fufpenfe, for the exercife of candour, or the effects of prejudice.
And to this point at leaft, the evangelifts
may be allowed to be good witneffes ; becaufe it is a point, in which exaggeration
or difguife would have been the other way.
Their accounts, if they could be fufpected
of falfehood, would rather have magnified,
than diminifhed, the effects of the miracles.

John vii. 21—31. " Jefus anfwered, and
faid unto them, I have done one work, and
ye all marvel --- If a man on the Sabbath-
day receive circumcifion, that the law of
Mofes fhould not be broken, are ye angry
at me, becaufe I have made a man every
whit whole on the Sabbath-day ? Judge not
according to the appearance, but judge
righteous judgment. Then faid fome of
them of Jerufalem, Is not this he whom
they feek to kill ? but lo, he fpeaketh boldly,
and

and they fay nothing to him; do the rulers know indeed that this is the very Chrift? *Howbeit we know this man, whence he is; but, when Chrift cometh, no man knoweth whence he is.* Then cried Jefus in the temple as he taught, faying, Ye both know me, and ye know whence I am; and I am not come of myfelf, but he that fent me is true, whom ye know not; but I know him, for I am from him, and he hath fent me. Then they fought to take him, but no man laid hands on him becaufe his hour was not yet come; *and many of the people believed on him, and faid, When Chrift cometh, will he do more miracles than thofe which this man hath done?"*

This paffage is very obfervable. It exhibits the reafoning of different forts of perfons upon the occafion of a miracle, which perfons of all forts are reprefented to have acknowledged as real. One fort of men thought, that there was fomething very extraordinary in all this; but that ftill Jefus could not be the Chrift, becaufe there was
a cir-

a circumftance in his appearance, which militated with an opinion concerning Chrift,
in which they had been brought up, and of
the truth of which, it is probable, they had
never entertained a particle of doubt, viz.
that " when Chrift cometh no man knoweth whence he is." Another fort were inclined to believe him to be the Meffiah.
But even thefe did not argue as we fhould;
did not confider the miracle as of itfelf decifive of the queftion, as what, if once allowed, excluded all farther debate upon the
fubject, but founded their opinion upon a
kind of comparative reafoning, " When
Chrift cometh, will he do *more* miracles
than thofe which this man hath done ?"

Another paffage in the fame evangelift,
and obfervable for the fame purpofe, is that,
in which he relates the refurrection of Lazarus: " Jefus," he tells us, (xi. 43, 44.)
" when he had thus fpoken, cried with a
loud voice, Lazarus, come forth; and he,
that was dead, came forth, bound hand and
foot with grave-clothes, and his face was
bound

bound about with a napkin. Jefus faith
unto them, Loofe him and let him go." One
might have expected, that at leaft all thofe
who ftood by the fepulchre, when Lazarus
was raifed, would have believed in Jefus.
Yet the evangelift does not fo reprefent it.
" Then many of the Jews which came to
Mary, and had feen the things which Jefus
did, believed on him; but *fome of them* went
their ways to the Pharifees, and told them
what things Jefus had done." We cannot
fuppofe that the evangelift meant, by this
account, to leave his readers to imagine that
any of the fpectators doubted about the
truth of the miracle. Far from it. Unqueftionably he ftates the miracle to have been
fully allowed: yet the perfons who allowed
it, were, according to his reprefentation, capable of retaining hoftile fentiments towards
Jefus. " Believing in Jefus" was not only
to believe that he wrought miracles, but that
he was the Meffiah. With us there is no
difference between thefe two things; with
them there was the greateft. And the difference is apparent in this tranfaction. If

St.

St. John has reprefented the conduct of the
Jews upon this occafion truly (and why he
fhould not I cannot tell, for it rather makes
againft him than for him), it fhews clearly
the principles upon which their judgment
proceeded. Whether he has related the
matter truly or not, the relation itfelf difcovers the writer's own opinion of thofe
principles, and that alone poffeffes confiderable authority. In the next chapter, we
have a reflection of the evangelift, entirely
fuited to this ftate of the cafe ; " but though
he had done fo many miracles before them,
yet believed they not on him*." The evangelift does not mean to impute the defect
of their belief to any doubt about the miracles, but to their not perceiving, what all
now fufficiently perceive, and what they
would have perceived had not their underftandings been governed by ftrong prejudices, the infallible atteftation, which the
works of Jefus bore, to the truth of his pretenfions.

***

* xii. 37.

The

The ninth chapter of St. John's gofpel contains a very circumftantial account of the cure of a blind man; a miracle fubmitted to all the fcrutiny and examination, which a fceptic could propofe. If a modern unbeliever had drawn up the interrogatories, they could hardly have been more critical or fearching. The account contains alfo a very curious conference between the Jewifh rulers and the patient, in which the point for our prefent notice, is their refiftance of the force of the miracle, and of the conclufion to which it led, after they had failed in difcrediting its evidence. "We know that God fpake unto Mofes, but as for this fellow we know not whence he is." That was the anfwer which fet their minds at reft. And by the help of much prejudice, and great unwillingnefs to yield, it might do fo. In the mind of the poor man reftored to fight, which was under no fuch biafs, felt no fuch reluctance, the miracle had its natural operation. "Herein," fays he, "is a marvellous thing, that ye know not from whence he is, yet he hath opened

4   mine

mine eyes. Now we know that God heareth not finners; but if any man be a wor-
fhipper of God, and doeth his will, him he
heareth. Since the world began was it not
heard, that any man opened the eyes of one
that was born blind. If this man were not
of God he could do nothing." We do not
find, that the Jewifh rulers had any other
reply to make to this defence, than that
which authority is fometimes apt to make
to argument, " Doft thou teach us ?"

If it fhall be enquired how a turn of
thought, fo different from what prevails at
prefent, fhould obtain currency with the
ancient Jews, the anfwer is found in two
opinions, which are proved to have fubfift-
ed in that age and country. The one was,
their expectation of a Meffiah, of a kind totally contrary to what the appearance of
Jefus befpoke him to be: the other, their
perfuafion of the agency of demons in the
production of fupernatural effects. Thefe
opinions are not *fuppofed* by us for the purpofe of argument, but are evidently recog-
nifed

nifed in the Jewifh writings, as well as in
ours. And it ought moreover to be confidered, that in thefe opinions the Jews of
that age had been from their infancy
brought up ; that they were opinions, the
grounds of which they had probably few of
them enquired into, and of the truth of
which they entertained no doubt. And I
think that thefe two opinions conjointly afford an explanation of their conduct. The
firft put them upon feeking out fome excufe to themfelves, for not receiving Jefus
in the character in which he claimed to be
received; and the fecond fupplied them
with juft fuch an excufe as they wanted.
Let Jefus work what miracles he would,
ftill the anfwer was in readinefs, " that he
wrought them by the affiftance of Beelze-
bub." And to this anfwer no reply could
be made, but that which our Saviour did
make, by fhewing that the tendency of his
miffion was fo adverfe to the views with
which this Being was, by the objectors
themfelves, fuppofed to act, that it could
not reafonably be fuppofed that he would

affift in carrying it on. The power difplayed in the miracles did not alone refute
the Jewifh folution, becaufe, the interpofi-
tion of invifible agents being once admitted,
it is impoffible to afcertain the limits by
which their efficiency is circumfcribed. We
of this day may be difpofed, poffibly, to
think fuch opinions too abfurd to have
been ever ferioufly entertained. I am not
bound to contend for the credibility of the
opinions. They were at leaft as reafonable
as the belief in witchcraft. They were opinions in which the Jews of that age had
from their infancy been inftructed: and
thofe who cannot fee enough in the force
of this reafon, to account for their conduct
towards our Saviour, do not fufficiently
confider how fuch opinions may fometimes
become very general in a country, and with
what pertinacity, when once become fo,
they are, for that reafon alone, adhered to.
In the fufpenfe which thefe notions, and
the prejudices refulting from them, might
occafion, the candid and docile and humble
minded would probably decide in Chrift's
favour;

favour; the proud and obstinate, together with the giddy and the thoughtless, almost universally against him.

This state of opinion discovers to us also the reason of what some choose to wonder at, why the Jews should reject miracles when they saw them, yet rely so much upon the tradition of them in their own history. It does not appear, that it had ever entered into the minds of those who lived in the time of Moses and the Prophets, to ascribe *their* miracles to the supernatural agency of evil Beings. The solution was not then invented. And the authority of Moses and the Prophets being established, and become the foundation of the national policy and religion, it was not probable that the later Jews, brought up in a reverence for that religion, and the subjects of that policy, should apply to their history a reasoning which tended to overthrow the foundation of both.

II. The infidelity of the gentile world,

and

and that more especially of men of rank and
learning in it, is resolvable into a principle,
which, in my judgment, will account for
the inefficacy of any argument or any evidence whatever, viz. contempt prior to examination. The state of religion amongst
the Greeks and Romans had a natural tendency to induce this disposition. Dionysius
Halicarnassensis remarks, that there were six
hundred different kinds of religions or sacred rites exercised at Rome *. The superior classes of the community treated them
all as fables. Can we wonder then, that
Christianity was included in the number,
without enquiry into its separate merits, or
the particular grounds of its pretensions?
It might be either true or false for any thing
they knew about it. The religion had nothing in its character which immediately
engaged their notice. It mixed with no politics. It produced no fine writers. It contained no curious speculations. When it did
reach their knowledge, I doubt not but that

* Jortin's remarks on Eccl. Hist. vol. i. p. 371.

it

it appeared to them a very ftrange fyftem—
fo unphilofophical—dealing fo little in argument and difcuffion, in fuch arguments
however and difcuffions as they were accuftomed to entertain. What is faid of
Jefus Chrift, of his nature, office, and miniftry, would be, in the higheft degree,
aliene from the conceptions of their theology. The redeemer, and the deftined judge,
of the human race, a poor young man executed at Jerufalem with two thieves upon a
crofs! Still more would the language, in
which the Chriftian doctrine was delivered,
be diffonant and barbarous to their ears.
What knew they of grace, of redemption,
of juftification, of the blood of Chrift fhed
for the fins of men, of reconcilement, of
mediation? Chriftianity was made up of
points they had never thought of; of terms
which they had never heard.

It was prefented alfo to the imagination
of the learned heathen, under additional difadvantage, by reafon of its real, and ftill
more of its nominal, connection with Ju-

Y 3

daifm.

daifm. It fhared in the obloquy and ridi-
cule, with which that people and their religion were treated by the Greeks and Romans. They regarded Jehovah himfelf only
as the idol of the Jewifh nation, and what
was related of him, as of a piece with what
was told of the tutelar deities of other countries: nay, the Jews were in a particular
manner ridiculed for being a credulous race;
fo that whatever reports of a miraculous nature came out of that country, were looked
upon by the heathen world as falfe and frivolous. When they heard of Chriftianity,
they heard of it as a quarrel amongft this
people, about fome articles of their own fuperftition. Defpifing therefore, as they did,
the whole fyftem, it was not probable that
they would enter, with any degree of ferioufnefs or attention, into the detail of its
difputes, or the merits of either fide. How
little they knew, and with what careleffnefs
they judged of thefe matters, appears, I
think, pretty plainly from an example of
no lefs weight than that of Tacitus, who,
in a grave and profeffed difcourfe upon the

7

hiftory

hiſtory of the Jews, ſtates that they wor-
ſhipped the effigy of an aſs*. The paſſage
is a proof, how prone the learned men of
theſe times were, and upon how little evidence, to heap together ſtories, which might
increaſe the contempt and odium in which
that people was held. The ſame fooliſh
charge is alſo confidently repeated by Plutarch †.

It is obſervable, that all theſe conſiderations are of a nature to operate with the
greateſt force upon the higheſt ranks; upon
men of education, and that order of the
public from which *writers* are principally
taken : I may add alſo, upon the philoſophical as well as the libertine character; upon
the Antonines or Julian, not leſs than upon
Nero or Domitian; and, more particularly,
upon that large and poliſhed claſs of men,
who acquieſced in the general perſuaſion,
that all they had to do was to practiſe the
duties of morality, and to worſhip the deity

---

* Tac. Hiſt. lib. v. c. 2. † Sympoſ. lib. iv. queſ. 5.

more

more patrio ; a habit of thinking, liberal as it may appear, which fluts the door againft every argument for a new religion. The confiderations above-mentioned, would acquire alfo ftrength, from the prejudice which men of rank and learning univerfally entertain againft any thing that *originates* with the vulgar and illiterate ; which prejudice is known to be as obftinate as any prejudice whatever.

Yet Chriftianity was ftill making its way: and, amidft fo many impediments to its progrefs, fo much difficulty in procuring audience and attention, its actual fuccefs is more to be wondered at, than that it fhould not have univerfally conquered fcorn and indifference, fixed the levity of a voluptuous age, or, through a cloud of adverfe prejudications, opened for itfelf a paffage to the hearts and underftandings of the fcholars of the age.

And the caufe which is here affigned for the rejection of Chriftianity, by men of

rank

rank and learning among the heathens,
namely, a ſtrong antecedent contempt, accounts alſo for their *ſilence* concerning it. If
they had rejected it upon examination, they
would have written about it. They would
have given their reaſons. Whereas what
men repudiate upon the ſtrength of ſome
prefixed perſuaſion, or from a ſettled contempt of the ſubject, of the perſons who
propoſe it, or of the manner in which it is
propoſed, they do not naturally write books
about, or notice much in what they write
upon other ſubjects.

The letters of the younger Pliny furniſh
an example of this ſilence, and let us, in
ſome meaſure, into the cauſe of it. From
his celebrated correſpondence with Trajan,
we know that the Chriſtian religion prevailed in a very conſiderable degree in the
province over which he preſided; that it had
excited his attention; that he had enquired
into the matter, juſt ſo much as a Roman
magiſtrate might be expected to enquire,
viz. whether the religion contained any opinions

nions dangerous to government; but that
of its doctrines, its evidences, or its books,
he had not taken the trouble to inform himfelf with any degree of care or correctnefs.
But although Pliny had viewed Chriftianity
in a nearer pofition, than moft of his learned countrymen faw it in; yet he had regarded the whole with fuch negligence and
difdain (farther than as it feemed to concern
his adminiftration), that, in more than two
hundred and forty letters of his which have
come down to us, the fubject is never once
again mentioned. If out of this number
the two letters between him and Trajan had
been loft, with what confidence would the
obfcurity of the Chriftian religion have been
argued from Pliny's filence about it, and
with how little truth?

The name and character which Tacitus
hath given to Chriftianity, " exitiabilis fuperftitio" (a pernicious fuperftition), and
by which two words he difpofes of the
whole queftion of the merits or demerits of
the religion, afford a ftrong proof how little
he

he knew, or concerned himfelf to know, about the matter. I apprehend that I fhall not be contradicted, when I take upon me to affert, that no unbeliever of the prefent age would apply this epithet to the Chriftianity of the New Teftament, or not allow that it was entirely unmerited. Read the inftructions given, by a great teacher of the religion, to thofe very Roman converts, of whom Tacitus fpeaks; and given alfo a very few years before the time of which he is fpeaking; and which are not, let it be obferved, a collection of fine fayings, brought together from different parts of a large work, but ftand in one entire paffage of a public letter, without the intermixture of a fingle thought, which is frivolous or exceptionable. " Abhor that which is evil, cleave to that which is good. Be kindly affectioned one to another, with brotherly love, in honour preferring one another. Not flothful in bufinefs, fervent in fpirit, ferving the Lord, rejoicing in hope, patient in tribulation, continuing inftant in prayer, diftributing to the neceffity of faints, given to hofpitality.

Blefs

Blefs them which perfecute you ; blefs, and curfe not ; rejoice with them that do rejoice, and weep with them that weep. Be of the fame mind one towards another : mind not high things, but condefcend to men of low eftate. Be not wife in your own conceits. Recompenfe to no man evil for evil. Provide things honeft in the fight of all men. If it be poffible, as much as lieth in you, live peaceably with all men. Avenge not yourfelves, but rather give place unto wrath ; for it is written, Vengeance is mine ! I will repay, faith the Lord : therefore, if thine enemy hunger, feed him ; if he thirft, give him drink ; for, in fo doing, thou fhalt heap coals of fire on his head. Be not overcome of evil, but overcome evil with good."

" Let every foul be fubject unto the higher powers, for there is no power but of God : the powers that be are ordained of God : whofoever therefore refifteth the power, refifteth the ordinance of God, and they that refift, fhall receive unto themfelves damnation.

damnation. For rulers are not a terror to good works, but to the evil. Wilt thou then not be afraid of the power? Do that which is good, and thou shalt have praise of the same, for he is the minister of God to thee for good: but if thou do that which is evil, be afraid, for he beareth not the sword in vain: for he is the minister of God, a revenger to execute wrath upon him that doeth evil. Wherefore ye must needs be subject, not only for wrath, but also for conscience sake: for, for this cause, pay ye tribute also, for they are God's ministers, attending continually upon this very thing. Render, therefore, to all their dues; tribute, to whom tribute is due; custom, to whom custom; fear, to whom fear; honour, to whom honour."

"Owe no man any thing, but to love one another; for he that loveth another hath fulfilled the law: for this, thou shalt not commit adultery, thou shalt not kill, thou shalt not bear false witness, thou shalt not covet, and if there be any commandment, it

is

is briefly comprehended in this saying, Thou shalt love thy neighbour as thyself. Love worketh no ill to his neighbour; therefore love is the fulfilling of the law."

"And that, knowing the time, that now is our salvation nearer than when we believed. The night is far spent, the day is at hand; let us therefore cast off the works of darkness, and let us put on the armour of light. Let us walk honestly as in the day, not in rioting and drunkennefs, not in chambering and wantonnefs, not in strife and envying *."

Read this, and then think of exitiabilis fuperftitio!!—Or if we be not allowed, in contending with heathen authorities, to produce our books against theirs, we may at leaft be permitted to confront theirs with one another. Of this " pernicious fuperftition," what could *Pliny* find to blame, when he was led by his office, to inftitute fomething like an examination into the conduct and

---

* Rom. xii. 9.—xiii. 13.

principles of the fect? He difcovered nothing, but that they were wont to meet together on a ftated day before it was light,
and fing among themfelves a hymn to Chrift
as a God, and to bind themfelves by an oath,
not to the commiffion of any wickednefs,
but not to be guilty of theft, robbery, or
adultery; never to falfify their word, nor to
deny a pledge committed to them, when
called upon to return it.

Upon the words of Tacitus we may build
the following obfervations:

Firft, That we are well warranted in calling the view, under which the learned men of
that age beheld Chriftianity, an obfcure and
diftant view. Had Tacitus known more of
Chriftianity, of its precepts, duties, conftitution or defign, however he had difcredited
the ftory, he would have refpected the principle. He would have defcribed the religion differently, though he had rejected it.
It has been very fatisfactorily fhewn, that the
" fuperftition " of the Chriftians confifted

in

in worshiping a person unknown to the
Roman calendar; and that the " pernicious-
ness" with which they were reproached,
was nothing else but there opposition to the
established polytheism: and this view of the
matter was just such a one as might be expected to occur to a mind, which held the
sect in too much contempt to concern itself
about the grounds and reasons of their conduct.

Secondly, We may from hence remark,
how little reliance can be placed upon the
most acute judgments, in subjects which they
are pleased to despise; and which, of course,
they from the first consider as unworthy to
be enquired into. Had not Christianity sur-
vived to tell its own story, it must have gone
down to posterity as a " pernicious superfti-
tion ;" and that upon the credit of Tacitus's
account, much, I doubt not, strengthened
by the name of the writer, and the reputation of his sagacity.

Thirdly, That this contempt prior to
examination,

examination, is an intellectual vice, from which the greateſt faculties of mind are not free. I know not, indeed, whether men of the greateſt faculties of mind are not the moſt ſubject to it. Such men feel themſelves ſeated upon an eminence. Looking down from their height upon the follies of mankind, they behold contending tenets waſting their idle ſtrength upon one another, with a common diſdain of the abſurdity of them all. This habit of thought, however comfortable to the mind which entertains it, or however natural to great parts, is extremely dangerous; and more apt, than almoſt any other diſpoſition, to produce haſty and contemptuous, and, by conſequence, erroneous judgments, both of perſons and opinions.

Fourthly, We need not be ſurpriſed at many writers of that age not mentioning Chriſtianity at all, when they, who did mention it, appear to have entirely miſconceived its nature and character; and, in conſe

quence of this mifconception, to have regarded it with negligence and contempt.

To the knowledge of the greateft part of
the learned heathens, the facts of the Chriftian hiftory could only come by report.
The books, probably, they had never looked into. The fettled habit of their minds
was, and long had been, an indifcriminate
rejection of all reports of the kind. With
thefe fweeping conclufions truth hath no
chance. It depends upon diftinction. If
they would not enquire, how fhould they
be convinced? It might be founded in truth,
though they, who made no fearch, might
not difcover it,

" Men of rank and fortune, of wit and
abilities, are often found, even in Chriftian
countries, to be furprifingly ignorant of religion, and of every thing that relates to it.
Such were many of the heathens. Their
thoughts were all fixed upon other things,
upon reputation and glory, upon wealth and
power,

power, upon luxury and pleafure, upon bufinefs or learning. They thought, and they
had reafon to think, that the religion of their
country was fable and forgery, an heap of
inconfiftent lies, which inclined them to
fuppofe that other religions were no better.
Hence it came to pafs, that when the Apoftles preached the gofpel, and wrought miracles in confirmation of a doctrine every
way worthy of God, many Gentiles knew
little or nothing of it, and would not take
the leaft pains to inform themfelves about
it. This appears plainly from ancient hiftory *."

I think it by no means unreafonable to
fuppofe, that the heathen public, efpecially
that part which is made up of men of rank
and education, were divided into two claffes;
thofe who defpifed Chriftianity beforehand,
and thofe who received it. In correfpondency with which divifion of character, the

* Jortin's Dif. on the Chrif. Rel. p. 66, ed. 4th.

writers

writers of that age would alfo be of two
claffes, thofe who were filent about Chriftianity, and thofe who were Chriftians. "A
good man, who attended fufficiently to the
Chriftian affairs, would become a Chriftian;
after which his teftimony ceafed to be Pagan, and became Chriftian *."

I muft alfo add, that I think it fufficiently proved, that the notion of magic was
reforted to by the heathen adverfaries of
Chriftianity, in like manner as that of diabo-
lical agency had before been by the Jews.
Juftin Martyr alledges this as his reafon for
arguing from prophecy, rather than from
miracles. Origen imputes this evafion to
Celfus; Jerome to Porphyry; and Lactantius to the heathen in general. The feveral paffages, which contain thefe teftimonies,
will be produced in the next chapter. It being difficult however to afcertain, in what degree this notion prevailed, efpecially amongft

* Hartley, Obf. p. 119.

the

the superior ranks of the heathen communities, another, and I think an adequate cause, has been assigned for their infidelity. It is probable that in many cases the two causes would operate together.

CHAP

CHAP. V.

*That the Christian miracles are not recited, or
appealed to, by early Christian writers
themselves, so fully or frequently as might
have been expected.*

I SHALL consider this objection, first, as
it applies to the letters of the Apostles, preserved in the New Testament; and secondly,
as it applies to the remaining writings of
other early Christians.

The epistles of the apostles are either hor-
tatory or argumentative. So far as they
were occupied, in delivering lessons of duty,
rules of public order, admonitions against certain prevailing corruptions, against vice, or
any particular species of it, or in fortifying
and encouraging the constancy of the disciples under the trials to which they were
exposed, there appears to be no place or
occasion

occasion for more of these references than we actually find.

So far as the epistles are argumentative, the nature of the argument which they handle, accounts for the infrequency of these allusions. These epistles were not written to prove the truth of Christianity. The subject under consideration was not that which the miracles decided, the reality of our Lord's mission; but it was that which the miracles did not decide, the nature of his person or power, the design of his advent, its effects, and of those effects the value, kind, and extent. Still I maintain, that miraculous evidence lies at the bottom of the argument. For nothing could be so preposterous, as for the disciples of Jesus to dispute amongst themselves, or with others, concerning his office or character, unless they believed that he had shewn, by supernatural proofs, that there was something extraordinary in both. Miraculous evidence, therefore, forming not the texture of these

Z 4   arguments,

arguments, but the ground and fubftratum, if it be occafionally difcerned, if it be incidentally appealed to, it is exactly fo much as ought to take place, fuppofing the hiftory to be true.

As a further anfwer to the objection, that the apoftolic epiftles do not contain fo frequent, or fuch direct and circumftantial recitals of miracles as might be expected, I would add, *that the apoftolic epiftles refemble in this refpect the apoftolic fpeeches,* which fpeeches are given by a writer, who diftinctly records numerous miracles wrought by thefe apoftles themfelves, and by the founder of the inftitution in their prefence; that it is unwarrantable to contend, that the omiffion, or infrequency, of fuch recitals in the fpeeches of the apoftles, negatives the exiftence of the miracles, when the fpeeches are given in immediate conjunction with the hiftory of thofe miracles; and that a conclufion which cannot be inferred from the fpeeches, without contradicting the whole

tenor

tenor of the book which contains them, cannot be inferred from letters, which, in this refpect, are fimilar only to the fpeeches.

To prove the fimilitude which we alledge, it may be remarked, that although in St. Luke's gofpel, the apoftle Peter is reprefented to have been prefent at many decifive miracles wrought by Chrift; and although the fecond part of the fame hiftory afcribes other decifive miracles to Peter himfelf, particularly the cure of the lame man at the gate of the temple (Acts iii. 1.), the death of Ananias and Sapphira (Acts v. 1.), the cure of Æneas (Acts ix. 40.), the refurrection of Dorcas (Acts ix. 34.); yet out of fix fpeeches of Peter, preferved in the Acts, I know but two, in which reference is made to the miracles wrought by Chrift, and only one in which he refers to miraculous powers poffeffed by himfelf. In his fpeech upon the day of Pentecoft, Peter addreffes his audience with **great** folemnity thus : " Ye men of Ifrael, hear thefe words; Jefus of Nazareth, a man approved of God among

you,

you, by miracles and wonders and figns, which God did by him in the midft of you, as ye yourfelves alfo know, &c. * " In his fpeech upon the converfion of Cornelius, he delivers his teftimony to the miracles performed by Chrift in thefe words : " We are witnefles of all things which he did, both in the land of the Jews, and in Jerufalem †." But in this latter fpeech no allufion appears to the miracles wrought by himfelf, notwithftanding that the miracles above enumerated, all preceded the time in which it was delivered. In his fpeech upon the election of Matthias ‡, no diftinct reference is made to any of the miracles of Chrift's hiftory, except his refurrection. The fame alfo may be obferved of his fpeech upon the cure of the lame man at the gate of the temple § ; the fame in his fpeech before the Sanhedrim ‖ ; the fame in his fecond apology in the prefence of that affembly. Stephen's long fpeech contains no reference whatever to

* Acts ii. 22. † x. 39. ‡ i. 15.
§ iii. 12. ‖ iv. 9.

miracles,

miracles, though it be expressly related of
him, in the book which preserves the speech,
and almost immediately before the speech,
" that he did great wonders and miracles
among the people *." Again, although
miracles be expressly attributed to St. Paul
in the Acts of the Apostles, first generally,
as at Iconium (Acts xiv. 3.), during the
whole tour through the Upper Asia (xiv.
27. xv. 12.), at Ephesus (xix. 11, 12.); secondly, in specific instances, as the blindness
of Elymas at Paphos †, the cure of the cripple at Lystra ‡, of the Pythoness at Philippi §, the miraculous liberation from pri-
son in the same city ‖, the restoration of
Eutychus ¶, the predictions of his ship-
wreck **, the viper at Milita ††, the cure
of Publius's father ‡‡; at all which miracles,
except the two first, the historian himself was
present: notwithstanding, I say, this positive
ascription of miracles to St. Paul, yet in the
speeches delivered by him, and given as de-,

* Acts vi. 8.   † xiii. 7.   ‡ xiv. 8.   § xvi. 16.
‖ xvi. 26.   ¶ xx. 10.   ** xxvii. 1.   †† xxviii. 6.
‡‡ xxviii 8.

livered

livered by him, in the fame book in which
the miracles are related, and the miraculous
powers afferted, the appeals to his own miracles, or indeed to any miracles at all, are
rare and incidental. In his fpeech at Antioch in Pifidia *, there is no allufion, but
to the refurrection. In his difcourfe at Mi-
letus †, none to any miracle; none in his
fpeech before Felix ‡; none in his fpeech
before Feftus §; except to Chrift's refurrection, and his own converfion.

Agreeably hereunto, in thirteen letters
afcribed to St. Paul, we have inceffant references to Chrift's refurrection, frequent references to his own converfion, three indu-
bitable references to the miracles which he
wrought ‖, four other references to the fame,
lefs direct yet highly probable ¶; but more
copious or circumftantial recitals we have
not. The confent, therefore, between St.
Paul's fpeeches and letters, is in this refpect

---

* Acts xiii. 16.   † xx. 17.   ‡ xxiv. 10.   § xxv. 8.
‖ Gal. iii. 5.   Rom. xv. 18, 19.   2 Cor. xii. 12.
¶ 1 Cor. ii. 4, 5. Eph. iii. 7. Gal. ii. 8. 1 Theff. i. 5.

fufficiently

fufficiently exact : and the reafon in both is
the fame ; namely, that the miraculous hiftory was all along *prefuppofed*, and that the
queftion, which occupied the fpeaker's and
the writer's thoughts, was this: whether,
allowing the hiftory of Jefus to be true, he
was, upon the ftrength of it, to be received
as the promifed Meffiah ; and, if he was,
what were the confequences, what was the
object and benefit of his miffion ?

The general obfervation which has been
made upon the apoftolic writings, namely,
that the fubject, of which they treated, did
not lead them to any direct recital of the
Chriftian hiftory, belongs alfo to the writings of the apoftolic fathers. The epiftle
of Barnabas is, in its fubject and general
compofition, much like the epiftle to the
Hebrews; an allegorical application of divers paffages of the Jewifh hiftory, of their
law and ritual, to thofe parts of the Chriftian difpenfation, in which the author perceived a refemblance. The epiftle of Clement was written for the fole purpofe of

5   quieting

quieting certain diffenfions that had arifen amongft the members of the church of Corinth; and of reviving, in their minds, that temper and fpirit of which their predeceffors in the gofpel had left them an example. The work of Hermas is a vifion; quotes neither the Old Teftament nor the New; and merely falls now and then into the language, and the mode of fpeech, which the author had read in our gofpels. The epiftles of Polycarp and Ignatius had, for their principal objeᒼ, the order and difcipline of the churches which they addreffed. Yet, under all thefe circumftances of difadvantage, the great points of the Chriftian hiftory are fully recognized. This hath been fhewn in its proper place *.

There is, however, another clafs of writers, to whom the anfwer above given, viz. the unfuitablenefs of any fuch appeals or references as the objeᒼion demands to the fubjeᒼs of which the writings treated, does

* Vol. i. p. 126—131.

not apply; and that is, the clafs of ancient
apologifls, whofe declared defign it was, to
defend Chriftianity, and to give the reafons
of their adherence to it. It is neceffary,
therefore, to enquire how the matter of the
objeftion ftands in thefe.

The moft ancient apologift, of whofe
works we have the fmalleft knowledge, is
Quadratus. Quadratus lived about feventy
years after the afcenfion, and prefented his
apology to the emperor Adrian. From a
paffage of this work, preferved in Eufebius,
it appears that the author did direftly and
formally appeal to the miracles of Chrift,
and in terms as exprefs and confident as we
could defire. The paffage (which has been
once already ftated) is as follows: "The
works of our Saviour were always confpicu-
ous, for they were real; both they that were
healed, and they that were raifed from the
dead, were feen, not only when they were
healed or raifed, but for a long time afterwards; not only whilft he dwelled on this
earth, but alfo after his departure, and for a

good

good while after it ; infomuch as that fome
of them have reached to our times *." Nothing can be more rational or fatisfactory
than this.

Juftin Martyr, the next of the Chriftian
apologifts whofe work is not loft, and who
followed Quadratus at the diftance of about
thirty years, has touched upon paffages of
Chrift's hiftory in fo many places, that a
tolerably complete account of Chrift's life
might be collected out of his works. In the
following quotation, he afferts the performance of miracles by Chrift, in words as
ftrong and pofitive as the language poffeffes:
" Chrift healed thofe who from their birth
were blind, and deaf, and lame ; caufing by
his word, one to leap, another to hear, and
a third to fee: and having raifed the dead,
and caufed them to live, he by his works
excited attention, and induced the men of
that age to know him. Who, however, feeing thefe things done, faid that it was a

* Euf. Hift. l. iv. c. 3.

magical

magical appearance; and dared to call him
a magician, and a deceiver of the people *."

In his firſt apology †, Juſtin expreſsly
aſſigns the reaſon for his having recourſe to
the argument from prophecy, rather than
alledging the miracles of the Chriſtian hiſtory: which reaſon was, that the perſons
with whom he contended would aſcribe
theſe miracles to magic; " leſt any of our
opponents ſhould ſay, What hinders, but
that he who is called Chriſt by us, being a
man ſprung from men, performed the miracles which we attributed to him by magical art." The ſuggeſting of this reaſon
meets, as I apprehend, the very point of the
preſent objection; more eſpecially when we
find Juſtin followed in it, by other writers
of that age. Irenæus, who came about forty
years after him, notices the ſame evaſion
in the adverſaries of Chriſtianity, and re-
plies to it by the ſame argument: " But, if

* Juſt. dial. p. 258. ed. Thirlby.

† Ap. prim. p. 48. ib.

Vᴏʟ. II.   A a   they

they shall say, that the Lord performed these things by an illusory appearance (φαντασιωδῶς), leading these objectors to the prophecies, we will shew from them, that all things were thus predicted concerning him, and strictly came to pass *." Lactantius, who lived a century lower, delivers the same sentiment, upon the same occasion. " He performed miracles---we might have supposed him to have been a magician, as ye say, and as the Jews then supposed, if all the prophets had not with one spirit foretold that Christ would perform these very things †."

But to return to the Christian apologists in their order; Tertullian—" That person whom the Jews had vainly imagined, from the meanness of his appearance, to be a mere man, they afterwards, in consequence of the power he exerted, considered as a magician, when he, with one word, ejected devils out of the bodies of men, gave sight

* Ir. l. ii. c. 57.   † Lact. v. 3.

I   to

to the blind, cleanfed the leprous, ftrengthened the nerves of thofe that had the palfy,
and laftly, with one command, reftored the
dead to life ; when he, I fay, made the very
elements obey him, affuaged the ftorms,
walked upon the feas, demonftrating himfelf to be the word of God *."

Next in the catalogue of profeffed apologifts we may place Origen, who, it is well
known, publifhed a formal defence of Chriftianity, in anfwer to Celfus, a heathen, who
had written a difcourfe againft it.   I know
no expreffions, by which a plainer or more
pofitive appeal to the Chriftian miracles can
be made, than the expreffions ufed by Origen ; " Undoubtedly we do think him to be
the Chrift, and the Son of God, becaufe he
healed the lame and the blind ; and we are
the more confirmed in this perfuafion, by
what is written in the prophecies, Then fhall
the eyes of the blind be opened, and the ears
of the deaf fhall hear, and the lame men fhall

* Tertull. Apolog. p. 20. ed. Priorii Par. 1675.

leap

leap as an hart. But that he alſo raiſed the
dead, and that it is not a fiction of thoſe who
wrote the Goſpels, is evident from hence,
that, if it had been a fiction, there would
have been many recorded to be raiſed up,
and ſuch as had been a long time in their
graves. But, it not being a fiction, few
have been recorded; for inſtance, the daughter of the ruler of a ſynagogue, of whom I
do not know why he ſaid, ſhe is not dead
but ſleepeth, expreſſing ſomething peculiar
to her, not common to all dead perſons; and
the only ſon of a widow, on whom he had
compaſſion, and raiſed him to life, after he
had bid the bearer of the corpſe to ſtop; and
the third Lazarus, who had been buried
four days." This is poſitively to aſſert the
miracles of Chriſt, and it is alſo to comment
upon them, and that with a conſiderable degree of accuracy and candour.

In another paſſage of the ſame author *,
we meet with the old ſolution of magic

* Or. con. Celſ. lib. ii. ſec. 48.

applied

applied to the miracles of Christ by the adversaries of the religion. "Celsus," saith Origen, "well knowing what great works may be alledged to have been done by Jesus, pretends to grant that the things related of him are true; such as healing diseases, raising the dead, feeding multitudes with a few loaves, of which large fragments were left." And then Celsus gives, it seems, an answer to these proofs of our Lord's mission, which, as Origen understood it, resolved the phenomena into magic; for Origen begins his reply, by observing, "You see that Celsus in a manner allows that there is such a thing as magic *."

It appears also from the testimony of St. Jerome, that Porphyry, the most learned and able of the heathen writers against Christianity, resorted to the same solution: "Unless," says he, speaking to Vigilantius, "according to the manner of the Gentiles, and

* Lard. Jewish and Heath. Test. vol. ii. p. 294, ed. quarto.

the

the profane, of *Porphyry* and Eunomius, you pretend that thefe are the tricks of demons *."

This magic, thefe demons, this illufory appearance, this comparifon with the tricks of jugglers, by which many of that age accounted fo eafily for the Chriftian miracles, and which anfwers, the advocates of Chriftianity often thought it neceffary to refute, by arguments drawn from other topics, and particularly from prophecy (to which, it feems, thefe folutions did not apply), we now perceive to be grofs fubterfuges. That fuch reafons were ever ferioufly urged, and ferioufly received, is only a proof, what a glofs and varnifh fafhion can give to any opinion.

It appears, therefore, that the miracles of Chrift, underftood, as we underftand them, in their literal and hiftorical fenfe, were pofitively and precifely afferted and appealed

* Jerome con. Vigil.

to by the apologifts for Chriftianity; which anfwers the allegation of the objection.

I am ready, however, to admit, that the ancient Chriftian advocates did not infift upon the miracles in argument, fo frequently as I fhould have done. It was their lot to contend with notions of magical agency, againft which the mere production of the facts was not fufficient for the convincing of their adverfaries: I do not know whether they themfelves thought it quite decifive of the controverfy. But fince it is proved, I conceive, with certainty, that the fparing-nefs with which they appealed to miracles, was owing neither to their ignorance, nor their doubt of the facts, it is, at any rate, an objection, not to the truth of the hiftory, but to the judgment of its defenders.

CHAP.

CHAP. VI.

*Want of universality in the knowledge and re-
ception of Christianity, and of greater clear-
ness in the evidence.*

OF a revelation which really came from God, the proof, it has been said, would in all ages be so public and manifest, that no part of the human species would remain ignorant of it, no understanding could fail of being convinced by it.

The advocates of Christianity do not pretend that the evidence of their religion possesses these qualities. They do not deny, that we can conceive it to be within the compass of divine power, to have communicated to the world a higher degree of assurance, and to have given to his communication a stronger and more extensive influ.... For any thing we are able to discern,

God

God *could* have fo formed men, as to have perceived the truths of religion intuitively; or to have carried on a communication with the other world, whilft they lived in this; or to have feen the individuals of the fpecies, inftead of dying, pafs to heaven by a fenfible tranflation. He could have prefented a feparate miracle to each man's fenfes. He could have eftablifhed a ftanding miracle. He could have caufed miracles to be wrought in every different age and country. Thefe, and many more methods, which we may imagine, if we once give loofe to our imaginations, are, fo far as we can judge, all practicable.

The queftion, therefore, is not, whether Chriftianity poffeffes the higheft poffible degree of evidence, but whether the not having more evidence be a fufficient reafon for rejecting that which we have.

Now there appears to be no fairer method of judging, concerning any difpenfation which is alledged to come from God, when

a queftion

a queſtion is made whether ſuch a diſpenſation could come from God or not, than by
comparing it with other things, which are
acknowledged to proceed from the ſame
council, and to be produced by the ſame
agency. If the diſpenſation in queſtion labour under no defects but what apparently
belong to other diſpenſations, theſe ſeeming
defects do not juſtify us, in ſetting aſide the
proofs which are offered of its authenticity,
if they be otherwiſe entitled to credit.

Throughout that order then of nature, of
which God is the author, what we find is a
ſyſtem of *beneficence*, we are ſeldom or ever
able to make out a ſyſtem of *optimiſm*. I
mean, that there are few caſes in which, if
we permit ourſelves to range in poſſibili-
ties, we cannot ſuppoſe ſomething more perfect, and more unobjectionable, than what
we ſee. The rain which deſcends from heaven is confeſſedly amongſt the contrivances
of the Creator, for the ſuſtentation of the
animals and vegetables which ſubſiſt upon
the ſurface of the earth. Yet how partially
and

and irregularly is it fupplied? How much of it falls upon the fea, where it can be of no ufe; how often is it wanted where it would be of the greateft? What tracts of continent are rendered defarts by the fcarcity of it? Or, not to fpeak of extreme cafes, how much, fometimes, do inhabited countries fuffer by its deficiency or delay?—We could imagine, if to imagine were our bufinefs, the matter to be otherwife regulated. We could imagine fhowers to fall, juft where and when they would do good; always feafonable, everywhere fufficient; fo diftributed as not to leave a field upon the face of the globe fcorched by drought, or even a plant withering for the lack of moifture. Yet does the difference between the real cafe and the imagined cafe, or the feeming inferiority of the one to the other, authorize us to fay, that the prefent difpofition of the atmofphere is not amongft the productions or the defigns of the Deity. Does it check the inference which we draw from the confeffed beneficence of the provifion? or does it make us ceafe to admire the contrivance?—

The

The obfervation, which we have exemplified
in the fingle inftance of the rain of heaven,
may be repeated concerning moft of the phenomena of nature: and the true conclufion
to which it leads is this, that to enquire what
the Deity might have done, could have done,
or, as we even fometimes prefume to fpeak,
ought to have done, or, in hypothetical cafes,
would have done, and to build any propofitions upon fuch enquiries againft evidence
of facts, is wholly unwarrantable. It is a
mode of reafoning, which will not do in natural hiftory, which will not do in natural
religion, which cannot therefore be applied
with fafety to revelation. It may have fome
foundation, in certain fpeculative *apriori* ideas
of the divine attributes; but it has none in
experience, or in analogy. The general character of the works of nature is, on the one
hand, goodnefs both in defign and effect;
and, on the other hand, a liability to difficulty, and to objections, if fuch objections
be allowed, by reafon of feeming incom-
pletenefs or uncertainty in attaining their
end. Chriftianity participates of this character

racter. The true fimilitude between nature and revelation confifts in this; that they each bear ftrong marks of their original; that they each alfo bear appearances of irregularity and defect. A fyftem of ftrict optimifm may neverthelefs be the real fyftem in both cafes. But what I contend is, that the proof is hidden from *us*; that we ought not to expect to perceive that in revelation, which we hardly perceive in any thing; that beneficence, of which we *can* judge, ought to fatisfy us, that optimifm, of which we *cannot* judge, ought not to be fought after. We can judge of beneficence, becaufe it depends upon effects which we experience, and upon the relation between the means which we fee acting, and the ends which we fee produced. We cannot judge of optimifm, becaufe-it neceffarily implies a comparifon of that which is tried, with that which is **not** tried; of confequences which we fee, with others which we imagine, and concerning many of which, it is more than probable we know nothing; concerning fome, that we have no notion.

If

If Chriftianity be compared with the ftate and progrefs of natural religion, the argument of the objector will gain nothing by the comparifon. I remember hearing an unbeliever fay, that, if God had given a revelation, he would have written it in the fkies. Are the truths of natural religion written in the fkies, or in a language which every one reads? or is this the cafe with the moft ufeful arts, or the moft neceffary fciences of human life? An Otaheitean or an Efquimaux knows nothing of Chriftianity; does he know more of the principles of deifm or morality? which, notwithftanding his ignorance, are neither untrue, nor unimportant, nor uncertain. The exiftence of the Deity is left to be collected from obfervations, which every man does not make, which every man, perhaps, is not capable of making. Can it be argued, that God does not exift, becaufe, if he did, he would let us fee him; or difcover himfelf to mankind by proofs (fuch as, we may think, the nature of the fubject merited), which no inadvertency could mifs, no prejudice withftand?

If

If Chriftianity be regarded as a providential inftrument for the melioration of mankind, its progrefs and diffufion refembles that of other caufes, by which human life is improved. The diverfity is not greater, nor the advance more flow in religion, than we find it to be in learning, liberty, government, laws. The Deity hath not touched the order of nature in vain. The Jewifh religion produced great and permanent effects: the Chriftian religion hath done the fame. It hath difpofed the world to amendment. It hath put things in a train. It is by no means improbable, that it may become univerfal; and that the world may continue in that ftate fo long as that the duration of its reign may bear a vaft proportion to the time of its partial influence.

When we argue concerning Chriftianity, that it muft neceffarily be true, becaufe it is beneficial, we go perhaps too far on one fide: and we certainly go too far on the other, when we conclude that it muft be falfe, becaufe it is not fo efficacious as we could have
fuppofed.

suppofed. The queftion of its truth is to be
tried upon its proper evidence, without de-
ferring much to this fort of argument, on
either fide. " The evidence," as Bifhop
Butler hath rightly obferved, " depends upon the judgment we form of human conduct, under given circumftances, of which it
may be prefumed that we know fomething;
the objection ftands upon the fuppofed conduct of the Deity, under relations with which
we are not acquainted."

What would be the real effect of that over-
powering evidence which our adverfaries require in a revelation, it is difficult to foretell ;
at leaft, we muft fpeak of it as of a difpenfation, of which we have no experience.
Some confequences however would, it is probable, attend this œconomy, which do not
feem to befit a revelation that proceeded
from God. One is, that irrefiftible proof
would reftrain the voluntary powers too
much ; would not anfwer the purpofe of trial
and probation ; would call for no exercife of
candour, ferioufnefs, humility, enquiry ; no

submiffion

submission of passions, interests, and prejudices, to moral evidence and to probable
truth; no habits of reflection; none of that
previous desire to learn, and to obey the
will of God, which forms perhaps the test of
the virtuous principle, and which induces
men to attend, with care and reverence, to
every credible intimation of that will, and to
resign present advantages and present plea-
sures to every reasonable expectation of pro-
pitiating his favour. " Men's moral probation may be, whether they will take due
care to inform themselves by impartial consideration; and, afterwards, whether they
will act as the case requires, upon the evidence which they have. And this, we find
by experience, is often our probation in our
temporal capacity *."

II. These modes of communication would
leave no place for the admission of *internal
evidence*; which ought, perhaps, to bear a
considerable part in the proof of every reve-

* Butler's Analogy, part ii. c. vi.

B b   lation,

lation, becaufe it is a fpecies of evidence,
which applies itfelf to the knowledge, love,
and practice of virtue, and which operates
in proportion to the degree of thofe qualities which it finds in the perfon whom it addreffes. Men of good difpofitions, amongft
Chriftians, are greatly affected by the impreffion which the fcriptures themfelves
make upon their minds. Their conviction
is much ftrengthened by thefe impreffions.
And this perhaps was intended to be one effect to be produced by the religion. It is
likewife true, to whatever caufe we afcribe it
(for I am not in this work at liberty to introduce the Chriftian doctrine of grace or
affiftance, or the Chriftian promife, "that,
if any man will do his will, he fhall know
of the doctrine, whether it be of God *,")—
it is true, I fay, that they who fincerely act,
or fincerely endeavour to act, *according* to
what they believe, that is, according to the
juft refult of the probabilities, or, if you
pleafe, the poffibilities in natural and reveal-

* John vii. 17.

ed

ed religion, which they themselves perceive, and according to a rational estimate of consequences, and, above all, according to the just effect of those principles of gratitude and devotion, which even the view of nature generates in a well-ordered mind, *seldom fail of proceeding farther.* This also may have been exactly what was designed.

Whereas may it not be said, that irresistible evidence would confound all characters, and all dispositions? would subvert, rather than promote, the true purpose of the divine councils, which is not to produce *obedience* by a force little short of mechanical constraint (which obedience would be regularity not virtue, and would hardly perhaps differ from that which inanimate bodies pay to the laws impressed upon their nature), but to treat moral agents agreeably to what they are; which is done, when light and motives are of such kinds, and are imparted in such measures, that the influence of them depends upon the recipients themselves? " It is not meet to govern rational free agents

in

in viâ by fight and fenfe. It would be no trial or thanks to the moft fenfual wretch to forbear finning if heaven and hell were open to his fight. That fpiritual vifion and fruition is our ftate in patriâ." (Baxter's Reafons, p. 357.) There may be truth in this thought, though roughly exprefled. Few things are more improbable than that we (the human fpecies) fhould be the high-eft order of beings in the univerfe; that ani-mated nature fhould afcend from the loweft reptile to us, and all at once ftop there. If there be claffes above us of rational intelli-gences, clearer manifeftations may belong to them. This may be one of the diftinc-tions. And it may be one, to which we ourfelves hereafter fhall attain.

III. But thirdly; may it not alfo be afked, whether the perfect difplay of a future ftate of exiftence would be compatible with the activity of civil life, and with the fuccefs of human affairs? I can eafily conceive that this impreffion may be overdone; that it may fo feize and fill the thoughts, as to

leave

leave no place for the cares and offices of men's several stations, no anxiety for worldly prosperity, or even for a worldly provision, and, by consequence, no sufficient stimulus to secular industry. Of the first Christians we read, " that all that believed were together, and had all things common ; and sold their possessions and goods, and parted them to all men, as every man had need ; and, continuing daily with one accord in the temple, and breaking bread from house to house, did eat their meat with gladness and singleness of heart *." This was extremely natural, and just what might be expected, from miraculous evidence coming with full force upon the senses of mankind: but I much doubt, whether, if this state of mind had been universal, or long continued, the business of the world could have gone on. The necessary arts of social life would have been little cultivated. The plough and the loom would have stood still. Agriculture, manufactures, trade, and naviga-

---

Acts ii. 44—46.

tion,

tion, would not, I think, have flourished, if they could have been exercised at all. Men would have addicted themselves to contemplative and ascetic lives, instead of lives of business and of useful industry. We observe that St. Paul found it necessary, frequently to recall his converts to the ordinary labours and domestic duties of their condition; and to give them, in his own example, a lesson of contented application to their worldly employments.

By the manner in which the religion is now proposed, a great portion of the human species is enabled, and of these, multitudes of every generation are induced, to seek and to effectuate their salvation through the medium of Christianity, without interruption of the prosperity, or of the regular course of human affairs.

CHAP.

CHAP. VII.

The supposed Effects of Christianity.

THAT a religion, which, under every form in which it is taught, holds forth the final reward of virtue, and punishment of vice, and proposes those distinctions of virtue and vice, which the wisest and most cultivated part of mankind confess to be just, should not be believed, is very possible ; but that, so far as it is believed, it should not produce any good, but rather a bad effect upon public happiness, is a proposition, which it requires very strong evidence to render credible. Yet many have been found to contend for this paradox, and very confident appeals have been made to history, and to observation, for the truth of it.

In the conclusions, however, which these writers draw, from what they call experi-

ence,

ence, two fources, I think, of miftake, may be perceived.

One is, that they look for the influence of religion in the wrong place :

The other, that they charge Chriftianity with many confequences, for which it is not refponfible.

1. The influence of religion is not to be fought for in the councils of princes, in the debates or refolutions of popular affemblies, in the conduct of governments towards their fubjects, or of ftates and fovereigns towards one another; of conquerors at the head of their armies, or of parties intriguing for power at home (topics, which alone almoft occupy the attention, and fill the pages of hiftory); but muft be perceived, if perceived at all, in the filent courfe of private and domeftic life. Nay more; even *there* its influence may not be very obvious to obfervation. If it check, in fome degree, perfonal diffolutenefs, if it beget a general probity

bity

bity in the tranfaction of bufinefs, if it produce foft and humane manners in the mafs
of the community, and occafional exertions
of laborious or expenfive benevolence in a
few individuals, it is all the effect which can
offer itfelf to external notice. The kingdom of Heaven is within us. That which
is the fubftance of the religion, its hopes
and confolations, its intermixture with the
thoughts by day and by night, the devotion
of the heart, the control of appetite, the ftea-
dy direction of the will to the commands of
God, is necefTarily invifible. Yet upon
thefe depend the virtue and the happinefs of
millions. This caufe renders the reprefentations of hiftory, with refpect to religion,
defective and fallacious, in a greater degree
than they are upon any other fubject. Religion operates moft upon thofe of whom
hiftory knows the leaft; upon fathers and
mothers in their families, upon men fervants
and maid fervants, upon the orderly tradef-
man, the quiet villager, the manufacturer at
his loom, the hufbandman in his fields.
Amongft fuch its influence collectively may
be

be of ineſtimable value, yet its effects in the
mean time little, upon thoſe who figure upon the ſtage of the world. *They* may know
nothing of it; they may believe nothing of
it; they may be actuated by motives more
impetuous than thoſe which religion is able
to excite. It cannot, therefore, be thought
ſtrange, that this influence ſhould elude the
graſp and touch of public hiſtory; for what
is public hiſtory, but a regiſter of the ſuc-
ceſſes and diſappointments, the vices, the
follies, and the quarrels, of thoſe who engage in contentions for power?

I will add, that much of this influence
may be felt in times of public diſtreſs, and
little of it in times of public wealth and ſe-
curity. This alſo increaſes the uncertainty
of any opinions that we draw from hiſtorical
repreſentations. The influence of Chriſtianity is commenſurate with no effects which
hiſtory ſtates. We do not pretend, that it
has any ſuch neceſſary and irreſiſtible power
over the affairs of nations, as to ſurmount
the force of other cauſes.

The

The Chriftian religion alfo acts upon public ufages and inftitutions, by an operation which is only fecondary and indirect. Chriftianity is not a code of civil law. It can only reach public inftitutions through private character. Now its influence upon private character may be confiderable, yet many public ufages and inftitutions, repugnant to its principles, may remain. To get rid of thefe, the reigning part of the community muft act, and act together. But it may be long before the perfons who compofe this body, be fufficiently touched with the Chriftian character, to join in the fuppreffion of practices, to which they and the public have been reconciled, by caufes which will reconcile the human mind to any thing, by habit and intereft. Neverthelefs, the effects of Chriftianity, even in this view, have been important. It has mitigated the conduct of war, and the treatment of captives. It has foftened the adminiftration of defpotic, or of nominally defpotic governments. It has abolifhed polygamy. It has reftrained the licentioufnefs of divorces. It has put

an

an end to the expofure of children, and the
immolation of flaves. It has fuppreffed
the combats of gladiators *, and the impurities of religious rites. It has banifhed, if
not unnatural vices, at leaft the toleration of
them. It has greatly meliorated the condition of the laborious part, that is to fay,
of the mafs of every community, by procuring for them a day of weekly reft. In
all countries, in which it is profeffed, it has
produced numerous eftablifhments for the
relief of ficknefs and poverty; and, in fome,
a regular and general provifion by law. It
has triumphed over the flavery eftablifhed
in the Roman empire: it is contending,
and, I truft, will one day prevail, againft
the worfe flavery of the Weft Indies.

A Chriftian writer †, fo early as in the

---

* Lipfius affirms, (Sat. b. i. c. 12) that the gladiato-
rial fhows fometimes coft Europe twenty or thirty
thoufand lives in a month; and that not only the men,
but even the women of all ranks, were paffionately fond
of thefe fhows. See Bifhop Porteus's Sermon XIII.

† Bardefanes ap. Eufeb. Præp. Evang. vi. 10.

second century, has testified the resistance which Christianity made to wicked and licentious practices, though established by law and by public usage. " Neither in Parthia, do the Christians, though Parthians, use polygamy; nor in Persia, though Persians, do they marry their own daughters; nor, among the Bactri or Galli, do they violate the sanctity of marriage; nor, wherever they are, do they suffer themselves to be overcome by ill-constituted laws and manners."

Socrates did not destroy the idolatry of Athens, or produce the slightest revolution in the manners of his country.

But the argument to which I recur is, that the benefit of religion being felt chiefly in the obscurity of private stations, necessarily escapes the observation of history. From the first general notification of Christianity to the present day, there have been in every age many millions, whose names were never heard of, made better by it, not only in their conduct, but in their disposition; and hap-

pier, not fo much in their external circumftances, as in that which is *inter præcordia*,
in that which alone deferves the name of
happinefs, the tranquillity and confolation
of their thoughts. It has been, fince its
commencement, the author of happinefs and
virtue to millions and millions of the human race. Who is there that would not
wifh his fon to be a Chriftian?

Chriftianity alfo, in every country in
which it is profeffed, hath obtained a fenfible, although not a complete influence, upon the public judgment of morals. And
this is very important. For without the occafional correction which public opinion receives, by referring to fome fixed ftandard
of morality, no man can foretell into what
extravagancies it might wander. Affaffina-
tion might become as honourable as duel-
ling; unnatural crimes be accounted as
venial, as fornication is wont to be accounted. In this way it is poffible, that many
may be kept in order by Chriftianity, who
are not themfelves Chriftians. They may
be

7

be guided by the rectitude which it communicates to public opinion. Their confciences may fuggeft their duty truly, and they may afcribe thefe fuggeftions to a moral fenfe, or to the native capacity of the human intellect, when in fact they are nothing more, than the public opinion reflected from their own minds; an opinion, in a confiderable degree, modified by the leffons of Chriftianity. " Certain it is, and this is a great deal to fay, that the generality, even of the meaneft and moft vulgar and ignorant people, have truer and worthier notions of God, more juft and right apprehenfions concerning his attributes and perfections, a deeper fenfe of the difference of good and evil, a greater regard to moral obligations and to the plain and moft neceffary duties of life, and a more firm and univerfal expectation of a future ftate of rewards and punifhments, than, in any heathen country, any confiderable number of men were found to have had *."

* Clark, Ev. Nat. Rev. p. 208, ed. v.

After

After all, the value of Chriftianity is not to be appreciated by its *temporal* effects. The object of revelation, is to influence human conduct in this life; but what is gained to happinefs by that influence, can only be eftimated by taking in the whole of human exiftence. Then, as hath already been obferved, there may be alfo great confequences of Chriftianity, which do not belong to it as a revelation. The effects upon human falvation, of the miffion, of the death, of the prefent, of the future agency of Chrift, may be univerfal, though the religion be not univerfally known.

Secondly, I affert that Chriftianity is charged with many confequences for which it is not refponfible. I believe that religious motives have had no more to do, in the formation of nine-tenths of the intolerant and perfecuting laws, which in different countries have been eftablifhed upon the fubject of religion, than they have had to do in England with the making of the game laws. Thefe meafures, although they have
the

the Chriftian religion for their fubject, are
refolvable into a principle which Chriftianity certainly did not plant (and which
Chriftianity could not univerfally condemn,
becaufe it is not univerfally wrong), which
principle is no other than this, that they
who are in poffeffion of power do what
they can to keep it. Chriftianity is anfwerable for no part of the mifchief which has
been brought upon the world by perfecution, except that which has arifen from *con-
fcientious* perfecutors. Now thefe perhaps
have never been, either numerous, or powerful. Nor is it to Chriftianity that even
their miftake can fairly be imputed. They
have been mifled by an error, not properly
Chriftian or religious, but by an error in
their moral philofophy. They purfued the
particular, without adverting to the general
confequence. Believing certain articles of
faith, or a certain mode of worfhip, to be
highly conducive, or perhaps effential to
falvation, they thought themfelves bound
to bring all they could, by every means,
into them. And this they thought, with-

out confidering what would be the effect of fuch a conclufion, when adopted amongft mankind as a general rule of conduct. Had there been in the New Teftament, what there are in the Koran, precepts authorizing coercion in the propagation of the religion, and the ufe of violence towards unbelievers, the cafe would have been different. This diftinction could not have been taken, or this defence made.

I apologize for no fpecies nor degree of perfecution, but I think that even the fact has been exaggerated. The flave trade deftroys more in a year, than the inquifition does in a hundred, or perhaps hath done fince its foundation.

If it be objected, as I apprehend it will be, that Chriftianity is chargeable with every mifchief, of which it has been the *occafion*, though not the motive; I anfwer, that, if the malevolent paffions be there, the world will never want occafions. The noxious element will always find a conductor. Any

point

point will produce an explosion. Did the applauded intercommunity of the Pagan theology preserve the peace of the Roman world? Did it prevent oppressions, proscriptions, massacres, devastations? Was it bigotry that carried Alexander into the East, or brought Cæsar into Gaul? Are the nations of the world, into which Christianity hath not found its way, or from which it hath been banished, free from contentions? Are their contentions less ruinous and sanguinary? Is it owing to Christianity, or to the want of it, that the finest regions of the East, the countries *inter quatuor maria*, the peninsula of Greece, together with a great part of the Mediteranean coast, are at this day a desart? or that the banks of the Nile, whose constantly renewed fertility is not to be impaired by neglect, or destroyed by the ravages of war, serve only for the scene of a ferocious anarchy, or the supply of unceasing hostilities? Europe itself has known no religious wars for some centuries, yet has hardly ever been without war. Are the calamities, which at this day afflict

it,

it, to be imputed to Chriftianity? Hath Po-
land fallen by a Chriftian crufade? Hath
the overthrow in France, of civil order and
fecurity, been effected by the votaries of
our religion, or by the foes? Amongft the
awful leffons, which the crimes and the miferies of that country afford to mankind,
this is one, that, in order to be a perfecutor,
it is not neceffary to be a bigot: that in
rage and cruelty, in mifchief and deftruction, fanaticifm itfelf can be outdone by infidelity.

Finally, if war, as it is now carried on
between nations, produce lefs mifery and
ruin than formerly, we are indebted perhaps to Chriftianity for the change, more
than to any other caufe. Viewed therefore
even in its relation to this fubject, it appears
to have been of advantage to the world.
It hath humanifed the conduct of wars; it
hath ceafed to excite them.

The differences of opinion, that have in
all ages prevailed amongft Chriftians, fall
very

very much within the alternative which has been ftated. If we poffeffed the difpofition, which Chriftianity labours, above all other qualities, to inculcate, thefe differences would do little harm. If that difpofition be wanting, other caufes, even were thefe abfent, would continually rife up, to call forth the malevolent paffions into action. Differences of opinion, when accompanied with mutual charity, which Chriftianity forbids them to violate, are for the moft part innocent, and for fome purpofes ufeful. They promote enquiry, difcuffion, and knowledge. They help to keep up an attention to religious fubjects, and a concern about them, which might be apt to die away in the calm and filence of univerfal agreement. I do not know that it is in any degree true, that the influence of religion is the greateft, where there are the feweft diffenters.

CHAP.

CHAP. VIII.

The Conclusion.

IN religion, as in every other fubject of human reafoning, much depends upon the *order* in which we difpofe our enquiries. A man who takes up a fyftem of divinity with a previous opinion that either every part muft be true, or the whole falfe, approaches the difcuffion with great difadvantage. No other fyftem, which is founded upon moral evidence, would bear to be treated in the fame manner. Neverthelefs, in a certain degree, we are all introduced to our religious ftudies under this prejudication. And it cannot be avoided. The weaknefs of the human judgment in the early part of youth, yet its extreme fufceptibility of impreffion, renders it neceffary to furnifh it with fome opinions, and with fome principles, or other. Or indeed, without much

6   exprefs

exprefs cafe, or much endeavour for this
purpofe, the tendency of the mind of man,
to affimilate itfelf to the habits of thinking
and fpeaking which prevail around him, produces the fame effect. That indifferency
and fufpenfe, that waiting and equilibrium
of the judgment, which fome require in religious matters, and which fome would wifh
to be aimed at in the conduct of education,
are impoffible to be preferved. They are
not given to the condition of human life.

It is a confequence of this fituation that
the doctrines of religion come to us before
the proofs; and come to us with that mix-
ture of explications and inferences from
which no public creed is, or can be, free.
And the effect which too frequently follows,
from Chriftianity being prefented to the underftanding in this form, is, that when any
articles, which appear as parts of it, contra-
dict the apprehenfion of the perfons to
whom it is propofed, men of rafh and confident tempers haftily and indifcriminately
reject the whole. But is this to do juftice,

either to themselves, or to the religion?
The rational way of treating a subject of
such acknowledged importance is to attend,
in the first place, to the general and substantial truth of its principles, and to that alone.
When we once feel a foundation; when we
once perceive a ground of credibility in its
history, we shall proceed with safety to enquire into the interpretation of its records,
and into the doctrines which have been deduced from them. Nor will it either endan-
ger our faith, or diminish or alter our motives for obedience, if we should discover that
these conclusions are formed with very different degrees of probability, and possess very
different degrees of importance.

This conduct of the understanding, dictated by every rule of right reasoning, will up-
hold personal Christianity, even in those
countries in which it is established under
forms, the most liable to difficulty and objection. It will also have the further effect of
guarding us against the prejudices which are
wont to arise in our minds to the disadvan-
tage

tage of religion, from obferving the numerous controverfies which are carried on
amongſt its profeſſors; and likewife of indu-
cing a fpirit of lenity and moderation in our
judgment, as well as in our treatment, of
thofe who ſtand, in fuch controverfies, upon
fides oppofite to ours. What is clear in
Chriſtianity we fhall find to be fufficient, and
to be infinitely valuable; what is dubious,
unneceſſary to be decided, or of very fubordinate importance; and what is moſt obfcure, will teach us to bear with the opinions
which others may have formed upon the
fame fubject. We fhall fay to thofe who
the moſt widely diſſent from us, what Au-
guſtine faid to the worſt heretics of his age;
" Illi in vos fæviant, qui nefciunt, cum quo
labore verum inveniatur, et quam difficile
caveantur errores - - - qui nefciunt, cum
quantâ difficultate fanetur oculus interioris
hominis - - - qui nefciunt, quibus fufpiriis et
gemitibus fiat, ut ex quantulacunque parte
poſſit intelligi Deus *."

* Aug. contr. Ep. Fund. cap. ii. n. 2, 3.

A judg-

A judgment, moreover, which is once pretty well fatisfied of the general truth of the religion, will not only thus difcriminate in its doctrines, but will poffefs fufficient ftrength to overcome the reluctance of the imagination to admit articles of faith which are attended with difficulty of apprehenfion, if fuch articles of faith appear to be truly parts of the revelation. It was to be expected beforehand, that what related to the œconomy, and to the perfons, of the invifible world, which revelation profeffes to do, and which, if true, it actually does, fhould contain fome points remote from our analogies, and from the comprehenfion of a mind which hath acquired all its ideas from fenfe and from experience.

It hath been my care, in the preceding work, to preferve the feparation between evidences and doctrines as inviolable as I could; to remove from the primary queftion all confiderations which have been unneceffarily joined with it: and to offer a defence of Chriftianity, which every Chrif-

tian

tian might read, without feeing the tenets in
which he had been brought up attacked or
decried : and it always afforded a fatisfaction
to my mind to obferve that this was practicable ; that few or none of our many controverfies with one another affect or relate
to the proofs of our religion ; that the rent
never defcends to the foundation.

The truth of Chriftianity depends upon
its leading facts, and upon them alone. Now
of thefe we have evidence which ought to
fatisfy us, at leaft until it appear that mankind have ever been deceived by the fame.
We have fome unconteftedand inconteftible
ble points, to which the hiftory of the
human fpecies hath nothing fimilar to offer.
A Jewifh peafant changed the religion of the
world, and that, without force, without
power, without fupport; without one natural
fource or circumftance of attraction, influence, or fuccefs. Such a thing hath not
happened in any other inftance. The companions of this perfon, after he himfelf had
been put to death for his attempt, afferted
his

his fupernatural character, founded upon his
fupernatural operations; and, in teftimony of
the truth of their affertions, *i. e.* in confequence of their own belief of that truth, and
in order to communicate the knowledge of
it to others, voluntarily entered upon lives of
toil and hardfhip, and, with a full experience of their danger, committed themfelves
to the laft extremities of perfecution. This
hath not a parallel. More particularly, a
very few days after this perfon had been
publicly executed, and in the very city in
which he was buried, thefe his companions
declared with one voice that his body was
reftored to life; that they had feen him,
handled him, eat with him, converfed with
him; and, in purfuance of their perfuafion
of the truth of what they told, preached
his religion, with this ftrange fact as the
foundation of it, in the face of thofe who
had killed him, who were armed with the
power of the country, and neceffarily and
naturally difpofed to treat his followers as
they had treated himfelf; and having done
this upon the fpot where the event took
place,

place, carried the intelligence of it abroad, in defpite of difficulties and oppofition, and where the nature of their errand gave them nothing to expect but derifion, infult, and outrage. This is without example. Thefe three facts, I think, are certain, and would have been nearly fo, if the Gofpels had never been written. The Chriftian ftory, as to thefe points, hath never varied. No other hath been fet up againft it. Every letter, every difcourfe, every controverfy, amongft the followers of the religion; every book written by them, from the age of its com-mencement to the prefent time, in every part of the world in which it hath been profeffed, and with every fect into which it hath been divided (and we have letters and difcourfes written by contemporaries, by witneffes of the tranfaction, by perfons themfelves bear-ing a fhare in it, and other writings follow-ing that age in regular fucceffion), *concur* in reprefenting thefe facts in this manner. A religion, which now poffeffes the greateft part of the civilifed world, unqueftionably fprang up at Jerufalem at this time. Some account

must

muſt be given of its origin; ſome cauſe aſſigned for its riſe. All the accounts of this
origin, all the explications of this cauſe,
whether taken from the writings of the early
followers of the religion (in which, and in
which perhaps alone, it could be expected
that they ſhould be diſtinctly unfolded) or
from occaſional notices in other writings of
that or the adjoining age, either expreſsly
alledge the facts above ſtated as the means by
which the religion was ſet up, or advert to
its commencement in a manner which agrees
with the ſuppoſition of theſe facts being
true, and which teſtifies their operation and
effects.

Theſe propoſitions alone lay a foundation
for our faith ; for they prove the exiſtence of
a tranſaction, which cannot even in its moſt
general parts be accounted for, upon any
reaſonable ſuppoſition, except that of the
truth of the miſſion. But the particulars,
the *detail* of the miracles or miraculous pretences (for ſuch there neceſſarily muſt have
been) upon which this unexampled tranſac-

tion

tion rested, and *for* which these men acted
and suffered as they did act and suffer, it is
undoubtedly of great importance to us to
know. We *have* this detail from the foun-
tain head, from the persons themselves; in
accounts written by eye-witnesses of the
scene, by contemporaries and companions of
those who were so; not in one book, but
four, each containing enough for the verification of the religion, all agreeing in the
fundamental parts of the history. We have
the authenticity of these books established by
more and stronger proofs than belong to
almost any other ancient book whatever,
and by proofs which widely distinguish
them from any others claiming a similar authority to theirs. If there were any good
reason for doubt concerning the names to
which these books are ascribed (which there
is not, for they were never ascribed to any
other, and we have evidence not long after
their publication of their bearing the names
which they now bear), their antiquity, of
which there is no question, their reputation
and authority amongst the early disciples of

6

the

the religion, of which there is as little, form
a valid proof that they muft, in the main at
leaft, have agreed with what the firft teachers
of the religion delivered.

When we open thefe ancient volumes, we
difcover in them marks of truth, whether
we confider each in itfelf, or collate them with
one another. The writers certainly knew
fomething of what they were writing about,
for they manifeft an acquaintance with local
circumftances, with the hiftory and ufages
of the times, which could only belong to an
inhabitant of that country, living in that age.
In every narrative we perceive fimplicity
and undefignednefs; the air and the language
of reality. When we compare the different
narratives together, we find them fo varying
as to repel all fufpicion of confederacy; fo
agreeing under this variety, as to fhew that
the accounts had one real tranfaction for
their common foundation; often attributing
different actions and difcourfes, to the perfon whofe hiftory, or rather memoirs of
whofe hiftory, they profefs to relate, yet

actions

actions and difcourfes fo fimilar, as very much to befpeak the fame character; which is a coincidence, that, in fuch writers as they were, could only be the confequence of their writing from fact, and not from imagination.

Thefe four narratives are confined to the hiftory of the founder of the religion, and end with *his* miniftry. Since however it is certain that the affair went on, we cannot help being anxious to know *how* it proceeded. This intelligence hath come down to us in a work purporting to be written by a perfon, himfelf connected with the bufinefs during the firft ftages of its progrefs, taking up the ftory where the former hiftories had left it, carrying on the narrative, oftentimes with great particularity, and throughout with the appearance of good fenfe *, information and candour; ftating

---

* See Peter's fpeech upon curing the cripple (Acts iii. 18.), the council of the apoftles (xv.), Paul's difcourfe at Athens (xvii. 22.), before Agrippa (xxvi.). I notice thefe paffages, both as fraught with good fenfe, and as free from the fmalleft tincture of enthufiafm.

all along the origin, and the only probable
origin, of effects which unqueftionably were
produced, together with the natural confequences of fituations which unqueftionably
did exift ; and *confirmed*, in the fubftance at
leaft of the account, by the ftrongeft poffible
acceffion of teftimony which a hiftory can
receive, *original letters*, written by the perfon who is the principal fubject of the hiftory, written upon the bufinefs to which
the hiftory relates, and during the period,
or foon after the period, which the hiftory
comprifes. No man can fay that this altogether is not a body of ftrong hiftorical
evidence.

When we reflect that fome of thofe, from
whom the books proceeded, are related to
have themfelves wrought miracles, to have
been the fubject of miracles, or of fupernatural affiftance in propagating the religion,
we may perhaps be led to think, that more
credit, or a different kind of credit, is due
to thefe accounts, than what can be claimed
by merely human teftimony. But this is an
argument

argument which cannot be addreſſed to
ſceptics or unbelievers. A man muſt be a
Chriſtian before he can receive it. The inſpiration of the hiſtorical ſcriptures, the nature, degree, and extent of that inſpiration,
are queſtions undoubtedly of ſerious diſcuſſion, but they are queſtions amongſt Chriſtians themſelves, and not between them and
others. The doctrine itſelf is by no means
neceſſary to the belief of Chriſtianity, which
muſt, in the firſt inſtance at leaſt, depend
upon the ordinary maxims of hiſtorical credibility *.

In viewing the detail of miracles recorded
in theſe books, we find every ſuppoſition
negatived, by which they can be reſolved
into fraud or deluſion. They were not ſecret, nor momentary, nor tentative, nor
ambiguous ; nor performed under the ſanc-
tion of authority, with the ſpectators on
their ſide, or in affirmance of tenets and
practices already eſtabliſhed. We find alſo

---

* See Powell's Diſcourſes. Diſc. xv. p. 245.

the

the evidence alledged for them, and which evidence was by great numbers received, different from that upon which other miraculous accounts reft. It was contemporary, it was publifhed upon the fpot, it continued; it involved interefts and queftions of the greateft magnitude; it contradicted the moft fixed perfuafions and prejudices of the perfons to whom it was addreffed; it required from thofe who accepted it, not a fimple indolent affent, but a change, from thenceforward, of principles and conduct, a fubmiffion to confequences the moft ferious and the moft deterring, to lofs and danger, to infult, outrage, and perfecution. How fuch a ftory fhould be falfe, or, if falfe, how under fuch circumftances it fhould make its way, I think impoffible to be explained: yet fuch the Chriftian ftory was, fuch were the circumftances under which it came forth, and in oppofition to fuch difficulties did it prevail.

An event fo connected with the religion, and with the fortunes, of the Jewifh people,

as

as one of their race, one born amongſt them, eſtabliſhing his authority and his law throughout a great portion of the civilized world, it was perhaps to be expected, ſhould be noticed in the prophetic writings of that nation ; eſpecially when this perſon, together with his own miſſion, cauſed alſo to be acknowledged, the divine original of their inſtitution, and by thoſe who before had altogether rejected it. Accordingly we perceive in theſe writings, various intimations *concurring* in the perſon and hiſtory of Jeſus, in a manner, and in a degree, in which paſſages taken from theſe books could not be made to concur, in any perſon arbitrarily aſſumed, or in any perſon, except him, who has been the author of great changes in the affairs and opinions of mankind. Of ſome of theſe predictions the weight depends a good deal upon the concurrence. Others poſſeſs great ſeparate ſtrength : one in particular does this in an eminent degree. It is an entire deſcription, manifeſtly directed to one character and to one ſcene of things : it is extant in a writing, or collection of

D d 3 writings,

writings, declaredly prophetic; and it applies
to Chrift's character, and to the circumftances of his life and death, with confiderable precifion, and in a way which no diverfity of interpretation hath, in my opinion, been able to confound. That the advent of Chrift, and the confequences of it,
fhould not have been more diftinctly revealed in the Jewifh facred books, is, I think, in
fome meafure accounted for by the confideration, that for the Jews to have forefeen
the fall of their inftitution, and that it was
to merge at length into a more perfect and
comprehenfive difpenfation, would have
cooled too much, and relaxed, their zeal for
it, and their adherence to it, upon which
zeal and adherence the prefervation in the
world of any remains, for many ages, of
religious truth, might in a great meafure
depend.

Of what a revelation difclofes to mankind, one, and only one, queftion can properly be afked, " Was it of importance to
mankind to know, or to be better affured
of ?"

of?" In this question, when we turn our thoughts to the great Christian doctrine of the resurrection of the dead, and of a future judgment, no doubt can possibly be entertained. He who gives me riches or honours does nothing; he who even gives me health does little, in comparison with that which lays before me just grounds for expecting a restoration to life, and a day of account and retribution: which thing Christianity hath done for millions.

Other articles of the Christian faith, although of infinite importance when placed beside any other topic of human enquiry, are only the adjuncts and circumstances of this. They are however such as appear worthy of the original to which we ascribe them. The morality of the religion, whether taken from the precepts or the example of its founder, or from the lessons of its primitive teachers, derived, as it should seem, from what had been inculcated by their master, is, in all its parts, wise and pure; neither adapted to vulgar prejudices,

D d 4   nor

nor flattering popular notions, nor excufing
eftablifhed practices, but calculated, in the
matter of its inftruction, truly to promote
human happinefs, and, in the form in which
it was conveyed, to produce impreffion and
effect; a morality which, let it have proceeded from any perfon whatever, would
have been fatisfactory evidence of his good
fenfe and integrity, of the foundnefs of his
underftanding and the probity of his defigns; a morality, in every view of it, much
more perfect than could have been expected from the natural circumftances and character of the perfon who delivered it; a morality, in a word, which is, and hath been,
moft beneficial to mankind.

Upon the greateft therefore of all poffible
occafions, and for a purpofe of ineftimable
value, it pleafed the Deity to vouchfafe a
miraculous atteftation. Having done this
for the inftitution, when this alone could fix
its authority, or give to it a beginning, he
committed its future progrefs to the natural
means of human communication, and to the
influence

influence of thofe caufes by which human
conduct and human affairs are governed.
The feed being fown, was left to vegetate;
the leaven being inferted, was left to fer-
ment; and both according to the laws of
nature: laws, neverthelefs, difpofed and
controlled by that Providence which con-
ducts the affairs of the univerfe, though by
an influence infcrutable, and generally un-
diftinguifhable by us. And in this, Chriftianity is analogous to moft other provifions
for happinefs. The provifion is made; and
being made, is left to act according to laws,
which, forming part of a more general fyftem, regulate this particular fubject, in common with many others.

Let the conftant recurrence to our obfervation, of contrivance, defign, and wifdom
in the works of nature, once fix upon our
minds the belief of a God, and after that
all is eafy. In the councils of a Being poffeffed of the power and difpofition which
the Creator of the univerfe muft poffefs, it
is not improbable that there fhould be a
future

future ftate; it is not improbable that we fhould be acquainted with it. A future ftate rectifies every thing; becaufe if moral agents be made, in the laft event, happy or miferable, according to their conduct in the ftation, and under the circumftances in which they are placed, it feems not very material by the operation of what caufes, according to what rules, or even, if you pleafe to call it fo, by what chance or ca- price, thefe ftations are affigned, or thefe circumftances determined. This hypothefis, therefore, folves all that objection to the divine care and goodnefs, which the promif- cuous diftribution of good and evil (I do not mean in the doubtful advantages of riches and grandeur, but in the unqueftion- ably important diftinctions of health and ficknefs, ftrength and infirmity, bodily eafe and pain, mental alacrity and depreffion) is apt on fo many occafions to create. This one truth changes the nature of things: gives order to confufion: makes the moral world of a piece with the natural.

Never-

Neverthelefs, a higher degree of affurance than that to which it is poffible to advance this, or any argument drawn from
the light of nature, was neceffary, efpecially
to overcome the fhock, which the imagination and the fenfes receive, from the effects
and the appearances of death; and the ob-
ftruction which from thence arifes to the
expectation of either a continued or a future exiftence. This difficulty, although of
a nature, no doubt, to act very forcibly, will
be found, I think, upon reflection, to refide
more in our habits of apprehenfion, than in
the fubject; and that the giving way to it,
when we have any reafonable grounds for
the contrary, is rather an indulging of the
imagination, than any thing elfe. Abftract-
edly confidered, that is, confidered without
relation to the difference, which habit, and
merely habit, produces in our faculties and
modes of apprehenfion, I do not fee any
thing more in the refurrection of a dead
man, than in the conception of a child; except it be this, that the one comes into his
world with a fyftem of prior confcioufneffes

about

about him, which the other does not: and
no perfon will fay, that he knows enough
of either fubject to perceive, that this circumftance makes fuch a difference in the
two cafes, that the one fhould be eafy, and
the other impoffible ; the one natural, the
other not fo. To the firft man the fucceffion of the fpecies would be as incompre-
henfible, as the refurrection of the dead is
to us.

Thought is different from motion, per-
ception from impact: the individuality of a
mind is hardly confiftent with the divifibi-
lity of an extended fubftance ; or its voli-
tion, that is, its power of originating motion, with the inertnefs which cleaves to
every portion of matter, which our obfervation or our experiments can reach. Thefe
diftinctions lead us to an *immaterial* principle : at leaft, they do this; they fo negative the mechanical properties of matter, in
the conftitution of a fentient, ftill more of a
rational being, that no argument, drawn
from thefe properties, can be of any great
weight

weight in oppofition to other reafons, when the queftion refpects the changes of which fuch a nature is capable, or the manner in which thefe changes are effected. Whatever thought be, or whatever it depend upon, the regular experience of *fleep* makes one thing concerning it certain, that it can be completely fufpended, and completely reftored.

If any one find it too great a ftrain upon his thoughts, to admit the notion of a fubftance ftrictly immaterial, that is, from which extenfion and folidity are excluded, he can find no difficulty in allowing, that a particle as fmall as a particle of light, minuter than all conceiveable dimenfions, may juft as eafily be the depofitary, the organ, and the vehicle of confcioufnefs, as the congeries of animal fubftance, which forms a human body, or the human brain; that, being fo, it may transfer a proper identity to whatever fhall hereafter be united to it; may be fafe amidft the deftruction of its integuments; may connect the natural with the fpiritual,

the

the corruptible with the glorified body. If
it be faid, that the mode and means of all
this is imperceptible by our fenfes, it is only
what is true of the moft important agencies
and operations. The great powers of nature are all invifible. Gravitation, electri-
city, magnetifm, though conftantly prefent,
and conftantly exerting their influence ;
though within us, near us, and about us ;
though diffufed throughout all fpace, over-
fpreading the furface, or penetrating the
contexture of all bodies with which we are
acquainted, depend upon fubftances and actions, which are totally concealed from our
fenfes. The Supreme Intelligence is fo
himfelf.

But whether thefe, or any other attempts
to fatisfy the imagination, bear any refemblance to the truth, or whether the imagination, which, as I have faid before, is the
mere flave of habit, *can* be fatisfied, or not ;
when a future ftate, and the revelation of a
future ftate, is not only perfectly confiftent
with the attributes of the Being who governs
the

the univerfe ; but when it is more ; when
it alone removes the appearances of contra-
riety, which attend the operations of his will
towards creatures capable of comparative
merit and demerit, of reward and punifhment ; when a ftrong body of hiftorical evidence, confirmed by many internal tokens
of truth and authenticity, gives us juft reafon to believe that fuch a revelation hath
actually been made ; we ought to fet our
minds at reft with the affurance, that, in the
refources of creative wifdom, expedients
cannot be wanted to carry into effect what
the Deity hath purpofed : that either a new
and mighty influence will defcend upon the
human world, to refufcitate extinguifhed
confcioufnefs ; or that, amidft the other
wonderful contrivances with which the univerfe abounds, and by fome of which we
fee animal life, in many inftances, affuming
improved forms of exiftence, acquiring new
organs, new perceptions, and new fources
of enjoyment, provifion is alfo made, though
by methods fecret to us (as all the great
proceffes of nature are), for conducting the

6   objects

objects of God's moral government, through the neceſſary changes of their frame, to thoſe final diſtinctions of happineſs and miſery, which he hath declared to be re-ſerved for obedience and tranſgreſſion, for virtue and vice, for the uſe and the neglect, the right and the wrong employment, of the faculties and opportunities, with which he hath been pleaſed, ſeverally, to entruſt, and to try us.

THE END.

* 9 7 8 3 3 3 7 0 2 6 0 4 2 *